INNOVATIONS
Infant and Toddler Development

D1404475

Kay's Acknowledgments

When I was in elementary school, I developed an interest in young children—I like watching them, helping them, and playing with them. I had many opportunities to do so at home, in the neighborhood, and at my church, where I hung out often at the nursery. One day, I told my mother that I liked working with kids. That was the day my child development training began. My mother, who was a professor in home economics/child development at the local university, calmly and quietly explained to me that "kids" are baby goats. Human offspring are called "children." Like so many of her lessons, I didn't think too much about the response at the time. Later, as I pursued my interest in young children, I came to understand and embrace the reverence and respect she had for all children and for the amazing and wonderful process of growth and development. She deserves credit for sparking the inspiration that resulted in this book.

Since then, there have been many other lessons learned about the transactional nature of growing and developing. Some of these lessons came from adults who taught me, like Ruth Highberger, Ph.D. at the University of Tennessee at Knoxville, who supervised me while I learned more, like Mary Rachel Armstrong at the University of Tennessee at Martin, Lucy C. Biggs in the Department of Head Start Training at the University of Tennessee, Knoxville, Mary Pyman, Ph.D. at Incarnate Word College in San Antonio, Texas, Joan Terry, Ed.D., and Robert Gratz, Ed.D. at Southwest Texas State University. Still more understanding about development came from the wonderful teachers with whom I have had the privilege to work with both in and out of the classroom. With them I learned to trust my teaching instincts and developed teaching skills and abilities that were worth sharing with others.

But, it is those "children" my mother enticed me to learn more about who have had the most impact on my understanding and insight into child development. There were many—Tara, James, Kristy, Jon, Jason, Ian, Heather Rae, the triplets, Joshua, Michael, Peter, Jaci, Jeff, Kaylee, Mary Katherine, Nick, Brent, Melanie, Bradley, Kinsey, Ali, Holly, Joseph, Emma, Bobby, William, Darcie, Keri, Jennifer, Shannon, Kyle, Elizabeth, Christopher, James, Daniel, Dusty, Sarah, Dixie, Amanda, Grant, Taylor, Lorin—and I thank them all for the many meaningful and important lessons.

Special thanks goes out to Sharon Spillman who coordinated photo shoots for this book, to Masami Mizukami, Lisa Meinen, and other staff who ably took photographs, and the parents and staff of Kandystripe Academy and HeartsHome Early Learning Center, who shared their beautiful children with us. Particularly, we thank their directors, Judy Mayfield-Scott and Kaye Anderson at Kandystripe, and Carla Gwinn at HeartsHome, for putting up with our intrusions.

During the last 18 months, I have been on a sort of sabbatical in Italy. During this time, there were a few special people who provided wonderful places to be as I researched and wrote this book. My appreciation goes to Stefano Paggetti and Elizabetta Nasi and their daughters Bianca and Susanna, who made us feel so much like family that we returned again and again to Parano; to Walter Mari and Paola Pannacci and their children Francesca, Lorenzo, and Alessandro, who shared the best home-harvested olive oil I have ever tasted and made us feel like part of the family in Le Cassella—especially Paola, who opened doors to every school in Rancolfo and the immediate area for me to visit and spend time learning; to Gun Lundgrin Cesarini, who shared her love of writing and home-cured olives with us in Panicale; and Marco Lucatello and Sylvia Ristori and their girls Michela and Noami, and Luca Pedocchi and Sandra Ristori and their son Lorenzo, who were our first resources for living Italian-style. They helped us make the transition gently, with much support.

Finally, thanks to my husband, Larry, who spent his sabbatical supporting me while this book was written. He spent hours coaxing balky computers, hassling with international email connections that should have worked but didn't, and feeding and caring for me. He was more patient than he should have been when the beauty of the Italian people, food, and countryside called us both, but could not lure me away until I was done.

Linda's Acknowledgments

I am fortunate to come from a very loving and supportive family. My sister Marie is 11 years younger. Because of her (and my mother's and father's trust) I was able to spend long periods of time realizing that young children are by far the most interesting part of the universe. My interest has grown with my amazing nephews (my sister Patti's children), my wonderful niece Amy (Marie's daughter), and, of course, the two most intriguing children (now teenagers) I have ever known, my own John and Kevin. Other children whom I have known through the years have only added to my understanding and interest.

I am grateful to the many individuals who have supported my professional growth and enriching experiences. They also helped make my interest in children grow and mature.

Thanks to Kay for her endurance, insight, and remarkable ability to communicate the intricate mysteries of child development. Thanks to Larry for understanding the importance of this book and that it had to be written.

Infant &Toddler
DEVELOPMENT

Illustrations:
Joan Waites and
K. Whelan Dery
Photographs: Kay Albrecht,
Masami Mizukami, René Summers,
Lisa Meinen, Gwendolyn Calhoun
and CLEO Photography

Kay Albrecht / Linda G. Miller

Copyright

© 2001, Kay Albrecht and Linda G. Miller
Published by Gryphon House, Inc., 10726 Tucker Street, Beltsville, MD, 20705 or PO Box 207, Beltsville, MD 20704-0207.
Call us at 800-638-0928.
Visit us on the web at www.gryphonhouse.com.

All rights reserved.

No part of this publication, except for the forms, may be reproduced, stored in a retrieval system, or transmitted, in any form or by any means, electronic, mechanical, photocopying, microfilming, recording, or otherwise, without permission of the publisher. Requests for permission to make copies of any part of the work should be mailed to Gryphon House, Inc.

Illustrations: Joan Waites and K. Whelan Dery
Photographs: Kay Albrecht, Masami Mizukami, René Summers, Lisa Meinen, Gwendolyn Calhoun, and CLEO Photography.
Cover photographs: © 2000, Artville

Library of Congress Cataloging-in-Publication Data

Albrecht, Kay M.
   Innovations : infant & toddler development / Kay Albrecht, Linda G. Miller; illustrations, Joan Waites and K. Whelan Dery.
     p. cm.
   Includes bibliographical references and index.
   ISBN 0-87659-259-0
   1. Infants—Development. 2. Toddlers. 3. Child development. 4. Early childhood education. I. Title: Infant & toddlers development. II. Title: Infant and toddler development. III. Miller, Linda G. IV. Title.

HQ774 .A634 2001
305.232--dc21

                                        2001051219

Bulk Purchase

Gryphon House books are available at special discount when purchased in bulk. Special editions or book excerpts also can be created to specification. For details, contact the Director of Sales at the address or phone number on this page.

Dedication

To Trey and Angi, who taught me so much as they grew up.—Kay

To John and Kevin, because being your mom is the most certain desire I have ever had in my life. Thanks to my love, Mike, who made motherhood possible.—-Linda

Disclaimer

The publisher and the authors cannot be held responsible for injury, mishap, or damages incurred during the use of or because of the information or activities in this book. The authors recommend appropriate and reasonable supervision at all times based on the age and capability of each child.

Table of Contents

Chapter 7: Expressing Feelings with Parents, Teachers, and Friends 305

Appendix 343

References 361
Index 367

Introduction

Innovations: Infant and Toddler Development advocates using early childhood knowledge to understand behavior as a window to the context of each child. This understanding, in turn, leads to opportunities for supporting developmental maturation and creating opportunities for children to learn and for teachers to teach. The outcome of this approach is developing and implementing best practices that are not only grounded in theory and research but also individualized to fit each child.

A large body of knowledge informs the practice of early childhood education (Bredekamp & Copple, 1997). Acquiring an understanding of this knowledge base is crucial to teaching children successfully, particularly children less than three years of age (Mooney, 2000). In ***Innovations: Infant and Toddler Development***, the term infant is used for children from birth to 18 months, and the term toddler is used for children from 18 months to 36 months.

This book is written for teachers who come into this profession through divergent paths. It is designed for teachers who are beginning their teaching careers and want to expand their understanding of what they will need to know to do their jobs effectively. It is also written for teachers who entered the professional ranks from the applied side—learning by doing in the classroom—who are now ready to understand the "whys" behind good teaching. And, finally, it is written for teachers who have had professional early childhood training that needs updating to reflect the dramatic increase in our understanding of child development and early childhood education that has occurred in the last few years.

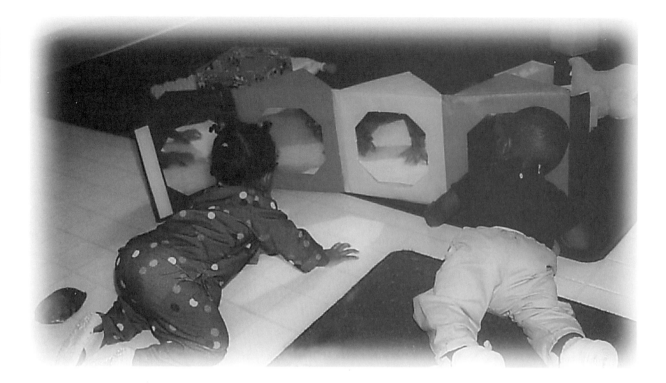

Innovations: Infant and Toddler Development is also targeted to another key group—those teachers who are working with young children in programs and who are challenged by the increasing complexity of the job that early childhood educators do. Teaching is not easy. Besides the real problems of low pay, wage stagnation, lack of status, poor regulation, and isolation, children are coming into programs with behaviors and developmental issues that require increased knowledge, understanding, skills, and abilities to address. In particular, teachers report that children are having problems with peers, experiencing delayed development, having difficulty acquiring normative developmental skills, exhibiting difficulty in managing aggression, experiencing delays in developing self-regulation, and so on. Children's behavior in early childhood programs serves as evidence of these emerging problems.

To address this reality, teachers must be even better connected to the knowledge base that contributes ideas, rationales, explanations, and insight about early childhood education and the best practices that emerge from what we know. Although we continue to uncover new knowledge and understanding as a result of research and reflective practice, what we already know can be used as a foundation for innovation in the classroom. It serves as a platform from which insightful, reflective teachers can design and implement teaching strategies and plans that support children's continued developmental progress. We are as interested in what teachers do and how they do it as we are in expanding teachers' understanding of theory or research. This preference for integration of knowledge and practice permeates ***Innovations: Infant and Toddler Development***.

As strong as our knowledge base is, we find that many myths and misconceptions about growth and development are widely held in the early childhood teaching field. Sometimes these misconceptions are based on cultural or historic misunderstandings; sometimes they are based on previous knowledge that has not been updated; sometimes they emerge from concerns and fears of teachers in the classroom; and sometimes they are the result of biases that have not been identified and discussed. Whatever the reason, we have attempted to identify these myths and misunderstandings and correct them with the best information we have at this time. Certainly, this information will need updating again. That is the nature and the transactional process between learning and growing—an exciting process that is very much like the human developmental experience.

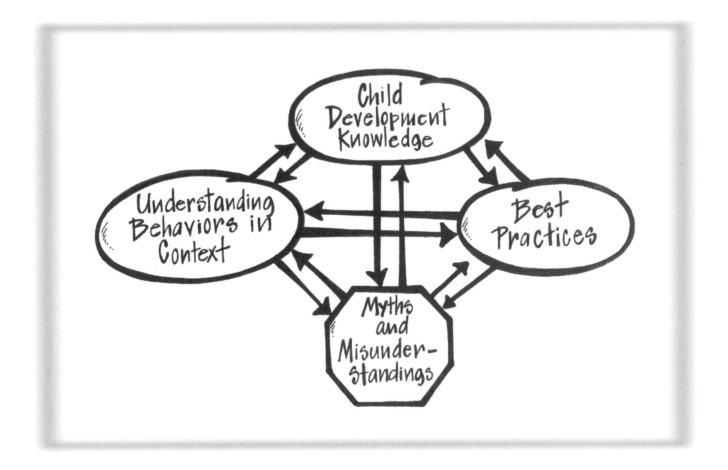

Thus, as the diagram illustrates, early childhood professionals are involved in the dynamic interactions between child development knowledge, best practices, myths and misunderstandings, and understanding behaviors in context. This view encompasses a level of complexity appropriate for issues in care and early education.

References

Bredekamp, S. & C. Copple. (1997). *Developmentally appropriate practice in early childhood programs, Revised edition.* Washington DC: National Association for the Education of Young Children (NAEYC).

Mooney, C.G. (2000). *Theories of childhood: An introduction to Dewey, Montessori, Erickson, Piaget, and Vygotsky.* St. Paul, MI: Redleaf Press.

Innovations: Infant and Toddler Development

INTRODUCTION

What Is Child Development?

Child development is a field of study that seeks to understand all aspects of human growth and development from birth until adulthood. It is a part of a larger discipline, known as developmental psychology, which seeks to describe what happens as humans develop throughout the life cycle.

What Is a Theory?

Child development scientists use many different techniques to investigate, describe, and explore the nature of human development. One important tool for this endeavor is the creation of theories. Theories are frameworks to organize and give meaning to ideas and actions, and to guide decisions. Once proposed, theories are often tested by research to provide confirmation and suggest practices for implementation.

Theories help us organize the complexity of development into manageable ideas that describe, explain, and predict behavior in young children. Sometimes theories try to explain development comprehensively, looking across the entire process. At other times, theories only describe discrete portions of the developmental process.

Which Theories Explain Child Growth and Development?

Historically, three major strands of theories contribute to explanations about how children grow and develop. The first strand views development as a result of the innate biological makeup of the child. Growth and development is then just a process of waiting and watching as the child follows her biological programming.

The second major strand views development as a result of environmental influences on the child. The child comes into the world waiting for experience to influence what will become of her.

The third major strand views the process of development as influenced both by biological heredity (or nature) and environment (nurture), as well as by the dynamic interplay between the two. Interactional theories, as they are called, view development as much more complex than the nature or nurture strands.

Recently, interactional theories have embraced additional components of influence. The expanded role of culture in child growth and development is beginning to be explored and understood. In addition, the role the child plays in her own development is also being explored. Finally, theoretical work in the interactional point of view has begun to embrace the centrality of relationships in how children grow and develop.

Categories of Theories that Contribute to Child Development Knowledge

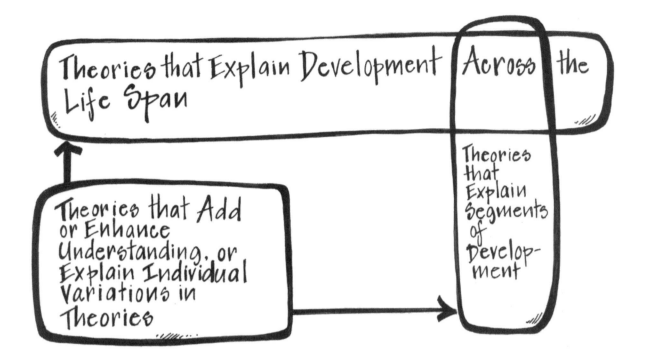

Theories that Explain Development Across the Life Span	Theories that Explain Segments of Development	Theories that Add or Enhance Understanding, or Explain Individual Variations
Examples • Maslow's Hierarchy of Needs • Erickson's Theory of Psycho-social Development • Brain Growth and Development	**Examples** • Parten's Stages of Play • Attachment Theory • Greenspan's Theory of Emotional Development	**Examples** • Bronfenbrenner's Ecological Systems Theory • Gardner's Theory of Multiple Intelligences • Vygotsky's Socio-cultural Theory

Theoretical Roots of Child Development Theories

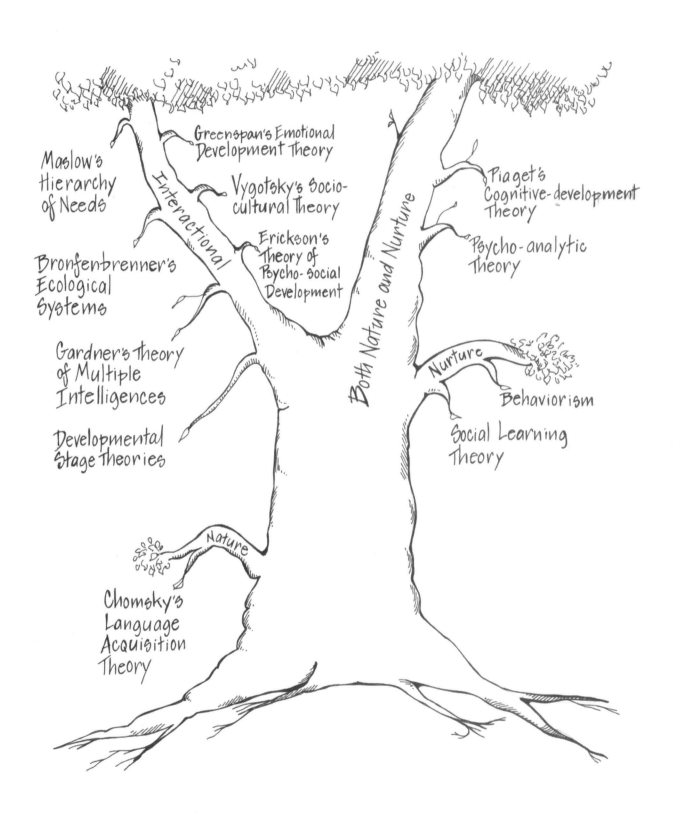

Greenspan's Emotional Development Theory

Maslow's Hierarchy of Needs

Interactional

Vygotsky's Socio-cultural Theory

Piaget's Cognitive-development Theory

Erickson's Theory of Psycho-social Development

Both Nature and Nurture

Psycho-analytic Theory

Bronfenbrenner's Ecological Systems

Gardner's theory of Multiple Intelligences

Nurture

Behaviorism

Social Learning Theory

Developmental Stage Theories

Nature

Chomsky's Language Acquisition Theory

The Innovations: Infant and Toddler Development Approach

Innovations: Infant and Toddler Development is grounded in theories that view human development as a dynamic, sequential, and cumulative process. But this view is not adequate to explain the individual nature of development and the uniqueness of each child. It must be supplemented with theories that view human development as occurring within the context of interactions— with significant others, with the social, cultural, and physical environment, and with the biological predispositions of individual genetics. Taken together, developmental and interactional theories are informative and useful for parents and teachers.

The developmental view is a tradition within early childhood education, forming the foundation of how we think children grow and develop. More recently, early childhood has benefited from increased documentation of the impact of the early years on development, an improved understanding of the importance of nurturing relationships, and clearer information about the impact of these relationships on children's development.

An increase in our knowledge and understanding of how children learn has also occurred. The long-held views of children as active learners who construct their own knowledge and understanding of the world are rapidly being amended with insights from neuroscience about sensitive periods of brain development.

Chapter 1 looks at the underlying principles of developmental and interactional theory. The goal is to help teachers understand the contribution of these theoretical points of view, concepts, and ideas for understanding infant and toddler development.

Developmental Theory of Infant and Toddler Development

Principles of Developmental Theory

Which of the following diagrams do you think best represents the way infants and toddlers develop?

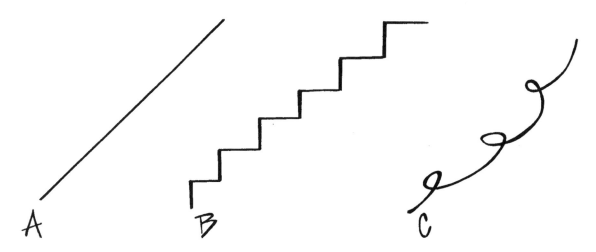

Based on what child development scientists now know, the answer is C. Development is a continuous though uneven cycle—a cycle of ever-increasing skills and abilities in which each period of growth is often preceded by a brief, sometimes turbulent regression. Guided by a set of underlying principles, developmental theory helps explain the amazing changes that take place during the first three years of life.

The first principle of developmental theory is that human development is integrated. All domains of development—physical, emotional, social, and intellectual (which includes language and cognition) are interrelated. Development or growth in one area influences and is influenced by development and growth in another (Bredekamp & Copple, 1997). This fundamental principle is understood by early childhood educators, who see children's development in light of the whole child.

The second principle is that growth follows a universal and relatively predictable sequence. Milestones of development are observable and are used to track children's progress along the growth continua. The relative predictability of development can be seen in each area of development—physical, social, emotional, and intellectual, including cognitive and language development. For example, in the physical area, development proceeds from sitting to crawling to pulling to a stand to walking. Almost every child follows this sequence of development.

The third principle of development is that each child has an individual pattern and timing of growth. Although the sequence is relatively predictable, each child's individual progress through the sequence is subject to variation and uniqueness. For example, one child may pull to a stand and walk at 7–8 months while another may do so at 12–13 months and still another at 17–18 months.

This principle refers to the sporadic and uneven nature of development. Developmental growth seems to be uneven or come in spurts. A child might work on physical development until she can pull to a stand and walk and then move on to language development or cognitive skill acquisition. Or, a child might make no observable developmental progress at all for a few weeks and then all of a sudden make major strides in several domains, seemingly all at once. This component of development illustrates the uniqueness of each child (Perry, 2000).

The Five Principles of Developmental Theory

- All human development is integrated.
- Growth follows a universal and relatively predictable sequence.
- Each child has an individual pattern and timing of growth.
- Development proceeds from the simple to the complex and from the general to the specific.
- Development is a complex interplay of biological, environmental, cultural, social, and interactional experiences.

The third principle of developmental theory explains why age is such a poor predictor of developmental stage and can rarely be used to identify or understand the developmental status of any individual child. Each child's prenatal and birth experience, personality, temperament, preferred approach to learning, type and variation in experiences, interests, strengths, needs, family structure and background, expectations of culture, motivation, energy level, health status, and so on, is individual and contributes to the child's unique pattern and timing of growth. This principle explains the differences among and between children who are the same chronological age.

A fourth principle of developmental theory is that development proceeds from the simple to the complex and from the general to the specific. Simple skills must be acquired before more complex ones can build upon them. For example, children typically eat first with their fingers before attempting to use a spoon or fork. Controlling fingers is a simpler task than controlling an extension of the fingers, in this case, the fork. Once the fingers develop into effective feeding implements, then using an extension of the fingers becomes a possibility for the child to master.

Development proceeds from behavioral knowledge to symbolic or representative knowledge. Children learn to do things long before they can

describe them with language or represent them with pictures or in writing. For example, children can understand and respond appropriately to words like "go bye-bye" before they are able to use those words functionally in speech and verbal interactions.

This trend of increasing complexity in development is predictable and leads to greater organization and internalization of skills and abilities (Bredekamp & Copple, 1997). Parents and teachers can see this principle at work as children become more independent, more able to do things for and by themselves, more self-controlled, and more able to coordinate their behaviors with the expectations of the people around them.

The fifth principle highlights the impact of biological, environmental, cultural, social, and interactional experiences on development. The interplay between these contexts and experiences influences not only the general direction of development but also the short- and long-term outcomes for children.

These principles are the foundation of the developmental approach. Teachers need a thorough understanding of these important concepts to serve as a foundation for their work with young children and their families.

Interactional Theories of Infant and Toddler Development

Principles of Interactional Theory and How Children Learn

Intimate, reciprocal, synchronous relationships form the foundation and core of healthy development. This first principle of interactional theory addresses the type of affective or emotional environment necessary for healthy development. Brazelton and Greenspan (2000) consider warm, nurturing interactions to be the first irreducible need of young children. Others point to the profound effect that these relationships have on how children grow up and what they learn (Berk, 1999; Shonkoff & Phillips, 2000).

The second principle is that interactions take place in and are influenced by a variety of different contexts, including social and cultural contexts. As individuals, we each live within our own culture. These social and cultural contexts determine how individuals communicate with each other (verbally and non-verbally), how they touch, and what behavioral expectations are present. The context within which interactions occur, to a large extent, controls and shapes the interactions.

The third principle of interactional theory states that there is a dynamic relationship between biological heredity and experience. This interplay is continuous and influences development throughout the lifespan. Although genetics are fixed at conception, optimal experiences during the early childhood years serve as the key to unlock biological potential at sensitive periods during children's development. Further, experiences can serve as compensating factors, mediating early deprivation or mistreatment.

> **The Five Principles of Interactional Theory**
>
> ◆ Intimate, reciprocal, synchronous relationships form the foundation and core of healthy development.
> ◆ Interactions take place in and are influenced by a variety of different contexts, including social and cultural contexts.
> ◆ There is a dynamic relationship between biological heredity and experience.
> ◆ Interactions between children and the social, cultural, and physical worlds direct children's learning.
> ◆ Play is the interactive medium of development.

The fourth principle tells us that interactions between children and the social, cultural, and physical worlds direct children's learning, allowing them to construct their own knowledge and understanding. No matter how knowledgeable we are as teachers, we cannot GIVE children knowledge and understanding. Instead, they BUILD their own, using who they are, what previous experiences they have had, what relationships they have, what learning styles they use, and what interest level they have at the moment.

The fifth principle is that play is the interactive medium of development. Emotional, social, physical, and intellectual growth takes place within the context of play that occurs with objects and materials, in interactions with peers, and as facilitated by supportive adults.

Integrating Interactional and Developmental Theories

Tasks

Development is a lifelong task. It begins in infancy and continues throughout the life span. There are many different ideas about how humans develop into capable, productive, functional adults. ***Innovations: Infant and Toddler Development*** proposes six life tasks that begin in infancy and continue as development emerges. Each life task is grounded in theory and the resulting practices that have emerged from developmental and interactional theory and research, and from our current understanding of how children learn.

In some cases, the tasks for infants are different than the tasks for toddlers, illustrating that different stages of development pose different maturation,

Interactional Theories **Developmental Tasks** **Developmental Theories**

learning, and interactional challenges. In others, the task continues to develop throughout the first three years of life, with each maturation, skill acquisition, and interactional accomplishment building on and being influenced by the previous one.

Developmental Tasks by Age

Birth   6 Months   12 Months   18 Months   24 Months   30 Months   36 Months

Separating from Parents ———————▶ Transitioning to School ———————————▶

Connecting with School & Teacher ▶ Making Friends ————————————————▶

Relating to Self & Others———————————————————————▶ Exploring Roles

◀——————————— Communicating with Parents, Teachers, and Friends ———————▶

Moving Around ————————————▶ Problem-solving ——————————————▶

◀————————————————— Expressing Feelings ———————————————————▶

When viewed this way, emerging development is not an event to be celebrated and forgotten. Instead, today's development influences how tomorrow's development proceeds.

These tasks and their supporting curricula are featured in ***Innovations: The Comprehensive Infant Curriculum*** and ***Innovations: The Comprehensive Toddler Curriculum*** (Albrecht & Miller, 2000). These resources can be used in conjunction with *Innovations: Infant and Toddler Development* to provide high-quality and appropriate school experiences for infants and toddlers.

Dealing with Behaviors: The *Innovations* Model

More than anything else, the goal of this book is to help teachers address behaviors. Often, when behaviors present themselves, adults view the behavior as a problem and seek solutions to eliminate or stop the behavior. This approach, which has its roots in behaviorist theory, usually doesn't work and may create additional problematic behaviors.

Instead, *Innovations: Infant and Toddler Development* proposes a different model for dealing with behaviors. When used by sensitive teachers as a teaching and curriculum development strategy, the model leads to increased developmental understanding and a feeling that teachers can, in fact, facilitate further growth, development, and learning, while influencing the child's behavior. Teachers accomplish this by the partnerships they form with parents or significant others, their interactions with parents and children, the experiences and activities they plan for children, the environments they create, and their insightful educational intervention.

Curriculum is defined here in its broadest sense. Curriculum is everything that can contribute to the child's development and the teacher's relationship with the child and the family. This is a paradigm shift—a move away from a view of curriculum as simply the activities that teachers plan for children—toward a comprehensive view that includes much more. The *Innovations* view of curriculum includes:

- An understanding of the developmental tasks of childhood
- An understanding of the theories that support these tasks, observations, and assessments of children's age, stage, play interests, play themes, and so on
- An understanding of theory, research, and best practices that emerge from knowledge of child development
- The interactive experiences between children and all of the significant adults in their lives
- Opportunities to teach that are planned by adults and embedded in interactions and activities
- Parent involvement and participation
- A well-prepared environment
- The specific activities and experiences planned for children by their teachers

Our hope is that this conceptualization moves curriculum (what we do with, to, and for children in school) out of the narrow range that leads to evaluating children's competence solely by standardized testing, toward a more comprehensive approach that embraces many different ways of knowing and learning.

Developmental Tasks

Observations and Assessment

Child Development

Interactive Experiences

Teaching

Parent Participation and Involvement

Environment

Activities and Experiences

The **Innovations** *Model—Phase I: Collect Data*

The **Innovations** model has four phases that lead to developing an individualized curriculum plan to address the identified behavior (See page 30). The first phase is to collect data. Information is gathered from observation, input from parents, and assessment.

Because development is integrated and contextual, careful observation provides information about the child in the settings where the behavior is present, including the classroom, the playground, the hallway during transitions, the home setting, and the bus or car on the way home. The goal of these observations is to gather substantive information to increase understanding of the behavior—where, why, and how it happens, with whom it occurs, what the behavior looks like, and how the multiple contexts of the child's life influence the what, when, where, how, and why of behavior.

Then, teachers seek insight and input from parents. Sometimes parents see the same behavior at home; other times they don't. Sometimes the behavior concerns parents, and sometimes it does not. Sometimes conversations with parents reveal other explanations or sources of problematic behavior. Regardless, discussions with parents can lead to further understanding about the child and the behavior.

Assessment forms the last source of information sought in the first phase. Often, behaviors are harbingers of change—indicators that something is about to happen developmentally for the child. Looking at indicators of developmental age and stage can shed light on the upcoming change. Further, developmental growth is usually preceded by regression as the child attempts to reorganize to accommodate the new growth. Although regressions are often brief, they can be turbulent and difficult. Identifying regressions is a crucial part of assessment data.

The result of this data-gathering process is a better picture of the behavior, grounded in the developmental uniqueness of the individual child. With this data, the model continues.

The **Innovations** *Model—Phase II: Increase Understanding*

The next phase is to increase understanding of the behavior and to collaborate with others who may be able to help. It starts with exploration of theory, research, and the knowledge base that supports our profession, research into the current understanding of best practices, and further exploration of the cultural context of the child and family.

Where does one find such information? Many sources of information are available. Some of the most helpful include:

- National Association for the Education of Young Children (NAEYC). NAEYC publishes **Young Children**, a bi-monthly journal for care and early education professionals and administers the accreditation program under the auspices of the National Academy of Early Childhood Programs. It is also a membership and advocacy organization.
- **Early Childhood Research Quarterly**, a quarterly publication of theoretical, analytical, and applied research.
- **Child Care Information Exchange**, a publication for teachers and directors or program administrators of care and early education programs.
- **Early Childhood Today**, a publication of Scholastic, Inc., for teachers and program administrators.
- Education Resources Information Center (ERIC), a national information center providing access to an extensive body of education-related literature.
- National Child Care Association, a national association of independent operators of early childhood programs.
- Center for Early Childhood Leadership at National-Louis University, dedicated to enhancing the management skills, professional orientation, and leadership capacity of early childhood educators.
- **Texas Child Care**, a quarterly magazine for teachers.
- Association for Childhood Education International (ACEI), which publishes **Childhood Education**, a bimonthly journal covering research, practice, and public policy. ACEI is also a membership organization that promotes sound educational practice from infancy to adolescence.
- High/Scope Educational Research Foundation, publishes the results of longitudinal research projects and materials that reflect the High/Scope educational philosophy.
- Related websites. (See Appendix page 357.)

Complete contact information is included in the Appendix on pages 357-358.

With the results of this research in hand, it is time to seek collaborative support from others. Collaboration can take many forms. It may include, for example, observations of the child and the teacher in the classroom, dialog with a teacher who has had experience with similar behaviors in her or his classroom, or therapeutic consultation from other helping professionals.

The **Innovations** Model—Phase III: Analyze, Synthesize, and Reflect

This is the most important phase. Analyzing, synthesizing, and reflecting lead the way to developing appropriate curriculum to address the behavior.

The analyzing, synthesizing, and reflecting process may be different for every teacher. Sometimes it is a personal process that can only be completed alone. More frequently, it is a collaborative one, facilitated by a mentor, a respected peer, or occasionally, by a protagonist—someone who creates cognitive conflict that results in reconsidering one's approach, position on an issue, or ideas about behavior.

The outcome of this process is almost always more questions that need to be answered or researched. Then, as the reflective process continues and the data collection and research continue, usually a fork in the road will emerge that gives teachers a direction in which to proceed or an approach to follow.

Some of the behaviors that children exhibit have intuitive responses that are within the response realm of almost every adult. For example, when a toddler falls down, adults usually pause to observe the child's physical reaction to the fall, watch to see the intensity of the emotional reaction, and then decide whether to encourage the child to hop up and brush off or to go over and render comfort and aid. This split second of analysis illustrates that the steps of the process can be done rather quickly and directly.

However, some behaviors emerge from a much more complicated picture or do not respond to intuitive teaching or interactive approaches. When this is the case, proceeding through the steps of the model works.

Notice that in this model, behavior is viewed as neutral—neither problematic nor desirable, neither good nor bad. Although behaviors may be challenging, disturbing, interesting, puzzling, cute, worrisome, or distressing, the model proposes to explore the underlying reasons or explanations for behavior for the purpose of developing a plan to support growing and learning. Labeling the behavior is not the purpose.

Several challenging behaviors are analyzed using this model. The behaviors that are addressed are ones that every infant and toddler teacher faces at some time in her career—crying, biting, adjustment difficulty, aggression, learning to toilet, and not talking. Take a look at pages 85-87 in Chapter 2, 135-137 in Chapter 3, 187-189 in Chapter 4, 239-241 in Chapter 5, 297-299 in Chapter 6, and 335-337 in Chapter 7. These sections of the book seek real solutions for real children, teachers, and behaviors.

The **Innovations** *Model—Phase IV: Plan Curriculum*

The curriculum plans that emerge from this process are rich with options to help children grow and develop, learn new skills, and reorganize their behavior at a higher level. Planning and implementing effective teaching strategies and curricula broaden understanding of the behavior and lead teachers to consider more than just stopping or eliminating it. When behaviors are viewed in this way, the result is almost always a path that helps both children and teachers grow.

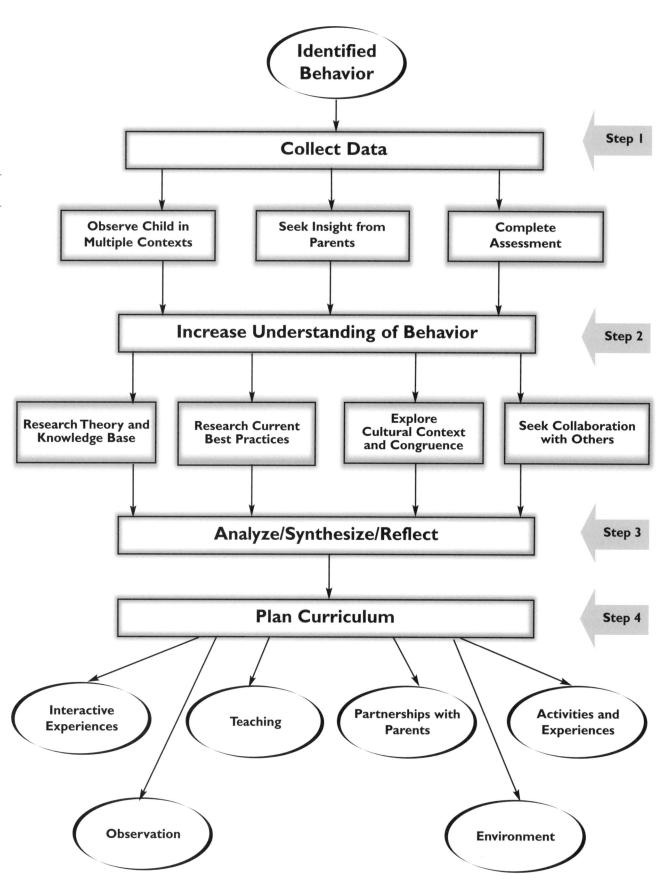

The Innovations Model

Myths or Misunderstandings

Accurate understanding of the knowledge base of care and early education sometimes requires that educators confront myths and misunderstandings that have somehow become a part of cultural context of teaching (Mooney, 2000; Shonkoff & Phillips, 2000). Sometimes these beliefs are widely held, yet inaccurate.

Innovations: Infant and Toddler Development addresses these myths and misunderstandings directly, pinpointing the points of view and detailing the reasons to question the validity of these ideas or practices.

The discussion of myths or misunderstandings is designed to encourage teachers to think about why they do what they do. Are their teaching practices and approaches really grounded in what we know, or not? In many cases, the myths or misunderstandings raise more issues and questions—indicating the transactional nature of our work with young children.

Summary

Both interactional and developmental theories help explain human development. Developmental theory posits that human development is a dynamic, sequential, and cumulative process. Interactional theory views human development as proceeding within the context of interactions—with significant others; with the social, cultural, and physical environment; and with the biological predispositions of individual genetics. *Innovations: Infant and Toddler Development* views human development from both a developmental and interactional point of view.

Developmental Theory

Infant and toddler development is a continuous though uneven cycle—a cycle of ever-increasing skills and abilities in which each period of growth is often preceded by a brief, sometimes turbulent regression. The following principles are the foundation of the developmental approach.

- Principle One—Human development is integrated. All domains of development—physical, emotional, social, and intellectual (language and cognition) are interrelated.
- Principle Two—Growth follows a universal and relatively predictable sequence.

▶ Principle Three—Each child has an individual pattern of timing of growth. Although the sequence is relatively predictable, each child's progress through the sequence is subject to variation.

▶ Principle Four—Development proceeds from the simple to the complex and from the general to the specific. Children learn to do things long before they can describe them with language or represent them with pictures or in writing.

▶ Principle Five—The interplay between contexts and experiences influences not only the general direction of development, but also the short- and long-term outcomes for children.

Interactional Theory

Intimate, reciprocal, synchronous relationships form the foundation and core of healthy development. The following principles show how interactional theory supports development.

▶ Principle One—Warm, nurturing interactions are the first irreducible need of young children.

▶ Principle Two—Interactions take place in a variety of contexts including social and cultural contexts.

▶ Principle Three —There is a dynamic relationship between biological heredity and experience.

▶ Principle Four —Children construct their own knowledge and understanding of the world. Interactions between children and the social, cultural, and physical worlds direct children's learning.

▶ Principle Five —Play is the interactive medium of development.

Tasks

Development is a task that spans a person's entire life. ***Innovations: Infant and Toddler Development*** proposes six life tasks that begin in infancy and continue as development emerges. The tasks for infants and toddlers are shown in the chart, "Developmental Tasks by Age" on page 23.

What Is Curriculum?

Innovations: Infant and Toddler Development proposes a broad view of curriculum. Within this model, curriculum is defined in its broadest sense. Curriculum is everything that can contribute to child development and the teacher's relationship with the child and the family.

Innovations: Infant and Toddler Development proposes a different model for dealing with children's behaviors. The **Innovations** model for dealing with behavior has four phases that lead to developing an individualized curriculum plan to address the identified behavior. The four phases of the model follow:

▶ Phase I: Collect Data—Information is gathered from observation, input from parents, and assessment. The result of this data-gathering process is a better picture of the behavior grounded in the developmental uniqueness of the individual child.

▶ Phase II: Increase Understanding—Next, the teacher seeks to increase understanding of behavior and to collaborate with others who may be able to help.

▶ Phase III: Analyze, Synthesize, and Reflect—Analyzing, synthesizing, and reflecting lead the way to developing appropriate curriculum to address the behavior. The outcome of this process is almost always more questions that need to be answered or researched.

▶ Phase IV: Plan Curriculum—Curriculum plans are then completed to address the child's behavior in the context of supportive and appropriate plans for activities and experiences, interactions, teaching opportunities, partnerships with parents, the environment, and continued observation and assessment.

Questions and Activities

1. What are the underlying principles of developmental theory? Give an example of how each principle can be recognized in each of the five areas of development (physical, social, emotional, cognitive, and language.)
2. Explain the following statement: "Children build their own knowledge." Give examples of ways children do so.
3. How does the teacher's definition of curriculum shape what she or he plans for young children?

References

Albrecht, K. & L.G. Miller. (2000). **Innovations: The comprehensive infant curriculum.** Beltsville, MD: Gryphon House.

Albrecht, K. & , L.G. Miller. (2000). **Innovations: The comprehensive toddler curriculum.** Beltsville, MD: Gryphon House.

Berk, L.E. (1999). *Infants and Children.* Boston: Allyn and Bacon.

Brazelton, T.B. & S.I. Greenspan. (2000). *The irreducible needs of children: What every child must have to grow, learn, and flourish.* Cambridge, MA: Perseus.

Bredekamp, S. & C. Copple. (1997). *Developmentally appropriate practice in early childhood programs, Revised edition.* Washington DC: National Association for the Education of Young Children (NAEYC).

Mooney, C.G. (2000). *Theories of childhood: An introduction to Dewey, Montessori, Erickson, Piaget, and Vygotsky.* St. Paul, MI: Redleaf Press.

Perry, B.D. (2000). Emotional development: The developmental hot zone. *Early Childhood Today*, Nov./Dec. Scholastic.

Shonkoff, J.P. & D.A. Phillips (Eds.). (2000). *From neurons to neighborhoods: The science of early childhood development.* Washington, DC: National Academy Press.

Glossary

Child Development—A field of study that seeks to understand all aspects of human growth and development from birth until adulthood. It is a part of a larger discipline, known as developmental psychology, that describes what occurs in the maturation process across the life span.

Curriculum—Defined in **Innovations** as everything that can contribute to the child's development and the teacher's relationship with the child and the family.

Developmental Domains—Interrelated areas of development, including physical, emotional, social, and intellectual (which includes language and cognition).

Developmental (or Life) Tasks—Tasks that children must accomplish in order to continue the developmental process as proposed by **Innovations: Infant and Toddler Development.**

Developmental Theory—Views child development as a series of relatively predictable stages of development that build on one another.

Interactional Theory—Views child development as taking place in the context of and as a result of interactions children have with other people, the environment, and the larger society.

Myths or Misunderstandings—Inaccurate beliefs that are part of the cultural context of teaching.

NAEYC (National Association for the Education of Young Children)—The largest professional association for early childhood educators, which publishes **Young Children**, a quarterly journal for care and early education professionals; administers the accreditation program under the auspices of the National Academy of Early Childhood Programs; and publishes the Early Childhood Research Quarterly.

Theory—Explanatory framework that organizes and gives meaning to ideas and actions, and also guides decisions within a discipline of study.

CHAPTER 2
Separating from Parents and Transitioning to School

INTRODUCTION

In Albrecht and Miller's *Innovations: The Comprehensive Infant Curriculum* and *Innovations: The Comprehensive Toddler Curriculum*, the developmental process is conceptualized as a series of life tasks that begin in infancy and continue through toddlerhood. These major tasks reflect the integrated nature of development as maturation and skill acquisition merge with the interactional and transactional experiences of living and learning within one's cultural context.

Focusing on the integrated (rather than the segregated) nature of development makes sense. It lessens the pressure on skill acquisition and content knowledge as the only measures of children's success and replaces it with a richer, broader, and more appropriate emphasis for the early years without losing the focus on the individual child.

Innovations: Infant and Toddler Development continues this tradition, providing the theory, research, and best practice outcomes of the large body of knowledge of the early childhood field. Current knowledge, research, and best practices create the opportunity for teachers to form a foundation of understanding of how children mature, grow, develop, and learn.

Developmental Tasks: Separating and Transitioning

Separating is a crucial developmental task negotiated during the first three years of life. Separating is also the first step in the process of becoming an autonomous, independent person. Children's success in moving through the developmental task of separating has lifelong implications. When children have positive and supported experiences with separation, they learn to trust the human world in which they live. If they have frustrating and unresponsive experiences with separating, they will learn to mistrust this new world. Basic trust in the world as a responsive, caring place creates a sense of security upon which development can unfold.

The toddler years are marked by many transitions that continue the lifelong task of learning to separate from home and connect to the larger world. As infants become toddlers, the number of separations and connections increases, requiring children to practice and perfect the task of transitioning among and between many different settings, experiences, and interactions.

The foundation formed by the experiences of separating and transitioning contributes to the subsequent path of development. It also forms the foundation for success with other life tasks.

Separating

Birth itself is the first separation experience an infant has—separating from the warm, protective uterine environment of the mother's body to experience the world outside. After this first experience, separating becomes a regular and frequent occurrence for infants: separating from the breast or bottle when feeding time is over, separating from Mom or Dad when holding time is over, separating from warm clothing to take a bath, separating from a familiar position to be moved around, and so on. Separating continues as infants learn to separate from favorite people, from home, and from favorite things such as toys or security items.

Transitioning

The task of separating that begins in infancy continues into toddlerhood with the task of transitioning. Toddlerhood—the period from 18 months to 3 years—is an exciting and challenging period for children and, often, for their parents and teachers. Marked by an emerging sense of self as separate and independent, this developmental period is given a wide variety of labels, such as the terrible twos, "tantrumming" twos, tumultuous twos, the search for autonomy, or the declaration of independence.

Transitions during the toddler years can be small and simple, or big and challenging. Transitions from baby bed to toddler bed, from being the only child to having a sibling, from depending on others to meet most of your needs to meeting your own needs, are all examples of transitions that occur during this period. As the number of transitions increases, toddlers may feel uncertain about them, often vacillating between viewing the change as exciting, then feeling overwhelmed. Toddlers may react to this uncertainty with increasingly resistant and oppositional behavior.

Many children enter formal early childhood education settings during this stage—expanding their interactive world dramatically. However, this expansion requires young children to learn new skills.

Chapter 2 focuses on the knowledge that is related to the tasks of separating and transitioning. A discussion of the best practices that emerge from this knowledge is also included in this chapter. The chapter ends by applying this new understanding of theory and practice to a common behavioral challenge.

Knowledge

Many theories add to our knowledge of how very young children grow and learn. The following section introduces some of the most important theories and concepts that teachers need to know about how children separate from home and transition to school to be effective in teaching very young children. Theorists are introduced and their ideas are explained. Then, these ideas are applied and put into practice in the section on best practices. When teachers discover the close connections between the theoretical underpinnings of our knowledge and the application that theory suggests, they increase their ability to interpret and apply these ideas to their interactions with children.

Mahler's Theory of Identity Formation—Developing a Sense of Self

Birth is a culminating event—the result of a biological growth process that prepares infants physically to survive in the world. What follows this physical birth is a much longer and much more complicated psychological birth—the process of becoming an individual—a separate, fully functioning person with unique thoughts, feelings, personality, and abilities. For human beings, this process is a lifelong one that begins during infancy and toddlerhood and continues throughout the life cycle. The experiences and outcomes of this identity formation process influence each stage of development, with new growth building upon previous experiences and outcomes.

Mahler's theory of identity formation proposes that there are four stages in the psychological separation-individuation process (Mahler, Pine & Bergman, 1975). In the first stage, called pre-separation/individuation, babies "tune in" to their mother's rhythms. This results in a feeling or state of oneness with the mother called symbiosis. This brief period begins at birth and lasts until three months.

Psychological "hatching" comes next in a stage called differentiation, which lasts from four months until about nine months. Many changes occur during this stage. Infants begin to develop an interest in other things in the immediate environment including objects, lights, shadows, toys, and other people, besides the primary caregiver.

During this stage the important attachment link between the primary caregiver and the child occurs. Then, babies explore their own bodies, learning about their physical boundaries from improving motor movements and practice. These gains in skills fuel an interest in the environment and send babies on explorations away from their loved ones, resulting in the completion of the "hatching" process. The final change during this stage is the emerging awareness that others in the environment are not their mothers or primary caregivers. Usually apparent as the result of separation or stranger anxiety, this awareness of the separateness of their primary caregiver illustrates that the baby has a clear sense of self as separate.

During the next stage, called practice, children experiment and practice being away from their primary caregivers for increasingly longer periods of time, always maintaining visual and non-verbal contact as they explore. Called emotional refueling, this visual and non-verbal connection is crucial to developing the emotional skill of being apart. As the length of time the child is away from the primary caregiver increases, supported by refueling, the child's sense of self as separate grows. Slowly, periods of separation begin to be tolerated as the child copes with the loss of the primary caregiver through exploratory and dramatic play. This stage lasts from 10 to 15 months.

The final stage in Mahler's theory of identity formation is rapprochement. During this period, children eagerly share all of their discoveries, toys, experiences, skills, and objects with their primary caregivers and seek to be with and play with these important people most of the time. As this interest expands to include peers, conflicts from the emerging sense of autonomy and individuation lead to many difficulties, often with children wanting their important caregivers to "fix" all of their difficulties. This stage, which lasts from 16 to 24 months, ends with children carrying clear images of their primary caregivers in their minds. These images can be used to cope when these important people are not visually or physically available.

Now, let's look further at what identity formation and individuation look like during infancy and toddlerhood.

Mahler's Four Stages of Identity Formation

▶ Pre-Separation/ Individuation

▶ Differentiation

▶ Practice

▶ Rapprochement

Individuation in Infancy

At birth, infants and their mothers experience both physical and psychological closeness. Physical closeness is most evident in the amount of physical support the infant needs to be fed, comforted, held, and nurtured. Psychological closeness is evident in the ways that caregivers read and respond to the baby's cues and the way that babies initiate, react, and sustain interactions with their caregivers. Both infant and caregiver take an active part in creating both physical and psychological closeness.

Babies have much to learn during the beginnings of individuation. Early understandings about self emerge during infancy. These discoveries include both physical and emotional awareness (Mahler, Pine & Bergman, 1975). For example, babies learn that they are physically and emotionally connected to their mothers/caregivers while they nurse or drink a bottle. When feeding ends, babies learn that the physical connection has ended but that the emotional connection continues.

As babies discover that they are different and separate from their caregivers, they make another remarkable discovery—they can make things happen! This ability to act and to initiate is a crucial step in the individuation process. For example, infants discover early that they are able to keep nurturing interactions going with their caregivers by gazing, cooing, smiling, and using other communication strategies. Babies increase these behaviors to encourage caregivers to continue the nurturing interactions of holding and cuddling even after feeding is finished.

As infants mature, this ability to act and initiate is obvious as they begin to make things happen to themselves (such as clinging to a security item to calm oneself down), and to the environment (for example, crawling after a toy spotted across the room). Increasing physical skills allow babies to widen their exploration of the environment, changing their whole perspective. From this new vantage point, infants experience many opportunities to practice and perfect problem-solving, enhancing their feelings of competence as autonomous, capable individuals.

Mahler says individuation emerges from intimate, healthy, reciprocal relationships with caregivers. To progress in individuating, infants need the security of knowing that they are protected, watched, valued, respected, and loved by someone special. They give us many cues that this is the case. They look to caregivers to "check out" their actions. They return to the physical safety of their caregiver's arms when they are hurt, frightened, or overwhelmed by their emotions. They use their caregivers to help them negotiate hunger, fatigue, and illness.

Creating a balance—the knowledge and understanding of when to depend on caregivers and when to depend on your own abilities is at the heart of individuation. Children who emerge from infancy with a clear understanding of this balance are poised and ready to continue the individuation process in toddlerhood.

In toddlerhood, individuation adds some new twists. Toddlers who are confident of their physical separateness from their caregivers and secure in their abilities to make things happen and initiate action, begin to vacillate between being able to handle independence and autonomy and being unable to handle it.

Called rapprochement in the psychoanalytical literature, individuation during this period is characterized by a need for closeness, approval, intimacy, and emotional availability of caregivers on the child's terms (see page 39 on Mahler's theory). The toddler is now clear about his separateness and seeks to maintain it or sever it, depending on the situation. Toddlers often become bossy, demanding, resistant, negative, and sometimes even hostile and aggressive as they struggle with separateness.

Separations once again become an issue as toddlers learn that they are not really in control of their caregivers—that caregivers have an independent existence that is unrelated to what the toddler does. This results in even more attempts to influence caregivers at times of separation. Many cultural differences influence how children are encouraged to respond to separation anxiety. For some children, transitional objects, such as pacifiers, blankets, and stuffed animals are usually entrenched firmly in the child's coping strategies and are used often to facilitate recovery from stressful events.

Then, toddlers' exploration of the social world expands, and they discover social interactions as a way to extend their experiential worlds. Social interaction with other adults (besides parents and primary caregivers) and other children broadens their experiences with autonomous and independent behavior and gives toddlers opportunities to practice these new skills and abilities.

Fear of strangers and the unknown peaks during toddlerhood. Stranger anxiety has its roots in the ambivalence of self-identity and the awareness of separateness from parents and primary caregivers. Can I handle this new or strange experience alone, without support or help from primary caregivers, or not? As children successfully negotiate experiences with strangers and other fearful experiences with the help of their caregivers, self-confidence in handling novel situations and strangers develops.

Growth in language and cognition signals that children are achieving stable self-identities. Young children use spoken language to express independence and autonomy, get needs met, and communicate feelings with caregivers. They also use emerging cognitive skills to predict reunions with significant others.

Individuation is not over. It continues throughout the life span with many additional challenges and dilemmas. Yet, at the end of the second year, toddlers have accomplished major steps in the self-identity formation process. They are now able to see themselves as separate and different from their parents or primary caregivers. They feel and act autonomously and independently. And, they are able to interact with the social world around them in increasingly sophisticated ways. These behaviors are all indicators of success in the early individuation process.

Myth or Misunderstanding
NOT MUCH IS HAPPENING TO CHILDREN DURING THE FIRST THREE YEARS.

Susanna, a teacher with a bachelor's degree in early childhood education, was asked in an interview to talk about her favorite age group of children. She explained how she adored infants and toddlers because of their enthusiasm and innocence. Then, Susanna went on to say that she wanted to work with older children because they were learning so much more during the preschool years than infants and toddlers.

This teacher, though trained in early childhood education, had embraced the myth that older children are learning more than younger children. In fact, the most rapid growth and learning occur during the first three years of life. Babies begin life totally dependent on others to care for them. Then, they emerge from toddlerhood having perfected the physical skills of walking, the emotional skills of sustained attachment to others, the social skills of making friends and participating in groups, and a host of cognitive skills including communicating both verbally and non-verbally and thinking about a wide range of ideas and concepts. This change is not only one of the most dramatic of the life span, but also it is one of the most influential. Children's development during the first three years of life influences the direction of future development and the quality of the developmental experience. A great deal is happening to infants and toddlers and most of "what's happening" influences the kind of preschooler the child will become.

What should happen next? Discuss the advantages and disadvantages of placing Susanna with preschool children. What might the pitfalls be if she is offered a job with infants and toddlers?

Implications of Identity Formation for Separating from Home and Transitioning to School

Mahler's theory creates a blueprint for supporting children in the individuation process in schools. Children are sequentially moving through the individuation process with their teachers, just as they are with their primary caregivers at home. They use teachers as attachment figures and reference them to support exploration.

Children are learning lessons that are incorporated into their emerging sense of self throughout the separation/individuation process. Children receive and use the cues they get from important adults during the refueling process. This information helps them decide what to be afraid of, which behaviors are appropriate and which ones aren't, how well they communicated with their loved ones, whether they were successful in getting their needs met, which emotions can be safely expressed and at what intensity, and how engaging others feel they are.

The congruence between the process as it unfolds at home and the process as it unfolds at school is crucial to identity formation (Lally, 1995). When these two worldviews match, children's views of themselves stabilize and the identity formation process continues. If these views conflict, children's sense of self as it is emerging may be challenged or compromised by their experiences.

Maslow's Hierarchy of Needs

Maslow (1954) conceptualized a Hierarchy of Needs that serves as a backdrop to how children develop and learn across the life span. The theory proposes that basic needs are arranged in a hierarchical order and that higher order needs cannot be addressed without satisfaction of previous levels.

The first level of needs is related to physiological survival and well-being. Food, water, clothing, shelter, hygiene, and health care are examples of some of the basic needs of this level. The second level of needs relates to physical safety and psychological security. This includes safety from physical dangers and psychological needs, such as the need for touch and responsive nurturing from significant caregivers.

Needs relating to love and belonging form the third level of the hierarchy. Emotional support from a limited number of consistent, responsive adults and interactions with other children are both required to meet this need. This is a reciprocal need—one that is necessary to receive as well as to give. The need for self-esteem and self-worth is the fourth level of the needs hierarchy. When a feeling of love and belonging is established through emotional support, the child develops self-esteem and a feeling of self-worth.

Finally, the need to know and understand is the fifth level of Maslow's Hierarchy of Needs. Human beings cannot get to this level until needs have been met at all of the other levels.

Maslow's Hierarchy of Needs

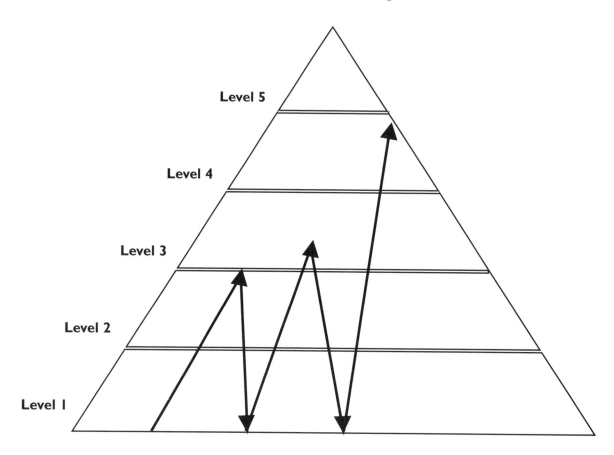

Maslow proposed that each need grows out of the satisfaction of the previous one and that the process of meeting needs can be regressive. In other words, if a child has progressed to the level of needing belonging and love, and suddenly is threatened physically by disease, his need level will revert from level three to level one until that need for physiological survival and well-being is once again satisfied.

Implications of Maslow's Hierarchy of Needs for Separating from Home and Transitioning to School

Maslow's theory has many implications for the tasks of separating and transitioning. If Maslow's ideas that one need must be met before growth can occur are correct, then meeting needs in order becomes a crucial consideration. Hungry or tired children will not be good candidates for stimulation or teaching. If children don't feel safe, they are unlikely to be interested in exploring an attractive environment. And, if children are not sure their caregivers will respond to them consistently, they are not likely to invest in establishing relationships.

Maslow's ideas about regression also are instructive for how children separate from home and transition to school. From this theoretical point of view, separating and transitioning can cause regression, resulting in the child regressing to an earlier level of need. Along with the regression, children will need to rebuild their sense of survival, feeling safe, or belonging before being able to move on.

Temperament

Regardless of the imprint of biology, environment, parents, and culture, every child is born with a personality—a temperament that guides and influences his approach to the world. Genetically determined, a child's temperament will manifest itself in a variety of character traits (Chess & Thomas, 1987). These stable differences in personality are a major consideration in predicting psychological difficulties later in life.

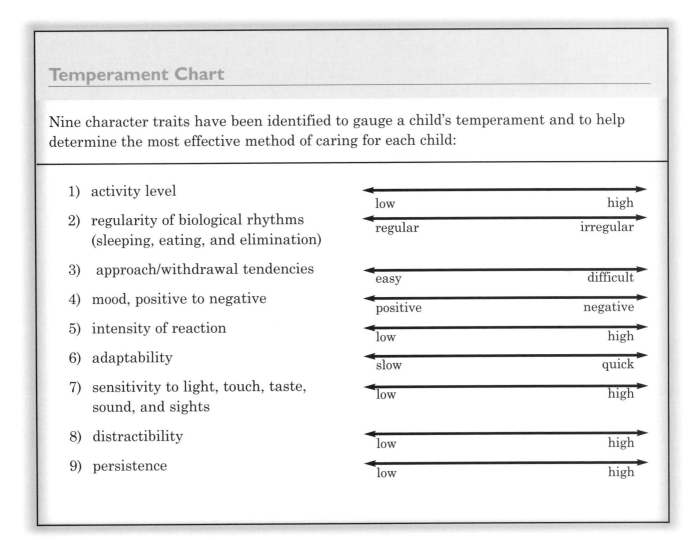

Temperament Chart

Nine character traits have been identified to gauge a child's temperament and to help determine the most effective method of caring for each child:

1) activity level — low ⟷ high

2) regularity of biological rhythms (sleeping, eating, and elimination) — regular ⟷ irregular

3) approach/withdrawal tendencies — easy ⟷ difficult

4) mood, positive to negative — positive ⟷ negative

5) intensity of reaction — low ⟷ high

6) adaptability — slow ⟷ quick

7) sensitivity to light, touch, taste, sound, and sights — low ⟷ high

8) distractibility — low ⟷ high

9) persistence — low ⟷ high

Each of these traits varies along a continuum. Teachers and parents can observe and identify where children are on each continuum. Psychologist Alicia Liebermann combined the characteristics of temperament into three groups and describes them as flexible, fearful, or feisty (California State Department of Education, 1990).

The Flexible Child—The traits of flexible children include regular biological rhythms, adaptability to change and new situations, low intensity, low sensitivity, and positive mood. In school, flexible children are easily recognizable but can be overlooked because they do not demand attention. It is important to the development of flexible children that adults devote attention to them even though they do not demand it.

The Fearful Child—Fearful children avoid new situations and are slow to warm to new people and experiences. Their cautious ways mean that adults must go slowly with them, allowing them to observe a new activity or situation before approaching it. Teachers also may need to introduce fearful children to new stimuli and only gradually withdraw their support as caution gives way to interest and enjoyment.

The Feisty Child—Feisty children have irregular rhythms and are very active, intense and easily distracted, sensitive, and moody. Feisty children run rather than walk, push the limits, and respond impulsively with intense emotions. Well-planned transitions are very important to feisty children who will resist being rushed. Feisty children need opportunities for active play, as well as a chance to experience quiet play when the mood strikes.

Myth or Misunderstanding
ALL CHILDREN ARE ALIKE.

This myth is a curious one. It doesn't take most teachers long to figure out that each of the children in their group is an individual—unlike all the others. Temperament, developmental uniqueness, biological predispositions, and experience all contribute to children being one of a kind. Yet, this myth persists. Perhaps it is related to the democratic tradition of the United States or to the fundamentally American idea of equality for all. Or, perhaps the attempts at homogeneous grouping in elementary education have perpetuated this misunderstanding.

Current thinking in care and early education views each child as an individual—a product of culture, genetic predispositions, the interactive experiences of childhood (in either direction, positive or negative), and developmental uniqueness, which are all further influenced by temperamental differences and experience. Developmentally appropriate practice encourages teachers to view development from this complex, yet more accurate point of view.

Discuss with another teacher or student the things that influenced your early development. Which were significant to your future growth and development?

Temperament is relatively stable, but not unchanging. Innate temperament is influenced by experience and these experiences can be compensating ones. For example, a fearful child can learn, with the help and support of caring adults, to approach new situations or to manage the fear of new experiences. Feisty children can learn to manage intense feelings and express them appropriately when supported by teachers in recovering from emotional outbursts. Flexible children can learn appropriate ways to ask for and receive needed attention even though the adults around them are busy. Sensitive parenting and teaching are mediating experiences that support children's temperamental characteristics.

Implications of Temperament for Separating from Home and Transitioning to School

Two implications of temperament for the tasks of separating and transitioning are clear. First, teachers have a wonderful opportunity to validate parents' knowledge of their child by exploring temperamental differences. Armed with this information, teachers can then respond to children in ways that are compatible with each child's unique temperamental style. Second, teachers can use their understanding of the child's unique temperament to get in synchrony with the child—approaching a fearful child slowly and with gentle communication, planning ways for feisty children to have individualized schedules, and attending to flexible children even when they don't demand attention.

Components of Developmental Uniqueness

Although children's development follows a relatively predictable, identifiable sequence, there are components of uniqueness within that sequence. One of the components is the child's pace of development—the pattern and timing of maturation and skill acquisition. This pattern varies within and across domains of development. The best example of this principle is seen in the onset of walking. One child might walk at 8–9 months, while another walks at 12–13 months, while still another walks between 16–17 months. All of these children moved sequentially through the steps of learning to walk within the time period they were expected to do so developmentally. However, each child's pace and timing were different.

The methods they used to perfect walking may also have been different. One child might have pulled up and cruised around anything and everything that could provide support for developing balance. Another might have worked only on perfecting stand-and-balance skills before attempting to take steps.

A second component of uniqueness is the child's integration of developmental domains. Development is integrated, with growth in one sphere closely tied to and influenced by development in other areas. For example, emotional development during toddlerhood influences children's ability to access and use social skills with friends, while social interest in what others are doing emerges from stability in emotional relationships.

Yet, the way children's domains of development are integrated varies. Children may have a dominant domain that leads the developmental process (Perry, 2000). For example, a child may mature or learn skills in one domain, such as the physical domain, before maturing or learning new skills in other domains.

Or, domains may dominate sequentially with a child learning new physical skills first, then emotional skills, then language skills, then cognitive skills, and then social skills. Or, domains may be so integrated that development proceeds in tandem in each area with parents and teachers noticing maturation or skill acquisition in all areas of development at the same time.

These subtle differences are important. Early indications of intelligences (Gardner, 1983) or learning styles (Scanlon, 1988), and risk factors (Shonkoff & Phillips, 2000), are often extrapolated from children's unique integration of developmental domains.

A third component of uniqueness is the sporadic and uneven nature of development. Developmental growth in children seems to come in spurts. A child might make no developmental progress at all for a few weeks. Then, all of a sudden the child may make major strides, acquiring new skills in several different areas seemingly all at once. Or, development may be steady and incremental—either within or across domains of development.

An example of uniqueness within domains might be the child who works hard on physical development until the ability to pull to a stand is acquired, then moves on to language development or cognitive skill acquisition, acquiring new skills in separate domains sequentially. An example across domains of development can be seen in the child who works on the growth in each developmental domain until maturation or skill acquisition is gained (learning to scoot on the tummy, to use one word to communicate needs, to find a hidden object when the hiding is observed, to begin to object to separation from the most familiar caregiver), then moves on.

Brain research has produced evidence that there are also biological components of uniqueness. When children's brains are developing, the process of synaptogenesis—the connecting of brain cells together in communicating neural pathways—is affected by experience. Some synaptogenesis is the result of experiences that the brain is biologically prepared to receive—genetically built-in pauses for external stimulation. Other synaptogenesis is dependent on experience from happenings and activities most children have as they grow and develop in the interactive world—that then triggers additional synaptic connections. Because each child's experiences (both experience-expectant and experience-dependent) are unique, they create a unique pattern of connections and neural pathways. As a result, no two brains form and strengthen exactly the same neural pathways (Shonkoff & Phillips, 2000; Shore, 1997).

Exploring Alternate Developmental Pathways

Variations in developmental growth are viewed as alternate developmental pathways—not deviant development but development that proceeds uniquely for one child as compared to other children. Children who never crawled or pulled to a stand before they crawled, or children with physical impairments (such as blindness and deafness) who still develop basic abilities to communicate or navigate their environments, illustrate the concept of alternate developmental pathways. They got to the same or similar place developmentally in a unique and different way. Because the components of uniqueness vary within the same child and across children, viewing these variations as alternate, yet normal development lessens the dependence on normative data as the measuring stick of developmental progress.

Implications of Developmental Uniqueness and Alternate Developmental Pathways for Separating from Home and Transitioning to School

One of the important roles of parents and teachers is to understand each child's developmental uniqueness and alternate developmental pathways. This knowledge is acquired through careful observations, insight shared by parents, and accurate assessment of the skills and abilities children have rather than focusing on the skills and abilities children don't have or can't do.

The need to understand the uniqueness of each child creates an ideal way to connect with parents and validate their important contribution to their child's care and early education. Together, teachers and parents can begin the journey to discover uniquenesses and alternate developmental pathways, cementing a mutual commitment to working together in the child's best interest.

Myth or Misunderstanding
SOME CHILDREN DEVELOP FASTER (OR SLOWER) THAN OTHERS DO.

She is "ahead" of her class. He is falling "behind" his peer group. She walked "before" her sister. These types of normative comparisons, which contrast one child to a group of children, are commonly made by parents and teachers in care and early education settings.

All children have unique patterns, timing, and paces of development. When presented normatively (as in comparing one child against the range of typically developing children), children get value-based labels such as "ahead" or "behind" rather than descriptive labels that identify children's competence and what they can "do" instead of what they can't or don't do. It is the job of parents and teachers to come to know and understand these naturally occurring variations in the pace and progress of development without labeling children or limiting their potential.

Identify the risks of normative comparisons. When can such comparisons be helpful?

Best Practices

Understanding of developmental and interactional theories informs the practices of infant and toddler teachers. Best practices reflect the integration and synthesis of knowledge joined with creative and thoughtful interpretation and implementation.

Each chapter of **Innovations: Infant and Toddler Development** proposes a number of best practices that support developmental tasks in the early childhood classroom. Some of these suggested practices are well grounded in the literature of our field and have wide support as the "best" practice at this time, often with extensive ideas for implementation. Others are ideas or suggestions that are recommended but that have not yet received wide attention.

Conduct Gradual Enrollments

One of the best ways to facilitate a child's adjustment to any new early childhood experience is to encourage the parents and the child to participate with the teacher in a gradual enrollment process. Gradual enrollment allows teachers to consider Maslow's ideas about need levels, develop an understanding of temperamental developmental uniqueness, and identify alternate developmental pathways, as well as give children time to begin the process of forming a relationship with the teacher. Young children have little experience with change and need time to adjust to new settings. Parents need to understand how new environments work and how teachers will handle the dynamic tasks of caregiving and early education. Gradual enrollment gives children, teachers, and parents time. Although there is no single correct way to do the gradual enrollment, most often it follows the steps outlined at left.

The Steps of Gradual Enrollment

1. The parent or a person familiar to the child brings him to school.
2. The child's things are put away in a labeled cubby.
3. The parent sits on the floor with the child or moves about the room allowing the child to play in the environment or watch the teachers, parents, and other children.
4. The child's teacher is near during this time but is not in a hurry to interact with the child. The teacher uses this time to observe the child and the parents in action as she or he continues to care for other children and follow the day's routine.
5. As the parent and child settle in, the parent can talk with the teacher as she or he moves about the room caring for other children. As this happens, the teacher's voice will become familiar to the child.
6. When the child needs feeding, diapering, or a nap, the parent proceeds with routine care. The teacher watches and observes.
7. Gradually, during subsequent visits or as the day progresses, the parent and the teacher reverse roles, with the parent becoming the observer and the teacher interacting directly with the child.

This approach is called inserviamento in the infant and toddler schools of Italy and is conducted both with individual children and with small cohort groups who begin their school experience together at the same time. Inserviamento is not only an adjustment and alignment time for infants and toddlers, but also a time for parents and teachers to get to know each other and the other children in the group as well as to form partnerships together for the education of the child (Gandini & Edwards, 2001).

Ideally, there are no prerequisites, standardized approach, or duration of gradual enrollment. It could take place over a week or so, with the parent and child staying one to two hours the first day and working up to a full day. It also could occur over a much longer period of time, depending on how the child and family are adjusting to the transition to school. Or, the process could be completed in a few days with additional plans for reconnections occurring as needed by the child, the parents, or the teachers.

Many parents are able to arrange this much time for transition. For those who can't, teachers and families can discuss variations. A family might be able to spend two days in gradual enrollment. Or, a well-known relative or family friend (like a grandparent or regular babysitter) may be able to provide the bridge between home and school. Or, the teacher might do a home visit or two to begin the relationship prior to starting school. Or, the parent might stay at school for the first hour or so, return for lunch and naptime, then stay a while at the end of the first few days. These types of arrangements give the child experience with the new environment before being left to cope in the new setting without support from his primary attachment figures.

Myth or Misunderstanding
PARENTS MAKE IT MORE DIFFICULT FOR CHILDREN TO ADJUST TO NEW SETTINGS.

Sam, a primary caregiver of a group of five toddlers, is preparing to add Ling Li to his group. After Ling Li's first visit to the classroom with her mother, Sam suggests that Ying Chu accept that her daughter is going to cry and that she go ahead and leave. He feels that the tears have to fall sometime, why not go ahead and get it over with now?

What Sam is missing is how Ling Li's mother can serve as her secure base as she becomes comfortable in the classroom and begins to develop a relationship with her new teacher. And, he is also missing that Ling Li is sensitive to her mother's cues about the classroom. If Ying Chu feels comfortable with the classroom and with Sam, she will communicate that comfort to Ling Li, facilitating the transition to school. Called social referencing, this skill is in place in most children before their first birthday and includes the ability to take cues from their primary caregivers and to use this information in deciding whether to continue to play or to stop and retreat to the safety of the caregiver's arms (Mahler, Pine & Bergman, 1975).

What should happen next? How can Sam's supervisor help him understand the support Ying Chu could provide?

Secondary Benefits of Gradual Enrollment

Although most schools do not require gradual enrollment, it is one of the most important components of the parent/school connection. It helps both parties understand what to expect. When parents are desperate to begin school immediately and cannot participate in the gradual enrollment process, they may have more difficulty adjusting to the school, complain more often, and drop out at a higher rate. This reality in itself is enough reason to consider gradual enrollment important. Dropping out of one school and moving to another, for whatever reason, requires the child to go through the adjustment process again, an experience that can cause anxiety and delay subsequent adjustment.

Further, parents who are unsuccessful in calibrating their expectations about their child's care and early education and who don't have the time to work cooperatively with the teacher to make sure the child's adjustment is well planned and implemented, may be less involved, have more complaints, conflicts, and misunderstandings. This makes creating a partnership between parents and teachers even more difficult.

Not providing an opportunity to gradually enroll a child in school also underestimates parents' interest in their children's adjustment to school. Many parents will be able to provide the gradual enrollment period, arranging it to fit the family's needs and resources. The lack of policies and procedures for gradually enrolling children puts schools in the position of responding institutionally to families and children. In doing so, schools create barriers and boundaries that impinge on the developing partnership with parents.

Don't skip gradual enrollment; it is the firm foundation upon which a mutual relationship between parents and teachers is built. It also gives infants and toddlers the time they need to adjust to new places, people, and stimulation.

Create Supportive Environments

Often, the transition from home and parents to school is a difficult one for children because the two environments are so very different. Imagine going from a closed, soft, dimly lit place with familiar smells to an open, sanitized one with bright lights and unfamiliar scents. No wonder the first week or more in a new school setting can be difficult! To create environments that support the developmental tasks of separating and transitioning, consider the following for both infants and toddlers:

Create a sense of calm. Creating a supportive environment begins with the use of carpets, curtains, blankets, and pillows to absorb sounds and keep them from bouncing off hard surfaces.

Include soft elements in the room. Soft elements help to make the environment more home-like. Cuddle toys like stuffed animals and terrycloth dolls give children items to hold and use to comfort themselves. Carpet on the floor, a quilt used during floor time, and cushions in the library also add softness.

Create a place for children's things. This gives parents and children a feeling of security and helps avoid lost articles. A cubby and a set of hooks provide a place for the diaper bag, diapers, extra clothing, security items from home, art projects, and notes between home and school. Family photographs may be kept in the cubby, covered with clear contact paper and placed low on the wall so toddlers can see them, or in the infant's crib. Maslow's theory indicates that this might contribute to a child's or family's need level, providing a sense of belonging.

Establish a predictable environment. Infants and toddlers need a predictable environment with both novel and interesting features including color, texture, sensory experiences, and different toys. Novelty also can be accomplished through mirrors, art projects hanging on the walls, mobiles, activity bars and boxes, appropriate music, and sensory experiences, such as smell jars, flour activities, paints, and texture experiences.

A comfortable, calm pace throughout the day is an important part of a predictable environment. Major elements in the classroom, such as cribs, low carts, chairs, food preparation area, and changing area, stay the same.

Create spaces within the classroom with different functions. Because the individual needs of infants and toddlers vary over the period of the day or even weeks/months, different spaces are needed to meet these different needs. Create places to be alone, places to be near or with friends, and places to be with teacher.

Create places to be alone. This is especially important when children are transitioning in the very stimulating environments in which young children find themselves. Teachers can create these spaces without sacrificing visual supervision of all children. By breaking up large open spaces, teachers can create smaller, more intimate settings. Children will pursue activities of interest for relatively long periods of time if they are not interrupted. The smaller spaces help keep interruptions to a minimum. Low carts, large soft blocks, toy bars, and activity areas can help create the places to play without interruption. Mahler's ideas about individuation view the opportunity to feel close to and connected to the primary caregiver and the teacher as conducive to identity formation. Further, Maslow's Hierarchy of Needs supports starting with the basics.

Myth or Misunderstanding
ENVIRONMENTS FOR INFANTS AND TODDLERS DON'T MATTER MUCH.

Cara's classroom shows her interest in keeping many toys and materials available to infants and toddlers. There are boxes of toys stacked in the corners, toy boxes full to overflowing, and paper sacks full of discarded items just waiting to be converted into interesting toys and materials to stimulate her children.

What Cara does not see is the amount of stimulation and distraction created by the mounds of clutter and collections. She is unaware that children need order in their environments to be able to determine what to explore and what to ignore (Lowman & Ruhmann, 1998). Environments teach (Edwards, Gandini & Forman, 1998). We want children to experience novelty in the toys and materials they play with and predictability in the location of important resources and the availability of sensitive adults. Clutter, disorganization, and broken toys are roadblocks to these important experiences.

What should happen next? Make an improvement plan for Cara's classroom environment with actions that need to be taken.

Create places to be with friends. Children develop a multi-sensory interest in the world around them. Spectator sports are very popular in the infant and toddler classroom—watching what other children are doing, watching what adults are doing, listening to sounds and noises, sensing changes in smells in the classroom, and touching friends who are nearby. Provide enough space to squirm and roll around, perhaps to scoot or crawl while playing.

Infants who are not yet mobile have little to say about where they are in the environment. Teachers are responsible for providing changes in scenery, position, and stimulation. Examples of changes in scenery include:

- Moving the child from a soft blanket on the floor to a baby bouncer that moves when the baby's arms and legs are wiggled
- Moving the baby from the blanket on the floor to the arms of the teacher, so the baby can look around and orient to a part of the classroom that wasn't visible from his back
- Laying babies side by side, so they can see each other when they turn their heads from side to side, discovering their friends, and so on

Changes in position help infants use new muscles as well as see new things. Babies need to be moved from back to stomach or stomach to back. They may like being able to sit with support from pillows or horseshoe rings so they can scan the environment or watch the activity of the classroom. They may enjoy practicing weight bearing to strengthen legs with the support of their teacher's arms.

Children also like changes in stimulation sources. Bouncing in warm water or on bubble wrap in a jumper provides very different experiences. Bouncing while you watch your friends is very different from bouncing while your teacher counts your bounces and applauds your strong leg muscles.

Toddlers are mobile and able to choose specific toys for play. Provide a variety of toddler toys, including manipulatives, puzzles, dolls, blocks, and books arranged on low shelves. Toddlers will choose, play with, and discard many toys as they play. Use clear containers that are labeled with a picture of the contents and the name of the objects. Putting toys in their appropriate containers can be a game at the end of play.

Create meltdown places. Toddlers need meltdown places, places where they can be alone while they regain composure. These spaces should be carpeted and away from sharp edges of furniture. While children are losing control and then getting it back, teachers must be able to see them and support them. Sometimes, even something as simple as sitting in a cardboard box can give a toddler the feeling of being alone and of being able to regroup emotionally and physically.

Create opportunities for different perspectives. Children often observe before they are able to join in an activity. Different perspectives are helpful. Multiple levels in the environment are one way to provide places for infants and toddlers to be away from others and still observe the action. A raised platform or even foam blocks joined together can create this perspective. Additionally, windows in walls, in doors, and between classrooms provide young children an opportunity to participate in one of their favorite activities—watching other children, adults, cars, animals, and the environment.

Create opportunities to climb. As soon as they are mobile, children enjoy actively exploring their environment. They like to climb and improve their climbing skills rapidly during toddlerhood. Although toddlers are growing and changing physically, they are still top-heavy. This can be a problem when climbing. Provide low climbing pieces of equipment and a cushioned fall zone both indoors and outdoors.

Create ways to decrease and increase stimulation. Teachers must be able to increase and decrease the level of activity and stimulation in the classroom. Decreasing the amount of light, or increasing it, or providing incandescent as well as florescent and full-spectrum lighting are examples of ways to change stimulation levels. Adding quiet music, removing all background noise, and replacing it with sounds of nature are others. Check your classroom to see which of these dimensions are under your control and can be managed as needed.

Create places to be with teacher. This allows the kind of intimate communication and face-to-face contact that Gerber and Johnson (1997) and Greenspan (1999) term "falling in love with baby." Such intimacy helps create a feeling of security. Diapering and eating experiences allow the teacher and child to enjoy one-on-one time. Create places that allow children to have precious time alone with their teacher. Intimacy creates strong bonds between the teacher and the child and is valuable, brain-stimulating curriculum!

Invest in Observation

Good teachers build an understanding of each child in their group by being good observers. Observation informs practice and serves as the foundation for matching the educational process to emerging development. This goodness of fit is crucial for maximizing infant and toddler potential. Without it, children rarely experience true learning moments. So powerful is the investment in observation that it is considered transformational to the teaching process (Curtis & Carter, 2000).

Observing as a teaching role is embedded throughout *Innovations: Infant and Toddler Development*. The thorough, accurate, systematic collection and organization of observational information about individual children in the context of classroom will both enlighten and inform all aspects of teaching. Observation serves as a foundation for matching teaching and curriculum to individual children.

During the developmental tasks of separating and transitioning, observation is directed at understanding two areas:

1) each child's components of uniqueness or alternate developmental pathways, and
2) each child's temperamental characteristics.

Understanding each child's components of uniqueness may require continued observation, while studying the temperamental characteristics of each child may be uncovered more directly.

Observe to Uncover Components of Uniqueness and Alternate Developmental Pathways for Each Child

The first goal of observation is to uncover the components of uniqueness and alternate developmental pathways of each child (see page 50 for a discussion of the components of developmental uniqueness). Understanding each child's pace and timing of development in each domain (physical, social, emotional and intellectual, which includes language and cognition), and understanding the relationship between developmental domains are important areas of observation. The integration illuminates learning styles and understanding of each child's pattern of fits and spurts that accompany growth.

Observe for Temperamental Differences

The second goal of observation is to uncover each child's temperamental characteristics. Temperament is innate—part of the child's biological personality. An understanding of temperament leads teachers to improve the goodness of fit between their interactions and the child's unique temperamental needs. And, temperamental differences are not unalterable (Chess & Thomas,

1987). Sensitive teaching and parenting practices can impact temperament. For example, helping a fearful child develop coping strategies for managing his hesitancy in new situations may decrease discomfort with new situations and influence the child's response to novel situations.

Validate What Moms and Dads Know

Many parents feel insecure in their roles as their child's first and most important teachers. Some parents try to read everything possible on child rearing and development to try to overcome their feelings of uncertainty and inadequacy. Others try to turn the responsibility for parenting over to teachers, asking teachers to make decisions that are really parenting decisions. Teachers can help parents by validating the extensive knowledge they have about their child and supporting their parental roles.

Teachers and parents have different views. Parents view the school world through their child's experience; teachers view the school world through the eyes of the group. Further, teachers often disagree with how parents are handling parenting issues because home strategies or techniques often differ from those used at school. Teachers who disagree with parents may find it difficult to validate parents.

Despite the fact that children may spend more waking time in the company of their teacher, parents still have a more profound effect on infants than any other factor. In fact, parents have the most influence on their children's development (Shonkoff & Phillips, 2000). So, when parents want to know what they can do to help their children, embrace their interest and encourage them to stay involved in their child's school and to enjoy being the most influential people in their child's life.

Actively Facilitate Adjustment

How Long Will Adjustment Take?

Many parents view the first few days of a child's school experience as an indication of how things will be when the child completes the adjustment process. Unfortunately, for infants and toddlers, the initial experience is just the beginning. Children who are just beginning school may take months to complete the transition process. In general, though, most children are well on their way in about six weeks.

What should parents expect as the adjustment process unfolds? For one- to three-month-olds, the initial visit to school may be exciting and interesting or overwhelming. Good school environments are home-like and comfortable but are also more stimulating than home environments. Depending on the baby's temperament, the response could be interest and curiosity or anxiety and over-stimulation. Babies at this age may initially resist routines like sleeping and eating, or they may shut down and sleep during the entire experience.

For three- to nine-month-olds, the novel environment will probably be engaging, particularly if Mom or Dad is facilitating the experience. The most common reaction to the adjustment process is to be so interested in the new environment that routines like sleeping and eating are interrupted. Don't panic if this occurs. A typical schedule will return as the novelty wears off. Expect this part of adjustment to take as much as two weeks.

Children who start school when they are 9- to 14-months old seem to need the longest adjustment period. Separation and stranger anxiety, perfectly normal stages in the development of attachment, increase the infant's reluctance toward new experiences and the baby's need to have Mom or Dad close. Children who are at this age or stage may need as much as six weeks to complete the transition to school.

Myth or Misunderstanding
WE HAD A GOOD DAY SO THE CHILD MUST BE "ADJUSTING."

Both parents and teachers often have unrealistic expectations about transitions for very young children. Parents sometimes expect children to act just like they act at home in the new setting and are confused when their child clings, cries, or refuses to play. Teachers sometimes resist making the investment in a new child until they are sure things are going to work out and the child will stay.

Adjustment is a process that takes place over time. The amount of time can rarely be prescribed before the process begins to unfold. Teachers, program directors, principals, administrators, and parents are all partners in making the process work for each child. They are also responsible for insuring that policies and procedures are in place to support children who may have a harder time with transitions than those who make the transition easily, as well as providing extra support for teachers as they invest in helping new children adjust.

Plan a staff meeting to address this issue with teachers. Focus your plans on ways teachers can help parents be realistic.

Starting school between 14 and 18 months is usually met with enthusiasm or concern, depending on the infant's temperament, stage of attachment, and experience with new environments. The good news about this age is that infants are usually easy to distract and redirect into interactions and play after Mom or Dad leaves.

Children who are 18–24 months old are often very uncomfortable in new settings and resist participating.

They may cling to their parents and refuse to join in activities. Give children who are in this age group plenty of time to stay close and watch while they get comfortable with the new setting. Provide nonverbal support if they do venture out (smile, nod your head, or hold a hand and go along.) Expect to see "tank-up behavior"—venturing out, then coming back for comfort and support, then venturing out again.

Children who are 24–30 months old may be cautious about new settings with new people, but their curiosity and interest in the environment are often enough to overcome their anxiety. Encouragement from familiar adults is usually all that is needed to bridge the gap. Or, a child may love the new setting the first time—exhibiting no resistance at all. Then, after a brief time, they will be ready to leave or not want to return. When this occurs, parents need to stay close during the next visit and teachers need to persist in supporting participation.

Children who are 30–36 months old usually look forward to new experiences, particularly when other children are involved. It is still important to support transitions by having parents share time together in the new setting and by supporting exploration of the new environment using positive nonverbal cues to serve as a social reference to the child that things are going well.

Developmental uniqueness will make every transition different. Temperamental characteristics may make transitions easier or more difficult. Be alert to these differences and adjust gradual enrollment to address or accommodate them.

Why Does Facilitating Adjustment Matter?

Facilitated experiences have significance for children for the rest of their lives. Secure attachments to significant adults (including teachers) can compensate for early deprivation and stressful experiences caused by poverty, unskilled parenting, abuse, or neglect (Schweinhart, Barnes & Weikart, 1993).

Make a Plan to Facilitate Adjustment

Teachers can involve parents in facilitating adjustment. Remind them to be patient with the process. It will take a while for children to adjust. This is normal and should be expected. Encourage parents to stay in close touch with their child's teacher. Good communication helps everyone succeed in adjusting. Help parents talk about their concerns and explore how the teacher is helping the child adjust at school.

Encourage parents to begin transitions with shorter days. Shorter days in the new environment with new people are usually easier for everyone. And, remind parents to persist—to celebrate small steps toward progress as they happen, building confidence that the process really is unfolding.

Use Supportive Teaching Behaviors to Facilitate Adjustment

What can teachers do to facilitate adjustment? Here are some ideas.

Individualize responses. Work hard to individualize responses to each child's cues. Congruence between the children's nonverbal cues and teachers' quick, appropriate responsiveness will reassure children and support the emerging relationship between children and their teachers (Kovach & Da Ros, 1998).

Clearly differentiate the teacher's role from the parents' role. Boundaries between infant and toddler teachers and the families they serve are often blurred. Both seem to do the same thing during different times of the day. But the roles are not the same. Teachers need to differentiate carefully for parents the nature of the teaching role. Teachers listen to parents, suggest solutions, raise issues, point out alternatives, and provide resources to parents. These are appropriate roles for teachers.

Directing child rearing or insisting on specific expectations (for example, requiring the parent to take away the bottle on the first birthday) are examples of inappropriate roles for teachers. Think about the following questions to help choose appropriate boundaries.

- Who should be the first person to share the emergence of a new skill or change in growth? Parent or teacher?
- Who should decide when it is time to start solid food? Parent or teacher?
- Who should determine strategies for helping children sleep through the night? Parents or teacher?
- Who should be responsible for replacing disposable diapers or formula when the supply at school is depleted? Parent or teacher?

There are many other questions to ask, and there is no absolute right answer to any of these questions. Situations will vary, and teachers need to be aware of carefully differentiating between the parenting role and the teaching role. Success in creating these boundaries will help facilitate the child's adjustment by clarifying both the teacher's and the family's unique roles.

Myth or Misunderstanding
TEACHERS REPLACE PARENTS WHILE CHILDREN
ARE IN SCHOOL SETTINGS.

It is not uncommon to hear teachers quietly wish that they could keep children's parents from having quite so much impact. These feelings may be caused by seeing the parents' lack of parenting skills or from feelings of competition between the caregiver and the parents.

What we know is that teachers can and do join the child's attachment network, developing a relationship that has many of the important characteristics of the parent's relationship with the child (Howes, 2000). Many, but not all. So, while it is true that teachers fill important nurturing and interactive roles with children during the school day, parents remain the most important people in the child's attachment network and maintain this pre-eminence throughout the child's life, regardless of the length of time away from these important people during the school day.

And, we know that responsive teachers can serve to offset and remediate some of the consequences of maternal depression, poor parenting skills, or lack of readiness to be responsive parents (Shonkoff & Phillips, 2000). But these interventions may not "take" unless teachers also support parents in improving their abilities. In other words, parents or primary caregivers matter most—and teachers can protect, compensate, and support children who are at risk from inadequate or poor family functioning by forging partnerships with parents that create opportunities to increase and expand parents' skills and abilities.

Make a list of boundaries that may be difficult for parents and for teachers to recognize and honor.

Bring the child's parents into the classroom. There are many ways to bring parents into the classroom. Parent participation activities encourage parents to be involved in their children's lives at school. Plan participation activities such as mid-day reunions, get-acquainted teas, and "happy hour" parent meetings. **Innovations: The Comprehensive Infant Curriculum** *and* **Innovations: The Comprehensive Toddler Curriculum** *have many other ideas for parent participation.*

Teachers also can bring parents into the classroom representationally — creating ways for children to stay in touch. Photographs of family members can be mounted on construction paper, covered with clear contact paper, and posted in the child's crib or on the wall in the toddler classroom. Individual pictures of family members can be laminated for toddlers to carry around or used to make accordion books to place where infants can see their parents' faces as they play on the floor. Parents can audiotape songs and fingerplays to be played for children at school, bringing the sound of Mom or Dad's voice into the classroom.

Myth or Misunderstanding
HAVING IMAGES OF PARENTS IN THE CLASSROOM JUST REMINDS CHILDREN TO MISS THEM.

This myth, like many, has its roots in behavior. A perfectly happy toddler who is playing with blocks looks over to the family photo carefully laminated at eye level on the wall and begins to cry as he realizes that his parents are not with him. Some teachers feel the easiest thing to do would be to remove the reminder—take away the photo until the child is better adjusted.

Infants and toddlers use photographs, pacifiers, and other security items as substitutes for the important people in their lives who may not be there during the school day. As they use these "crutches," they are better able to regulate the intense feelings that separation from parents and familiar settings causes (Jalongo, 1987).

Removing the stimulus (in this case the photo) doesn't improve the child's emotional regulation. Repeated experiences with separation, a responsive teacher to fill the gap while parents are gone, and the relief of reunions are "curriculum"—opportunities for children to master and regulate these intense feelings in the close presence of supportive and responsive alternative caregivers.

Convince a reluctant co-worker to keep photos of parents accessible to children.

Consider arrivals and departures as transitions for the child and the family.
Everything in a child's life is a transition, so teachers need to expect arrival
and departure times to be transitions and encourage parents to see arrivals
and departures in this light. Some transitions are handled better than others.
Teachers can help parents realize that arrival and departure times can't be
abrupt and quick—transitions take time. In general, children, even very young
children resist being rushed or hurried. Knowing this, teachers and parents
can plan arrival and departure routines to accept this inevitable reality.

Encourage parents to create a separation and reunion ritual. The way the day
begins and ends for children is so important. It sets the tone for the day and
supports the task of learning to separate and reunite. Helping parents
establish a predictable way to separate and reunite with their child helps
children feel secure with the transition process. The following is a suggested
strategy for creating such rituals.

When parents come into the room, talk with them a minute as they put their
child's things away. Encourage parents to help the child settle in by spending
a few minutes interacting in the classroom setting—offering the child a toy to
play with or reading a book. Remind parents not to rush the separation
process. It may take as long as 15 minutes or so for the child to indicate that
he is ready for the next step in the transition process.

When it is time for the parent to leave, encourage the parent to tell you. This
transfers the responsibility for care and interaction
from the parent to the teacher, so you
won't have to figure out if the
parent is ready to leave or not.
Sometimes this will be a
physical transfer—the
child from the parent's
arms to yours;
sometimes it will
just be a verbal
transfer if the
child has made the
transition to play.

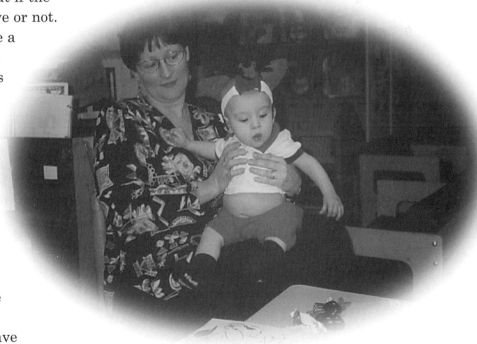

Help parents plan a
special ritual for
saying good bye—
three kisses and three
hugs, going over to a
goodbye window to wave
goodbye, and so on. Then help the

parent follow through in a way that works for him or her. Reassure parents that you will help the child if he needs support after they leave.

Reunions can follow a similar pattern. Encourage parents to cherish the reuniting process by spending a few minutes getting reconnected as soon as they return. They can sit down and watch what their child is doing and follow his lead about the pace of reuniting.

Predictable beginnings and endings of the day are important for parents, teachers, and children. Separations and reunions are easier for adults because we are more experienced in negotiating them. Children, particularly very young children, need help from both parents and teachers to make separations and reunions a pleasant part of their school experience.

Myth or Misunderstanding
HOW PARENTS LEAVE CHILDREN AT SCHOOL DOESN'T MATTER.

"I think I'll just sneak out while he is playing." This probably represents a sincere attempt by parents to make the leaving process easier on the child as well as on themselves. Usually it doesn't. When the child discovers that his parents have disappeared, trust in the abiding nature of the relationship can be damaged.

The leaving process matters. It can create comfort or crisis for children. Teachers can facilitate parents' understanding of the importance of leaving and uniting. When teachers support children's feelings during separation, help children anticipate reunions, and provide an alternative source of support and nurturing, children learn, over time, that their parents come back.

How would you discuss your concerns about leave-taking with a parent who wants to sneak out while the child is playing? Write a script to help you remember your plan.

Teach parents always to say goodbye. Leaving their child may be very hard for some parents. It might seem that leaving without saying goodbye could save parents and their infant or toddler from suffering through another separation. In fact, the opposite is true.

During the first three years of life, children learn that the world in which they live is a predictable and responsive place to be, or that it isn't. They learn this important lesson from their caregivers. Parents and teachers who provide sensitive, responsive, and predictable care are teaching children that they are trustworthy (see discussion on Erickson on page 98 of this book).

Parents can help children learn that although they may leave, it will never be without a goodbye kiss and hug and a promise to return. Young babies may not object too much to separations. If parents always say goodbye when their children are infants, during toddlerhood, when it really does matter, the toddler will remember the separation routine used over time and take comfort from the routine.

Encourage parents to call if their plans change and to develop backup plans. All parents at some point experience schedule interruptions and conflicts, which upset arrival and departure routines. Ask parents to let you know if this happens. Sometimes teachers can offset children's real discomfort about changes in schedule by preparing the child for the change. Even very young children know the sequence of which parent comes in first, then next, then next, and so on. When teachers know about plan changes, they can help children accept the increased time at the school without going into the "waiting" mode too soon.

Parents should also be encouraged to develop backup strategies before they need them and practice these routines, too. It's going to happen—a flat tire, a car accident, a last-minute work demand that can't be postponed, more traffic than you have ever seen, the downpour that floods every street leading to the school. If parents and teachers plan now for these situations, the backup plan will be an understood variation in the child's predictable routine.

Encourage parents to write down the plan and to discuss the plan with you. Practice it once or twice before it is needed. Then everyone will know what to do if the plan needs to be put into effect.

Use a Variety of Teaching Roles

Teachers use a wide variety of roles in their work with young children. During the developmental tasks of separating and transitioning, two of the most important roles are the teacher as observer and the teacher as facilitator. These roles take on specific characteristics during these developmental tasks.

The Teacher as Observer

As teachers participate in a gradual enrollment process and get to know the children with whom they will spend the day, much of their time is spent in observation. Observation, rather than interaction, is the primary strategy for getting to know new children and their families. Teachers observe to discover—

- The unique ways parents communicate with their children
- The ways parents interact with their children
- How children approach new stimulation
- A child's sense of personal space—whether being close to a new face is acceptable or unacceptable
- Children's interest in the physical world that is near them
- Comforting strategies used by parents that might be used by teachers
- Children's temperamental traits
- Children's developmental uniqueness or alternative developmental pathways

The Teacher as Facilitator

The role of facilitator emerges from the important task of planning and implementing gradual enrollment with children. The tasks of separating and transitioning are challenging ones for most children and families. When teachers see their role as facilitating this experience, rather than directing it, families are free to use their skills and abilities to help their children adjust.

This means that teachers check in with the parents often, asking if things are going well. They seek to discover ways to make the gradual enrollment fit the family better. In addition, they facilitate the expression of ideas, opinions, points of view that differ from their own, and find ways to facilitate the connection between the child and the teacher and the parents and the school.

Teaching Roles

Facilitator

Observer

Myth or Misunderstanding
PARENTS DON'T NEED ASSISTANCE MAKING THE TRANSITION TO SCHOOL.

This misunderstanding may emerge from the idea that parents generally select schools for their children and must feel that their choices are good ones for the family. But in reality, parents often have concern and anxiety about their selection of schools and their child's transition to the new setting. Feelings of inadequacy are common in parents, particularly as they embark on experiences for the first time or in new settings. They can be unsure of how to handle these experiences and may welcome input or support from teachers to help do so.

Parents benefit from relationships with teachers that validate the important role of parents as their child's first and most important teacher and from an honest discussion of ways to proceed that take the family's unique strengths and needs into consideration.

Make a list of ways to help parents overcome their concerns about transitions.

This facilitation can take many forms and, based on the astute observations during the process of gradual enrollment, can be modified to achieve a better fit along the way. Here are some areas for facilitation during the tasks of separating and transitioning:

- Facilitating the transition from outside the classroom to inside the classroom
- Helping parents understand where things go
- Facilitating the exchange of knowledge about the child from the parent to the teacher, including information about typical schedules, go-to-sleep routines, security items, favorite comforting strategies, ideas for encouraging interactions, and so on
- Facilitating the exchange of information about the cultural context of the child from the parents to the teacher
- Facilitating the identification of concerns, fears, anxieties, expectations for learning and growing, hopes for the child's development, parental development needs, and so on

Identify and Respond to Individual Differences

Individualize Schedules

During infancy, children are often on very different and individual schedules. For example, some children eat every three hours while others eat every four or five hours. During toddlerhood, schedules are often more similar, but individual children have different needs within similar schedules. For example, some children need one long nap a day while others need two or even three short ones.

Individual scheduling means letting the child's natural biological rhythms and temperament determine schedule rather than superimposing a common schedule on all children. Hidden in this situation is a marvelous tool for infant and toddler teachers. Imagine having three or four children who get hungry at the very same moment—or worse still, who need to be rocked to sleep at the same time. When teachers allow children to determine their own schedules, they are freed from this type of demand. Caregivers are still feeding, changing, and putting children to sleep, but instead of doing it all at once, they are doing it intermittently all day long.

The result is less stress for children having to wait to get their needs met and less pressure on teachers to meet multiple needs at once. To follow individual schedules, it is necessary to find out what the child's regular schedule is. Sometimes children's schedules are not very predictable. Even when this is the case, patterns emerge that teachers and parents can use to plan the day. Look for these patterns if the child's schedule isn't predictable.

Myth or Misunderstanding
LET'S GET THESE CHILDREN ON A SCHEDULE, THE SAME SCHEDULE.

A common misconception that persists in infant and toddler programs is that younger children need the same or similar things that older children need. If preschool children benefit from a common schedule, then surely infants and toddlers will, as well. If older children can enjoy having books read to them in a group, then surely infants and toddlers benefit from group book reading.

While it is true that most children respond to a predictable sequence in the daily routine, few infants and toddlers follow the same schedule as their peers, nor should they.

Part of children's learning is making sense of the bio-behavioral experiences they are having (Mahler, Pine & Bergman, 1975). What does that rumbling in my stomach mean? How can I change my position when my arm starts to hurt? Where did that light come from and what does it mean? Why can't I calm myself down? Can I stay awake until I finish my lunch?

Routines, not rigidly timed schedules, support children's emerging self-regulation skills. Predictable sequences of events accommodate children's individual needs for less or more rest, less or more activity, less or more food, less or more warm interaction all alone with a teacher, and so on. Understanding these variations within children is as important as understanding other components of developmental uniqueness.

How would you convince a new assistant teacher to use individualized schedules?

Maximize Interactions During Basic Care and Routines

Once the commitment is made to allow children to follow their own schedules, it is then easy to combine one-on-one interaction with routine activities. Time spent diapering, toileting, eating, and putting children to sleep is also used to stimulate and encourage social, emotional, physical, language, and cognitive growth.

Reciprocity—the give and take of interactions—is virtually guaranteed during routine care. It is really difficult to feed a baby unless the baby opens his mouth; hard to change a diaper on a wiggly toddler until you get his attention. Because reciprocal interactions are so important to the development of happy, healthy children, teachers who use routines to insure a healthy dose of reciprocal exchanges are making the most of the time spent on routine care by "ping-ponging"—getting a response and responding to children (Gordon, 1972). Maximizing routine experiences allows children to blossom and teachers to find time for one-on-one interchanges (Gerber, 1979; Gerber & Johnson, 1997.)

Myth or Misunderstanding

ROUTINES TAKE UP THE WHOLE DAY— THERE'S REALLY NO TIME TO TEACH.

Over the course of one day, a teacher with primary responsibility for 4 children will likely change 20 diapers, disinfect the changing area 20 times, administer 3 doses of medication, wash each child's hands 4 times, change 2 children's clothing, prepare snacks for 4 children 2 times, clean up 6 spills, serve 4 lunches, put on 4 pairs of shoes and socks, and many other routines (Hostetler, 1984).

"Teaching moments" are different for infants and toddlers. They almost always present themselves during interactions. When teachers are diapering, feeding children, or helping them calm down in preparation for a nap, they are "teaching." These moments can be maximized to extend or scaffold a child's learning while an observant teacher discovers additional "teaching moments" through observation and participation in children's play.

Identify and describe ways to help teachers turn routines into interactive experiences that enhance the relationship with the child or create opportunities to teach.

Respond Promptly to Crying

Crying children present a constant dilemma to their caregivers. If they respond promptly to crying, many feel they would spend all of their time responding to crying children with little time left for other tasks of fostering developmental growth. A good understanding of the consequences of letting children cry without prompt adult response will help adults approach crying children in the most helpful way.

Myth or Misunderstanding
RESPONDING QUICKLY TO A BABY'S CRY WILL SPOIL HIM.

This misunderstanding is a difficult one to understand. Parents often express this point of view, bolstered by traditions in their own families. Unfortunately, this point of view is often repeated and validated by teachers.

Research into this area has provided clear evidence that children who are held, cuddled, rocked, and so on when they are distressed, comfort more quickly than children who are not (Bell & Ainsworth, 1972) and cry for shorter periods of time if response to crying is prompt (Korner & Thoman, 1972). No research has documented that children need to cry a little while before being picked up or that responding promptly to crying increases crying.

How will you explain this idea to a parent who believes that children should cry for a little while before being picked up?

Children cry for a variety of reasons. Sometimes the cause is simple discomfort like a wet diaper or an empty stomach. Sometimes children cry because they are too hot or too cold. Pain, particularly pain caused by intestinal upsets, can result in intense crying. Teachers also know that some cries seem to have no identifiable cause. Dealing with crying that has no apparent cause can often be the most difficult situation to handle.

The issue of responding to crying children is complicated by a fairly prevalent, yet mistaken view that too much responsiveness may result in spoiled children (Mooney, 2000). Are children spoiled when teachers respond promptly to their cries? Do children who get this kind of attention cry more or less?

Also, research has provided us with an additional benefit of timely response to crying. Children often respond to holding by looking around and scanning the environment. When they are in this alert state, children are more likely to accept transition to another activity or being put down (Korner & Thoman, 1972).

When children's needs are met quickly when they cry, they learn to trust the world around them and the adults who care for them (Erickson, 1963). If they learn that they must cry loudly and persistently to get their needs met, they may well use crying behaviors instead of developing other coping strategies or self-management skills.

How can caregivers respond to crying? Obviously, if the adults are free to do so, the best cure for crying is to respond to the child, and hold, cuddle, soothe, and love him. Each prompt response will increase the likelihood that the child will come to trust his caregiver and learn other self-soothing skills.

But what if caring adults are not free to respond promptly? In school settings, it is not unusual for more than one child to cry and need attention at once. Try some of the following strategies if a crying child cannot be responded to immediately.

Move near the child. If he is in a crib, the sight of your face and soothing sounds from your voice may help. Comment on the situation and the reason you cannot help the baby at once. You might say, "I'm almost finished giving Melanie her bottle. As soon as I'm finished, I'll pick you up." Avoid comments such as, "You're all right." No crying child is all right. Crying infants are trying to communicate, even if the adults are unsure of what the message means.

If the child is mobile, move near him and sit down on the floor so the child can get close to you. Sometimes an elbow, knee, arm, or leg can provide the needed touch to calm a crying child even if you cannot pick him up. Again, use your voice to calm and soothe by talking quietly to the child or singing a favorite tune.

Myth or Misunderstanding
SECURITY ITEMS HAVE NO PLACE IN THE CLASSROOM.

Do security items belong in the classroom? Do they help children cope? Is the use of transitional items a good or a bad thing?

Group care for very young children is a relatively new phenomenon. Because of the newness of infant and toddler care, school models are often based on what is done with preschoolers rather than what is needed for infants and toddlers.

As children have left home care for school care, the requirements on them have increased. They are required to deal with more adults, more peers, and much more stimulation. At the same time, they are expected to be away from the most important people in their lives—their parents—for extended periods of time.

Security items serve to support children in coping with these demands, and as such, belong in infant and toddler programs. The need to use security items can be diminished, though, by low child-to-adult ratios, high levels of teacher responsiveness to emotional needs, well-planned physical environments, and activities and experiences that are neither frustrating or boring.

How can you help other children understand that security items are not toys for everyone to use?

Use a security item or favorite toy. Often a security item or favorite toy helps children calm themselves when you are unable to do so in person. There is no reason to limit access to these items unless you find yourself substituting them for adult attention. When you begin to look for a child's favorite toy or blanket, ask yourself if you can respond in person rather than presenting the substitute. If the answer is yes, then do it! No substitute is as good as the real thing.

Get information from other members of the attachment network. An excellent prevention idea for coping with crying is to get information about what works from other familiar people. Children often develop self-soothing behaviors in one context that can be used in other contexts.

Relax. Sometimes adults themselves contribute to the crying cycle. They can tense up and send messages about stress to children through voice tone and muscle tension. Some relaxation techniques that work are an important part of any caregiver's repertoire. Try slow, deep breaths, visualizing the child when he was happy and content, or systematic muscle relaxation to help break the cycle and get the crying under control.

Consider applying Maslow's Hierarchy (see page 45) or Erickson's stages (see page 98) to the crying behavior. It could be that cries are actually requests to meet higher order or stage needs—such as the need to belong or feel loved, or to feel confident and autonomous, rather than needing to meet security or safety needs. Including these kinds of ideas in the response to crying broadens the range of possible responses. Further, it gives caregivers opportunities to explore changes and growth that may have recently occurred.

Infants and toddlers cry to communicate. Promptly responding to crying and developing effective coping strategies to use when prompt response is not possible will lower the frequency and duration of crying. Responding appropriately to crying allows children to gain confidence that the adults who care for them will meet their needs.

Applying Theory and Best Practices

A large part of professional practice in the field of care and early education is synthesizing knowledge, research, and best practices into teaching actions and strategies. A goal of ***Innovations: Infant and Toddler Development*** is to help teachers apply theory, research, and best practices to real-life situations and behaviors in the infant and toddler classroom. Let's take a look at a common behavior that is a part of most children's experience in care and early education settings to see if the knowledge we have gained, the research we have reviewed, and/or the best practices we have explored give any suggestions of how the behavior might be handled by teachers in the classroom.

Separating and transitioning experiences for very young children are often accompanied by crying. This crying is associated with either the separation or transition or it is a result of experiences with other children and adults in the care and early education setting. So, let's begin exploring the integration of knowledge, research, and best practices by considering the implications of the topics covered in this chapter for children's crying behaviors at school.

Possibilities from Identity Formation for Crying

How might teachers understand and use the information on identity formation and individuation with crying that occurs in the classroom? From the discussion of identity formation and individuation (see page 39), several possibilities are presented that might help teachers understand crying behavior and consider what kind of teaching action or intervention might be appropriate.

The first possibility is that crying might have many different meanings. It could mean the obvious—the child needs physical care like feeding or diapering. Or, crying might mean the child is expressing a need for physical and psychological or emotional closeness to the teacher.

Another possibility is that the crying could come from the child's interest in acting and initiating. Having discovered that he can make things happen in the interactive world, the child may be trying out or practicing these new skills, checking to see if they produce the desired results. Or, the cry may result from frustration at not being able to make things happen and wanting help in acting or initiating from the teacher. Or, the cry may be a request for the caregiver to come over and share in the child's experience, thereby supporting the child in accomplishing the initiated action or activity. In all of these situations, the child is dependent on a response—an indication from his caregivers that the message sent has been received and that a response is on the way.

Individuation also helps us understand why caregivers' prompt, sensitive response is so important to children. The delicate balance a child maintains—seeking to do for himself when he can and depending on others when he can't is maintained only when calls for help (crying) are answered.

So, knowledge of identity formation creates possibilities for the teacher to look beyond the obvious need for physical care to other explanations for crying. In doing so, she is matching her response to the child's need, furthering his feelings of competence and self-reliance.

This theory also points to the crucial importance of connections between home and school and partnerships between parents and teachers. Children develop their self-identities in the context of culture (Lally, 1995). Culture influences child-rearing and caregiving practices, including how parents respond to children's behaviors. For crying, this means incorporating home practices into school practices. When teachers incorporate patterns of caregiving from home into school, children experience congruence in the cues they receive from visual and non-verbal refueling exchanges and from caregiving responses from teachers. When the way teachers respond looks and feels the same as the responses children receive at home, there is no conflict or incongruence for the child to experience.

Possibilities from Maslow's Hierarchy of Needs for Crying

Maslow's ideas about the Hierarchy of Needs offer an interesting point from which to view the crying. Perhaps the child is hungry, or has a dirty diaper, both indications of physiological needs that must be met. Or, the child could be uncomfortable in clothes that have become too small, threatening physical safety. Or, the child could be using crying to indicate a need for social interaction with Mom or Dad, or teacher, so that he can feel loved.

Infant and toddler teachers might want to keep Maslow's Hierarchy in mind as they try to determine the cause of crying. Often, a teacher's first impulse is to offer food or a bottle to a crying baby. Sometimes, the cry may be a request to meet higher order needs. This may be the case when crying ceases as soon as the caregiver picks the child up or when the child refuses the bottle when offered in favor of being close to the caregiver and being held.

As teachers manage their myriad tasks and roles, Maslow's ideas remind us of the complexity of teaching—that teachers are always in the role of considering a wide range of potentially appropriate responses to any given situation. Maslow's theory reminds us to open up the range of possibilities.

Possibilities from Temperament for Crying

Temperament gives us other possibilities about crying. For example, when a child is fussing as he tries to settle in for a nap, he may be signaling different messages to teachers or caregivers depending on his temperamental characteristics. A feisty child might need to roll around, tossing and turning to settle in and get comfortable. A flexible child might be telling the teacher that his stomach hurts—a warning sign that might need attention. Or, a fearful child might be signaling that the teacher moved away and stopped patting a little too soon and that the child needs a little more help to get to sleep.

Temperament is particularly applicable to crying. Some children cry; others wail. Some children cry for a few minutes; others can cry for hours. Crying deserves a response that is consistent with the child's temperament and respectful of the differences of temperament.

Possibilities from Developmental Uniqueness for Crying

Developmental uniqueness may also give us some clues about the crying. For example, if an infant has gone to sleep being rocked for the first nine months of his life, but suddenly starts to fidget and self-stimulate when the teacher rocks him, the teacher may be observing the early emergence of new skills—in this case, the ability to go to sleep with a little less support from rocking and cuddling.

As the child reorganizes at a new level of skill, he may need different things from his caregiver at different times. One child may need continued rocking for a little while, then a transition to the bed or cot to finish the job on his own. Another child may need to try it on his own, only to return to the comforting arms of his teacher to finish the process, perhaps taking five or six tries at each before settling down enough to sleep. Still another child might need the caregiver right there in view as he tries to go to sleep on his own, and failing to succeed, may need the rocking to continue once again.

Integrating Theory and Best Practices into Curriculum

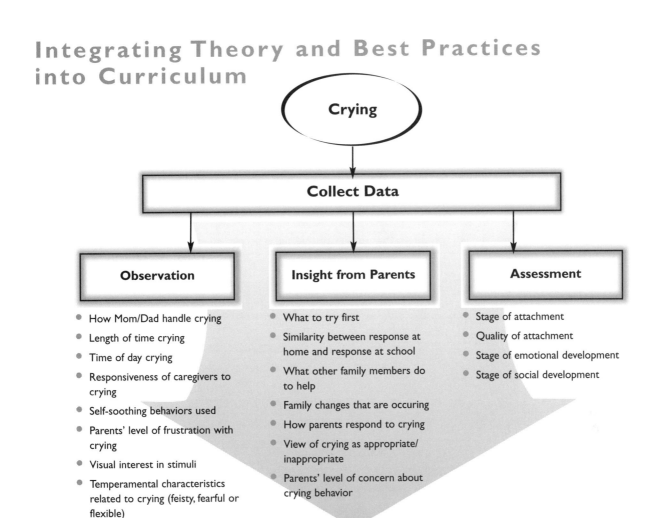

Crying

Collect Data

Observation

- How Mom/Dad handle crying
- Length of time crying
- Time of day crying
- Responsiveness of caregivers to crying
- Self-soothing behaviors used
- Parents' level of frustration with crying
- Visual interest in stimuli
- Temperamental characteristics related to crying (feisty, fearful or flexible)

Insight from Parents

- What to try first
- Similarity between response at home and response at school
- What other family members do to help
- Family changes that are occuring
- How parents respond to crying
- View of crying as appropriate/inappropriate
- Parents' level of concern about crying behavior

Assessment

- Stage of attachment
- Quality of attachment
- Stage of emotional development
- Stage of social development

Increase Understanding

Theory/Research Knowledge

- Maslow's Hierarchy (determine needs level)
- Stages of individuation
- Strategies to assess attachment quality
- Strategies to assess social development
- Strategies to assess emotional development

Best Practices

- Modify or adjust gradual enrollment
  -shorter day
  -more visits with parents
- Environments
  -lower stimulation in classroom before arrival
- Validate parents
  -have Mom show teacher how to soothe different cries
- Facilitate adjustment
- Individualize schedule
- Learn individual differences

Cultural Context and Congruence

- Assess "attunement" between Mom and baby
- Record sleep/wake/crying schedule to look for clues (both at home and school)
- Explore accommodation strategies to address context differences

Collaboration

- Ask family to consult with physician to rule out physical problem/illness
- Refer parents to psychologist to assess maternal depression
- Get ideas from other teachers who have had crying children
- Ask director to observe teacher and child together to look for clues about goodness of fit between child and teacher
- Conversations at staff meetings
- Identify expert to support teachers and parents; e.g., psychologist, master teacher, social worker, etc.

Possibilities

Parent Possibilities

Teacher-Initiated   Request family photos. Request shirt or nightgown.
Interview parent re: home practices for crying.

Parent Participation

Observe when Mom does routines. Ask parents to model responding to crying for teacher.
Ask parents to record lullaby. Slow down gradual enrollment and/or shorten day. Plan lunchtime visit

Innovations in Environments

Create special place to put baby down after all attempts to soothe fail.
Make special place familiar w/blanket from home and shirt from Mom or Dad.
Play lullaby after a few moments alone in special area.

Lower stimulation when crying occurs (turn off bright lights, lower volume of music, etc.).

Observation/Assessment Possibilities

Chart for crying
-self-soothing behaviors   -time of day
-length of crying   -amount of parent distress
-circumstances
Check need for physical care often (diapering, holding, feeding).
Monitor frustration w/activities and experiences.
Determine stage of attachment, stage of cognitive development, stage of emotional development.
Determine how Mom/Dad view crying behavior.

Interactive Experiences

Increase holding time for baby whenever possible.
Set up routines to be peaceful and not disruptive.
Triangulate w/ a toy to interact (play with toy to attract interest of baby).
Respond to crying w/ systematic approach.
Balance needs of other children with this child's needs.
Create opportunities to make things happen.
Share in experiences often by being close and present.
Match responses carefully to child's needs to develop competence.
Consider cries as communication.

Plan

Web

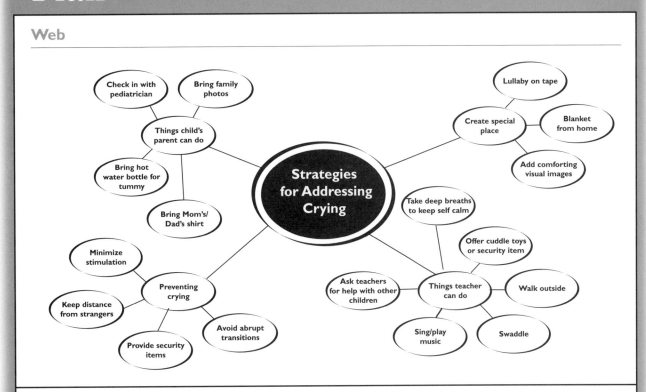

Dramatic Possibilities Mom or Dad's shirt or handkerchief

Art/Sensory Possibilities Warm water activity, try soothing sensory experiences

Curiosity Possibilities Duplicate items to replicate at home

Music Possibilities Parent lullaby

Movement Possibilities Avoid overstimulation (bouncing, tickling)

Literacy Possibilities Introduce favorite books from home, familiar fingerplays, Me! book

Outdoor Possibilities Take walks outdoors

Project Possibilities

Books	Picture File Pictures/Vocabulary
Familiar books from home Me! book Are You My Mother? by P.D. Eastman	Family photos

Rhymes & Fingerplays	Music/Songs	Prop Boxes
"Baby's Bath" Nursery rhymes from home "Baby's Nap"	"My Mommy Comes Back" Recording of parent singing lullaby "Rockabye Baby"	Babies prop box Mommies and Daddies prop box Mommy's or Daddy's Work prop box

Summary

Separating is a crucial developmental task negotiated during the first three years of life. Birth itself is the first separation experience an infant has—separating from the warm, protective uterine environment of the mother's body to experience the world outside. Separating is also the first step in the process of becoming an autonomous, independent person. When children have positive and supported experiences with separating, they learn to trust the world in which they live.

Infancy and toddlerhood are exciting and challenging periods for children, their parents, and teachers. As infants become toddlers, the number of separations and connections increases, requiring children to practice and perfect the important task of transitioning.

Identity formation or individuation involves developing a sense of self—as a separate, fully functioning person with unique thoughts, feelings, personality, and abilities. For human beings, this is a lifelong process. As children discover that they are different and separate from their parents and caregivers, they also discover that they can make things happen.

Children who are confident of their physical separateness from their caregivers and secure in their abilities to make things happen and initiate action, begin to vacillate between being able to handle independence and autonomy and being unable to handle it. Fear of strangers peaks during toddlerhood. Growth in language and cognition signals that children are achieving self-identities.

Maslow's Hierarchy of Needs serves as a backdrop for how children develop and learn. This theory explains the emotional needs that children are motivated to meet through their interactions with others. The levels are physiological survival and well-being, physical safety and psychological security, love and belonging, self-esteem and self-worth, and the need to know and understand.

Every child is born with a personality—a temperament that guides and influences his approach to the world. Leiberman (1990) described the types as flexible, fearful, and feisty.

Although children's development follows a predictable, identifiable sequence, there are components of uniqueness within that predictable sequence. These components are the child's pace of development, the child's integration of developmental domains, and the sporadic and uneven nature of development. Viewing these variations as alternate, yet normal, is important.

Best practices reflect the integration and synthesis of knowledge joined with creative and thoughtful interpretation and implementation. One of the best ways to facilitate a child's adjustment to any new early childhood experience is to encourage the parents and the child to participate with the teacher in a gradual enrollment process—with the parent and child staying one to two hours the first day and working up to a full day.

Other best practices include creating supportive environments, investing in observation, validating what Moms and Dads know, actively facilitating adjustment, using a variety of teaching roles, identifying and responding to individual differences, and maximizing interactions during basic care and routines.

Questions and Activities

1. How would you expect a child's temperament to impact each of the other areas of development: language, cognitive, emotional, physical, and play?
2. Why is it important to learn and understand a child's temperament? Give three examples of how this understanding will help in ordinary, day-to-day situations.
3. Children who are 9–14 months old seem to have the most difficulty adjusting to school. What difficulties would you expect? What could you do to support both the child and the parents during the transition?
4. Explain the role of the teacher as observer.
5. How can Maslow's Hierarchy of Needs help a teacher to interpret a toddler's behavior?
6. How would you decide whether a child is exhibiting a developmental delay or an alternate developmental pathway?
7. Pick a best practice from pages 53-81. Identify which theories support the practice. Discuss how with a colleague or mentor.

References

Albrecht, K. & L.G. Miller. (2000). *Innovations: The comprehensive infant curriculum.* Beltsville, MD: Gryphon House.

Albrecht, K. & L.G. Miller. (2000). *Innovations: The comprehensive toddler curriculum.* Beltsville, MD: Gryphon House.

Bell, S.M. & M.D.S. Ainsworth. (1972). Infant crying and maternal responsiveness. *Child Development,* 43, 1171-1190.

California State Department of Education. (1990). *Flexible, fearful, or feisty: The different temperaments of infants and toddlers.* Videotape. Sacramento, CA: Department of Education.

Chess, S. & A. Thomas. (1987). *Know your child.* New York: Basic Books.

Curtis, D. & M. Carter. (2000). *The art of awareness: How observation can transform your teaching.* St. Paul, MI: Redleaf Press.

Edwards, C., L. Gandini, & G. Forman. (1998). *The hundred languages of children: Advanced reflections.* Norwood, N.J: Ablex.

Erickson, E.H. (1963). *Childhood and society.* New York: Norton.

Gandini, L. & C.P. Edwards. (2001). *Bambini: The Italian approach to infant/toddler care.* New York: Teacher's College Press.

Gandini, L. & J. Goldhaber. (2001). Two reflections about documentation. In Gandini, L. and C.P. Edwards (Eds.), *Bambini: The Italian approach to infant/toddler care.* 121-145. New York: Teacher's College Press.

Gardner, H. (1983). *Frames of the Mind: The theory of multiple intelligences.* New York: Basic Books.

Gerber, M. (1979). *Resources for infant educarers: A manual for parents and professionals.* Los Angeles: Resources for Infant Educarers.

Gerber, M. & A. Johnson. (1997). *Your self-confident baby.* New York: Wiley.

Gordon, I. (1972). *Baby learning through baby play.* New York: St. Martin's.

Greenspan, S. (1999). *The six experiences that create intelligence and emotional growth in babies and young children.* Reading, MA: Perseus Books.

Hostetler, L. (1984). Public policy report: The nanny trap: Child care work today. *Young Children,* 39(2), 76-79.

Howes, C. (2000). Social development, family, and attachment relationships of infant and toddlers. In D. Cryer &T. Harms, (Eds.), *Infants and toddlers in out of home care* (87-113). Baltimore, MD: Brookes Publishing.

Jalongo, M.E. (1987). Do security blankets belong in preschool? *Young Children,* 42(3), 3-8.

Korner, A.F. & E.B. Thoman. (1972). Visual alertness in neonates as evoked by maternal care. *Journal of Experimental Psychology,* 10, 67-68.

Kovach, B.A. & P.A. Da Ros. (1998). Respectful, individual, and responsive caregiving for infants: The key to successful care in group settings. *Young Children,* 53 (3), 61-64.

Lally, J.R. (1995). The impact of child care policies and practices on infant/toddler identity formation. *Young Children,* 51 (1), 58-67.

Leiberman, A.F. (1993). *The emotional life of a toddler.* New York: The Free Press.

Lowman, L.H. & L. Ruhmann. (1998). Simply sensational spaces: The multi-S approach to toddler environments. *Young Children,* 53(3), 11-17.

Mahler, M.S., F. Pine, & A. Bergman. (1975). *The psychological birth of the human infant: Symbiosis and individuation.* New York: Basic Books.

Maslow, A. (1954). *Motivation and personality.* New York: HarperCollins.

Mooney, C.G. (2000). *Theories of childhood: An introduction to Dewey, Montessori, Erickson, Piaget, and Vygotsky.* St. Paul, MI: Redleaf Press.

Perry, B.D. (2000). Emotional development: The developmental hot zone. *Early Childhood Today,* Nov./Dec. Scholastic.

Scanlon, P. (1988). In search of excellent training: Tuning into right brain/left brain thinking. *Child Care Information Exchange,* 63, 7-11.

Schweinhart, L., H. Barnes, D. Weikart, W.S. Barnett, & A.S. Epstein. (1993). *Significant benefits: The High/Scope Perry Preschool study through age 27.* Monographs of the High/Scope Educational Research Foundation, No. 10. Ypsilanti, MI: The High/Scope Press.

Shonkoff, J.P. & D.A. Phillips (Eds.). (2000). *From neurons to neighborhoods: The science of early childhood development.* Washington, DC: National Academy Press.

Shore, R. (1997). *Rethinking the brain: New insights into early development.* NY: Families and Work Institute.

Glossary

Autonomy—Being independent and alone, trusting oneself for guidance.

Fearful Child—One of three major temperament types. Fearful children avoid new situations and are slow to warm to new people and experiences.

Feisty Child—One of three major temperamental types. Feisty children have irregular rhythms and are very active, intense and easily distracted, sensitive, moody.

Flexible Child—One of three major temperamental types. The traits of flexible children include regular biological rhythms, adaptability to change and new situations, low intensity, low sensitivity, and positive mood.

Gradual Enrollment—A strategy for adjusting to a new school situation that gives children, parents, and teachers time to get to know each other and to establish mutual reciprocal relationships.

Individuation—The process of becoming an individual—a separate, fully functioning person with unique thoughts, feelings, personality, and abilities.

Inserviamento—An enrollment and orientation approach used in the infant and toddler schools of Italy to facilitate adjustment of families and children to early education services.

Interaction—Social interchange between individuals or between objects, the environment, and individuals.

Maslow's Hierarchy of Needs—A theory that proposes that basic needs are arranged in a hierarchical order and that higher order needs cannot be addressed without satisfaction of previous levels.

Meltdown Places—Places where toddlers can be alone while they regain composure.

Myth—A commonly held belief not based in fact, research, or best practices. In **Innovations**, myths are used to illustrate commonly held beliefs about child development that can be better understood in the light of research and best practices.

Neural Pathways—Routes of connecting brain cells.

Rapprochement—Period of toddlerhood that is characterized by a need for closeness, approval, intimacy, and emotional availability of caregivers on the toddlers' terms.

Reciprocity—The give and take of interactions that is virtually guaranteed during routine care.

Reunion Ritual—A ritual for the reuniting process for parents and children.

Separation Ritual—A ritual for separating.

Social Referencing—Taking emotional cues from significant others about the physical, emotional, and social attributes of a situation and using the cues to modify behavior.

Synaptogenesis—Connecting of brain cells together in communicating neural pathways.

Tank-up Behavior—Venturing out, then coming back for comfort and support, then venturing out again.

Temperament—Characteristics of personality that guide and influence an individual's approach to the world.

Connecting with School and Teacher and Making Friends

Developmental Tasks: Connecting with School and Teacher and Making Friends

Connecting with School and Teacher

The complement of separating from the comfort and familiarity of home is connecting to the world outside the home. At many ages and stages during the first three years, it is the experience of connecting that bridges these two worlds. Connecting is a process, just like separating. It can begin with curiosity, confusion, interest, or wariness. And connecting takes time.

The infant's connection to others is facilitated by both caring, involved parents, and by warm, responsive interactions from the other new people she meets in the community. This connection is also affected by the infant's personal characteristics and by dynamic components of the ecological cultural context.

As the connection to others and community is considered, a fundamental reality becomes clear. Relationships are embedded in a cultural context. Everything that happens in children's lives takes place in this rich, complex, and changing cultural context. Any understanding of the relational components of development must consider this important point.

Making Friends

Toddlerhood marks the beginning of an exciting and challenging period in the lives of young children. Toddlers emerge from infancy with a considerable range of skills and abilities that are just beginning to be evident to adults. They have perfected the motor skills of getting around and eating and drinking without assistance. Toddlers have learned to comprehend a rather large number of words and are beginning to communicate their needs and wants with an ever-growing expressive vocabulary. And, toddlers are inquisitive about everything—wanting to interact, discover, manipulate, and explore everything in sight.

Along with this curiosity comes an emerging interest in the larger physical and social world. Exploration takes on new dimensions as the environment entices toddlers to look up as well as out, behind doors, out windows, and underneath objects, as well as at them. Viewing the room from a tabletop instead of from the floor is as interesting as viewing the underside of the table while lying on the floor.

Making friends becomes an important task once the connection with the social world is made. Peer relationships are important to children. The widening social world serves as the springboard for learning about secondary relationships that are as interesting and engaging as the important primary ones established in infancy.

Both adult and peer playmates become important as toddlers widen their social experience to include more than their attachment figures. Friendships begin to emerge as children integrate their experiences in the world of play.

Chapter 3 focuses on the important knowledge related to the developmental tasks of connecting to parents, teachers, and friends, and making friends. The best practices that emerge from this knowledge are then discussed. The chapter ends by applying this new understanding of theory and practice to a common behavioral challenge.

Knowledge

Bronfenbrenner's Ecological Systems Theory

Bronfenbrenner's ecological model of human development proposes that development occurs in the context of complex systems that influence, impact, and direct development. These systems are dynamic, as is the child's development occurring within them (Bronfenbrenner, 1979).

Four systems of influence are identified in Bronfenbrenner's theory—the microsystem, the mesosystem, the exosystem, and the macrosystem. The microsystem is composed of the child and the socio-cultural context of the family, including values, cultural practices, previous caregiving experiences, and reciprocal relationships between the child and her parents or frequent caregivers. The microsystem includes all of the activities and interactions in the child's immediate environment.

The mesosystem includes connections between the child and family and the neighborhood and other settings that foster development. The educational context and the interface between cultural, religious, ethnic, family composition, racial, and socioeconomic backgrounds are part of the mesosystem.

The exosystem is composed of the community and includes values and practices of schools, religious organizations, community agencies, and social groups. The macrosytem is composed of the broader society including economic resource allocation, business practices, employment, health and education priorities, government policies, demographic trends, and technological changes. The priority given to children by the community is usually evident at this level.

Howes proposed a theoretical model for social development that builds on Bronfenbrenner's ecological systems theory. The primary difference in this theory of social development "is the centrality of relationships in understanding development" (Howes, 2000, p. 88). This reconceptualization moves attachment relationships with extended family members, alternative caregivers, and peers much closer to the child into the microsystem. The emphasis is placed on the influence of a network of relationships, rather than simply the mother/child or parent/child relationship, which is more consistent with children's experiences.

The relationships between the family and their childcare arrangements are added to the social context (the mesosystem) of the child. The influences from relationships within the family and the relationship between the child and the quality of the childcare arrangements are considered key variables in the child's social development, and as such, are socializing agents.

At the exosystem level, Howes places the influence of culture as it is "understood and enacted by the child's caregivers" (Howes, 2000, p.93.) As caregivers understand, interpret, and enact caregiving routines, children learn important lessons about how adults view the child's cultural background and characteristics. These lessons influence social development.

Finally, society is placed at the macrosystem level, where social policy, racism, sexism, and beliefs about gender roles influence the social development of the child. A child's primary caregivers operate within these societal expectations, influencing how the child's social development proceeds.

Myth or Misunderstanding
ALL FAMILIES ARE ALIKE.

After going to community college, Jolee Walsh started working at Loving Care Learning Centers. She has always worked with toddlers, and really enjoys interacting with the different families in the community. Jolee is one of three children who all live in the same community. She got married two years ago to Gene and is expecting a baby in the summer.

When parents come to school to pick up their child, Jolee is always polite and calls them by the last name of their child. Sue Lee's parents are called Mr. and Mrs. Lee. The two women who pick up Juan Martinez, she calls Ms. Martinez.

In the examples above, Jolee is using her own view of family (two married parents with the same last name having two or three children of their own) as the foundation for interactions with the families she serves. She would never knowingly insult the families, but her own view of family leads her to assume that all families are like hers.

Children in Jolee's classroom are very likely to have different family compositions. Families come in many variations; biological unmarried mother and father who live together, biological mother with woman companion, adoptive mother and father, married biological mother and father with different last names, as well as the traditional married mother and father living in the same household.

All families are not alike. Teachers must pay great attention to these differences, incorporating views of all kinds of families, as well as their cultures and languages, into their teaching behaviors, social interactions, and curricula. Through mutual respect and sensitivity to each other's perspectives, teachers and parents can develop partnerships that support young children (Stonehouse, 1988).

What should happen next? Discuss the next steps in Jolee's professional development. If you were Jolee's colleague, how would you begin a discussion about this issue?

Implications of Ecological Systems Theory for Connecting with School and Teacher and Making Friends

Bronfenbrenner's systems have interesting implications for connecting with school and teacher and making friends. Ecological systems give teachers a view of the influences that impact the child as she accomplishes the developmental task. Here, the essence of what it means to be part of a family is evident. The type, quality, consistency, and approach of the central adults gives teachers clues about ways to connect the school experience congruently with the microsystem experience.

The mesosystem includes the neighborhood and the educational context. Here teachers can view teaching, the school, and the other children as socializing agents—sources of socialization experiences that might or might not be congruent with family and/or school culture.

Bronfenbrenner's ideas also alert teachers to their own biases, views, preferences, prejudices, and values. Teachers need to make sure they modify the lens they use to view the world of the child so that their own points of view don't cloud their understanding of the child's ecological context.

Erickson's Stages of Psycho-social Development

Erik Erickson proposed a stage theory of psycho-social development (Erickson, 1963). He viewed each stage as a struggle, a crisis to be negotiated before continuing to the next stage. The resolution of each crisis influenced the way the crisis of the next stage would unfold.

Erickson's contribution to what we know about the development of very young children hinges on the idea that development is cumulative, with each developmental step laying the foundation for the next and each future step forward being influenced by previous ones. He also believes that the foundation of emotional and social development is formed in the early childhood years.

The first stage of Erickson's theory is the struggle to develop a sense of trust in the interactive, physical, social, and cultural world. During the first year of life, babies discover that the world is a safe and responsive place to be or that it is not. The direction of this struggle has so much to say for developmental outcomes as children grow and develop. During this stage, children learn whether their needs will be met by caring and responsive caregivers, particularly when they are in distress. The outcome of learning that their needs will be met results in a growing sense of connection and attachment to their caregivers—a condition crucial to continued emotional development.

Children are also learning to understand and use their own skills and abilities to impact what happens to them. The result of these experiences is a sense of self-awareness and self-motivation—an "I can" and "I want to" attitude toward life.

A feeling of trust, instead of mistrust, grows when there is a good match between children and their caregivers. If caregivers "read" non-verbal cues and respond appropriately, children become more intentional with their communication and seek to perfect it. If caregivers misinterpret or misread cues, children experience frustration, responding by severing the communication or by increasing their unsuccessful attempts in an effort to get a response. A lack of success damages the developing relationship.

The second stage of Erickson's theory relates to feelings of autonomy versus shame and doubt. The struggle to hold on or to let go is evident in this stage. Feelings of autonomy (rather than shame and doubt) emerge from successful experiences with choosing when to hold on and when to let go, and from many successful experiences in letting go.

Erickson's Stages of Psycho-social Development

Age	Stage
0–1 year	Trust vs. Mistrust
2–3 years	Autonomy vs. Shame and Doubt
4–5 years	Initiative vs. Guilt
6–12 years	Industry vs. Inferiority
Adolescence	Identity vs. Role Confusion
Young Adulthood	Intimacy vs. Isolation
Middle Age	Generativity vs. Stagnation
Old Age	Ego Integration vs. Despair

Growth in physical development contributes to feelings of autonomy as children try and succeed at new endeavors like hopping, running, drawing, building with blocks and manipulatives, climbing, digging, and so on. Growth in language enables children to communicate their emotional needs successfully, resulting in less dependence by adults on gestural or non-verbal cues. Cognitive growth leads to the ability to wait just a moment and to make simple predictions about when something might happen.

Although most children have many successful experiences with autonomy, some don't. Erickson's theory offers hope for children whose early childhood experiences are less than optimal. Failure to resolve an early dilemma is not irreversible. Renegotiation of any stage is possible at later stages although Erickson cautioned that the renegotiation is not easy. For example, for children who do not develop a sense of trust, Erickson felt it was possible to help them renegotiate this struggle with consistent, responsive care. Over time the feelings of mistrust are replaced with ones of trust. It takes a long time for sensitive, responsive care to reverse the mistrustful trend than it would have taken to establish trust in the first place.

Erickson's theory is a good fit with ideas about development and learning occurring within the context of relationships. The identity crises of each stage are obviously worked out in relationships with important people within the child's world. Children's experience in resolving these struggles is tied closely to repeated interactive and behavioral sequences of caregiving that build to create feelings of one kind (trust, autonomy, and so on) or the other (mistrust, shame and doubt, and so on) (Howes, 2000).

Implications of Erickson's Theory of Psycho-social Development for Connecting to School and Teacher and Making Friends

Erickson's theory of psycho-social development lets teachers know that any time spent investing in building relationships is time well spent. The very first stage—Trust vs. Mistrust—has profound implications for all of the future relationships an individual will have during her lifetime.

Erickson's stages build on each other, and each struggle influences the next one. For this reason, teachers need to take a long-term view of the effects their relationships can have on the child. Crafting experiences that support feelings on the positive side of Erickson's crises benefits children.

Erickson cues teachers to view interactions as cumulative. All experiences matter, and the combination of experiences influences how children are able to negotiate future conflicts and struggles.

Through all of Erickson's stages, individuals are able to use both their own observations and those of others to help interpret the experience. This is especially important for young children as they use their experiences to form a view of themselves.

Additionally, Erickson's theory of psycho-social development shows teachers that they can affect how children approach, work through, and eventually resolve a conflict. Teachers form central relationships with children and are then able to influence the direction of a child's crisis resolution.

Attachment Relationships

Feelings of security and trust emerge in infants and toddlers when they have intimate, reciprocal, continuing relationships with adults. Secure attachment bonds serve important purposes for infants and toddlers. They allow children to develop a sense that the world is a responsive place. From this orientation, they are free to venture out into the environment, exploring the world and managing the stress that exploration can produce. Attachment facilitates feelings in infants and toddlers that they can make things happen in their physical, social, and emotional environments.

Most often, this relationship is with the mother, but there are networks of attachment relationships in most children's lives. Who fills this role is less important than the quality of the abiding relationships between the child and these special adults (Howes, 2000; Shonkoff & Phillips, 2000). Other adults who are part of the network of attachment relationships, like extended family members and teachers at school, also create important relationships with children that influence healthy growth and development and contribute to the child's emotional well-being.

Attachment Theory

Ideas about how infants form relationships with their caregivers are based on John Bowlby's ethological theory of attachment (Bowlby, 1982). This theory explains the way children develop important and complex emotional relationships with their parents and primary caregivers. Although this theory views the development of attachment as promoting survival, it also connects the quality of attachment relationships to children's capacity to feel secure enough to form and maintain other relationships.

Attachment theory explains the changes in children's attachment behavior across infancy and toddlerhood and explores the impact of secure attachment on development and learning.

Stages of Attachment

Ainsworth and her colleagues (1978) modified Bowlby's stage theory of attachment, proposing four stages of attachment, with one stage building upon another. These stages are characterized by behaviors that give clues to parents and teachers about where infants and toddlers are in the development of attachment relationships.

Stage 1 (Indiscriminate Attachment)—The first stage is called indiscriminate attachment. During Stage 1, which lasts from birth to four or five months, there is less difference in the way babies respond to adults. As long as they are fed when hungry and held when uncomfortable, infants allow a caring adult to meet their needs.

Infants during this stage are particularly sensitive and responsive to their mothers. This sensitivity begins during pregnancy as the baby is exposed to the mother's biological rhythms and the sound of her voice. As a result, the baby is born with a familiarity with the mother that is enhanced by new connections from sight, smell, and touch. So, mothers are typically able to calm and soothe their newborns more easily than others are. This preference for the mother continues as the attachment process unfolds.

Stage 2 (Discriminate Attachment)—This stage is called discriminate attachment. During this stage, which lasts from 5 months to about 11 or 12 months, babies begin to smile, babble, coo, and respond more quickly to the mother and other familiar adults. During this stage, infants show a definite preference for interaction and comforting from a familiar person—usually the child's mother and father or other frequent caregiver. Babies are learning that their needs will be met by a specific set of caring adults and that they can trust the world to be a responsive place.

Stage 3 (Separation Anxiety)—This stage is called separation anxiety. During the third stage of attachment, which lasts from 11 or 12 months to about 17 or 18 months, children begin to show clearly defined preferences for mothers and fathers and the most familiar caregiver. Friendliness toward unfamiliar adults goes away. Children in this stage of development will resist care or attention from unfamiliar adults. They move close to their parents or most frequent caregiver when new people enter the room and cry or resist separation when their parents and most frequent caregiver leave.

At the beginning of this stage, children believe that their parents and favorite teacher have simply disappeared; they do not know that these special people will come back from work or their break. Children learn that things that disappear still exist and will come back. Repeated positive experiences with separation and reunion and further developmental maturation help infants learn that parents and teachers will return later.

Stage 4 (Stranger Anxiety)—This stage is called stranger anxiety. During the fourth stage of attachment, which lasts from about 17–18 months to 24–25 months, fear of strange or unknown adults is present. The cautious behavior of Stage 3 infants is replaced with clinging, crying, and fearful responses to strangers and to separation. Children resist any overture by unfamiliar adults and show great distress when their parents or teacher leaves.

At the end of the fourth stage of attachment, children are usually venturing out into the social world, supported and secure in the stability of their primary relationships. But progress through the stages isn't guaranteed. Children's experience at each stage of attachment affects their progress through the next stage and their subsequent emotional development. If they experience consistent, responsive physical and emotional care from one or more significant adults who are fully invested in their relationship with the child, attachment security and attachment relationships are formed.

Components of developmental uniqueness and alternative developmental pathways suggest chronological ages to stages must be interpreted with individual differences in mind. This is particularly true for attachment behaviors. Individual children may show behaviors described in a stage well before the suggested age range of the stage, or may not show the behaviors until well after. It is the sequence of the pattern of behaviors that increases our understanding of emerging attachment, not the ages assigned to specific stages.

Myth or Misunderstanding
PARENTS WHO DON'T SPEND MUCH TIME WITH THEIR CHILDREN OPEN THE DOOR FOR TEACHERS TO FILL THEIR SHOES.

Martina stays at school each day for 12 hours. Her mom, who is a single parent, does shift work at the textile factory as a seamstress. When overtime is available, she always takes it. Martina eats breakfast, lunch, and afternoon snack at school. Martina's teacher, Miss Sharon, is worried because she stays at school so long. Sharon feels like Martina's mother doesn't spend enough time with her daughter.

Sharon makes every effort to spend extra time with Martina during the day, trying to fill her up with extra love that she feels the child's parent doesn't have the time to provide. She is beginning to feel more like Martina's mother than her teacher.

There are really two myths here. The first myth is that time together is the only measure of the parent-child relationship. In fact, it is the quality of the relationship that is of utmost importance (Howes, 2000; Shonkoff & Phillips, 2000).

The other myth is that teachers can step in and fill the role of parent. Although the relationship a young child has with her teacher is important, it never equals the relationship a child has with her parents or primary caregivers. Parents are a child's first and most important teachers. They have the most profound influence in their child's life. This is true even for children who experience long hours in alternative childcare arrangements (Shonkoff & Phillips, 2000).

Sharon can still help Martina by supporting her mother's skill at reading and responding sensitively to Martina's cues. She can validate that Martina's mother is the most important person in the world to her daughter. And, she can partner with Martina's mother to make sure she gets what she needs from her teacher during school hours. How can Sharon support the quality of the relationship between Martina and her mother?

Attachment as a Secure Base

If the development of attachment goes well, children use members of their attachment networks as a secure base from which to explore the environment and the people and things in it. When with these important people, children seek to stay near them, maintaining proximity, particularly in new or unfamiliar situations. When children are separated from their attachment figures, they protest and try to prevent the separation from happening.

When they are in familiar and comfortable situations, infants and toddlers venture out into the environment, explore it, and then return to touch base with these important attachment figures. The process of returning to this secure base refuels the child's interest and emotional readiness for further exploration.

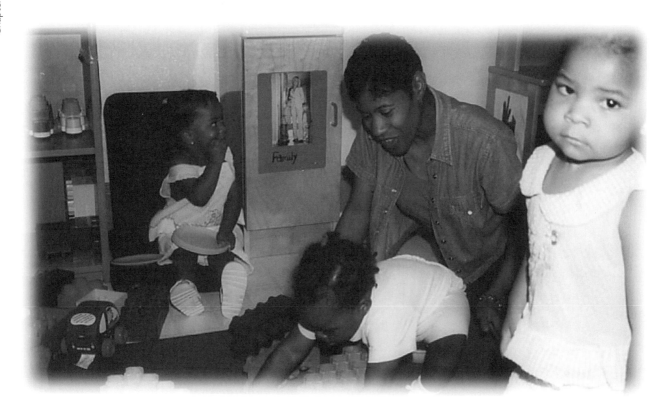

Children resist separation from their secure base. They object when the individuals who form their secure base leave, and they show increased anxiety if the separation is prolonged. Children who exhibit these behaviors are said to have a clear understanding of the reciprocity of their relationships with parents or primary caregivers and have come to trust in and depend on this emotional support. Without their secure base, they are unable to initiate and sustain the natural drive to construct knowledge through experience.

Implications of Attachment Theory for Connecting to School and Teacher and Making Friends

Children who have attachment security look and act very different from those who do not. They are more likely to become self-reliant toddlers and have a positive sense of self (Sroufe & Fleeson, 1986), have positive understandings of friendships (Cassidy, Kirsh, Scolton & Parke, 1996), show more advanced memory skills (Kirsh & Cassidy, 1997), and have better emotional self-regulation (Laible & Thompson, 1998).

These advantages appear to last throughout life. Children who were securely attached to their mothers or other primary caregivers are more independent as adolescents, have lower rates of mental illness, are more successful with friends, and do well in school (Schweinhart, Barnes, Weikert, Barnett & Epstein, 1993). There are physiological differences as well. Children who have attachment security respond differently to stressful situations than those who have not developed secure relationships. They produce less cortisol, a chemical produced by the body that can destroy brain cells and restrict synaptic development (Shonkoff & Phillips, 2000; Shore, 1997).

Peer Relationships

Making friends is one of the major tasks of childhood. The foundation for success in having friends and being friends is laid in the first three years of life. Success in peer relationships matters because it impacts how children view themselves and their place in the social world, predicts success with peer relationships in later life, and affects the type of children selected as friends during adolescence (Shonkoff & Phillips, 2000).

Knowledge about peer relationships is socially constructed (Piaget, 1962; Vygotsky, 1978). Like social development in general, interaction and experience with peers influences friendships. Peers help each other learn lessons about interactions that are different from the lessons learned within family relationships. They learn social skills like joining in play, sustaining play, resolving disagreements and conflicts, and maintaining relationships. They learn to make social comparisons—to evaluate themselves compared to others. These self-evaluation skills contribute to children's emerging sense of self as competent and capable, affecting identity formation and self-esteem. Children get a sense of belonging to a group beyond family from peer relationships (Rubin, 1980).

Early friendships begin with an interest in others, often observed in infants as young as two months. By nine months or so, children actively try to get and keep each other's attention. By 12 months, peer interactions increase in length and intensity as children begin to interact reciprocally with each other, taking turns in their interactions. To be able to move through these steps, infants need to be able to pay attention to selected parts of environmental stimulation, know how to take turns interactively, and be mutually responsive to others, all lessons first learned in important relationships with significant adults in their lives.

For toddlers, peer relationships are not always easy. As toddlers' interest in peers increases, so do the mistakes they make in keeping interactions between themselves and others going. Miscues derail play often as they bump into each other, take each other's toys, lose track of play ideas, or hurt each other.

An important condition of peer relationships for toddlers is familiarity. Toddlers find it easier to play successfully with familiar playmates who have compatible temperamental styles (Howes, Phillips, & Whitebrook, 1992). Children who stay in peer groups throughout the infant and toddler years remain friends and have increased social skills (Howes, 1988). Continuity of care creates the ideal setting for children to become better friends—by giving children time to become familiar and to succeed in working out conflicts and problems.

Conflict plays a big role in children's construction of peer relations, particularly among friends. When children are friends, they are more likely to stay and try to work out conflicts than if the conflicts occur among acquaintances or unfamiliar playmates (Shonkoff & Phillips, 2000). Conflicts are not necessarily negative experiences for children. When conflict occurs among friends, it can actually support emerging social competence as children try to work out strategies to continue to play together. These interruptions create experiences with negotiation and problem solving, and encourage children to figure out what will maintain their play.

Emotional, social, and cognitive competence affects peer relations. Secure emotional attachments create the emotional foundation for friendships to grow. Social skills such as the ability to gain entry into a play setting, join in play, and then sustain play by eliciting responses from others, helps friendships grow. The ability to communicate clearly, either with gestures or with language, and good observational abilities are cognitive competencies that enhance peer relations. Opportunity affects friendships, also. When there are many opportunities to play successfully with friends, peer relationships grow. Children also play more competently when they perceive their friends as similar. Being "like me" makes early friendships easier to initiate and maintain.

The environments in which peer relationships operate make a difference. When responsive, supportive adults provide coaching and clear ideas about inappropriate play behaviors, friendships and play mature (Rubin, 1980). When parents and teachers view helping peers interact and play successfully as a key parenting or teaching role, children are more successful in making and keeping friends.

Implications of Peer Relationships for Connecting to School and Teacher and Making Friends

The first implication of peer relationships for connecting to school and teacher and making friends is the importance of a secure emotional attachment to parents and alternative caregivers. The quality of the relationships between the children and their caregivers sets the stage for connections between friends. This investment by parents and teachers pays off as they gain the confidence and competence to expand their social worlds to include friends.

The social construction of peer relationships suggests that parents and teachers provide many opportunities for interactions between friends. Social skill acquisition takes repeated practice. Practice can be planned (by adults) or spontaneous interactions initiated by children. Frequency and regularity are as important as the length of time of play and the level of play.

Another implication is that continuity of care has benefits for peer relationships in addition to having benefits for children's emotional development. Familiar playmates make the best friends and continuity of care gives children opportunities to become familiar with one another over time.

Perhaps the most important implication is that emerging friendships need support from adults. Infants and toddlers do a better job of peer relations when adults help them figure out how to play together successfully. An important part of this early support is limits on hurting others and clear messages about appropriate and inappropriate ways to treat friends. When children receive supports, such as coaching, or options that might be explored, peers can play together more competently than they could play without support.

Best Practices

Invest in Establishing Relationships

Ongoing, nurturing relationships characterized by consistency and intimacy must be there—there are no short cuts (Brazelton & Greenspan, 2000). Everything good that happens to infants and toddlers happens in the context of abiding, mutual relationships. Investing in relationships with infants and toddlers and with the adults in their attachment network forms the foundation of accomplishing the goals and objectives for children in care and early education programs.

Implement Primary Teaching

Child development and early childhood literature is full of references to primary teaching as a strategy for facilitating the development of infants and toddlers during the first three years of life (Bernhardt, 2000; Cryer & Harms, 2000; Greenman & Stonehouse, 1996; Lally, 1995; Post & Hohmann, 2000; Raikes, 1996; Reisenberg, 1995). Primary caregiving usually focuses on the development of an intimate, sensitive, and reciprocal relationship between an infant or toddler and her most frequent alternate caregiver at school. Primary teaching is viewed here as a more comprehensive construct—one that offers schools the opportunity to develop close ties among parents, teachers, children, and school.

Powell (1998) supports this approach where schools work more inclusively with children and parents rather than constructing a separate parent involvement component. When primary teaching is viewed this way, it creates a true partnership with families, placing families at the center of the relationship, not on the periphery.

Primary teaching typically involves assigning each child to a special person to get to know at school. The primary teacher then spends her or his time gathering information and knowledge about the child's family, culture, unique temperament style, cues, schedule, and personality, so this teacher can be responsive and appropriate in her or his relationships with the child and the family.

Myth or Misunderstanding
WHEN CHILDREN GET ATTACHED TO THEIR
TEACHERS, IT ISN'T GOOD FOR PARENT/CHILD
ATTACHMENT.

Sam and Sheila Waites are owners and directors of a child care center in the suburbs of their community. Their school has an excellent reputation and has been in operation for 12 years. Sam and Sheila hesitantly started accepting infants into their program last year. They have been very concerned about the effect time away from home has on young children.

To keep babies from getting too attached to the teachers in the infant room, Sam and Sheila schedule rotations. Teachers work for four hours in the infant room and then four hours in the preschool room.

The misunderstanding here is that attachment to alternate caregivers is unhealthy for children. By not allowing babies to form strong attachments with teachers, Sam and Sheila may be putting children's emotional development at risk, rather than supporting and encouraging it (Cryer & Harms, 2000).

The intimate, sensitive, and reciprocal relationship between the teacher and the child influences healthy growth and development, especially emotional development. The concern that the mother/child relationship is harmed by separation from the mother is unfounded (Shonkoff & Phillips, 2000). The mother/child relationship remains important and is not diminished by developing other strong relationships.

Developing relationships takes time. When children are faced with rotating caregivers, they do not have the time they need to figure out the interactive style and approach of each teacher. This is also true of teachers. When they are faced with short or varied schedules, they are prevented from getting to know and understand the temperament, preferred interactive style, developmental uniquenesses, and other characteristics of each child.

Children in care and early education settings need a primary caregiver, someone who can get to know them over time. When teachers invest in becoming a part of children's attachment networks, they are in the position to support and encourage emotional development, specifically, and development in other domains as well.

What should happen next? How would you (as the teacher) bring your concerns to the Waites' attention? What alternatives would you suggest?

Components of Primary Teaching

There are three components of primary teaching. The first component is the relationship between the parents and the school. Because parents are the most significant people in a child's life, the relationship between the teacher and the parent is also paramount (Lally, 1995). Seeing each other as partners is an essential, yet complex component of early education. The parent/teacher/school relationship needs to have the same importance and develop the same amount of trust as the teacher's relationship with the child.

The second component of primary teaching is the responsive relationship between the child and teacher. Non-parental caregivers are considered part of the attachment network when they provide sustained physical and emotional care for the child and invest in an emotional relationship with the child (Cryer & Harms, 2000). When this relationship is based on careful observation of each child's individuality and on "a sense of personal and emotional involvement that is mutual" (Leavitt, 1994), caregivers are positioned to facilitate development.

Many researchers—Brazelton (1992), Erickson (1963), Gerber & Johnson (1997), Howes, Phillips & Whitebrook (1992), and Shore (1997)—have characterized the interactive relationship between caregivers and children as crucial. Young children need to know that the human world in which they live is a caring one that is responsive to their bio-behavioral needs.

The concepts of reciprocity and mutual trust include much more than just stimulating interactions (Gerber & Johnson, 1997; Kovach & Da Ros, 1998; McMullen, 1999). Characteristics are:

- Interacting with, rather than reacting to, children
- Working to read and interpret verbal and non-verbal cues
- Anticipating needs and wants
- Responding quickly and affectionately
- Waiting for cues from the child that she is ready for some action to take place
- Including the child's individuality and temperament in decisions about cue interpretation
- Including the child in the process of caregiving
- Having sensitivity to over- or under-stimulation of children from the environment and the people (and other children) in it
- Individualizing the schedule or pace of the day

When classrooms reflect these characteristics, trust between infants and toddlers and teachers naturally emerges (Gerber & Johnson, 1997; Howes & Hamilton, 1992).

Because each child is unique, primary teachers take the time to learn each child's unique qualities to foster positive communication. Teachers gather substantive information about the child from the parents and from observations of the child with his parents at school. This information gives the teacher a running start toward understanding each child's individuality, so the teacher's interactive style can match the emotional and social needs of the child.

The teacher-child relationship is based on mutual personal involvement between the child and the teacher that is reciprocal in nature. Reciprocity refers to the careful give and take of interactions between the child and the teacher and their mutual interdependence upon one another. Gordon (1970) calls this the "ping-ponging" of interactions—the child coos; the adult comments on the vocalization; the child coos longer and louder; the adult smiles and again comments.

Myth or Misunderstanding
CHANGES IN TEACHERS ARE GOOD FOR CHILDREN—CHANGE KEEPS THEM FROM GETTING TOO ATTACHED.

Morgan's mother and father are worried that she will get too attached to her teachers. There is a 12-year age difference between their middle child and Morgan. Morgan's mother stayed home with their other children, but now she has a job and plans to keep it. Her parents wanted Morgan to stay with her grandmother, but she recently entered a nursing home. That is why Morgan is now in child care.

The misunderstanding here is that attachment relationships with adults outside of the extended family unit are not good for children. Infants and toddlers develop multiple relationships within the family context and are able to do so as well in the school context (Howes, 2000).

When teachers and children have extended periods of time together, social and emotional development is supported. Further, consistent caregiving relationships in school enhances cognitive and language development, and supports the development of peer relationships.

What should happen next? Draft an article for the school newsletter to help parents understand this issue.

This conceptualization of the child and adult in an interactive and interdependent relationship is confirmed by many experts (Brazelton, 1992; McMullen, 1999). It isn't just the adult's response that makes the child respond or connect. The child is just as active a participant as the adult, engaging in continued or modified interaction by his vocalizations, and verbal and non-verbal responses.

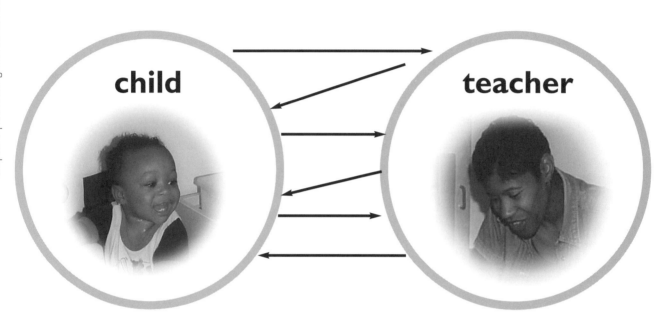

The third component of primary teaching is the balance between routines and interactions, and between stimulation and time alone. An unfortunate legacy of the early education movement is the mistaken idea that children need to have constant stimulation (Elkind, 2001). In reality, children need balance in this area. They need sensitive responses to routines; warm, caring, intimate interactions with a primary teacher; stimulation from the environment; toys, adults, and children in the environment; and, very importantly, uninterrupted time alone to integrate the experience.

Components of Primary Teaching

1. Mutual relationships between parent and teacher
2. Mutual teacher-child relationships
3. Balance between routines, interactions, stimulation, and time alone

Relationships between teachers and children are not formed overnight; they develop over time. The process of becoming familiar, learning each other's interactive styles, developing a joyful interest in each other's worlds, and learning to understand each other's communication style takes time (Fein, Gariboldi & Boni, 1993). Primary teaching leads children and their teachers to form such relationships by taking time with each step of the process and by not requiring the child or the teacher to be in a relationship "all at once."

Provide Continuity of Care

Continuity of care keeps all of the components of relationships intact over time. The teacher stays the same, the peers stay the same, and the context stays the same. In early childhood programs, it is worth the effort to maintain as many of these components as possible during the first three years (Albrecht, et al, 2001; Brazelton & Greenspan, 2000; Post and Hohmann, 2000).

Because it takes time to develop close, reciprocal relationships, teachers and children need long periods of time together. Continuity of care involves keeping all components of the child's experience continuous—the teacher, the other children in the group, and the context of the child's experience. Frequent moves of children to new classrooms with new teachers disrupt the relationship-building process, forcing everyone (child, parent, and teacher) to start over again and again.

Philosophically and experientially, primary teaching extends the length of time a teacher and her or his group of children stay together in the same place. Changing any of the components of continuity is approached cautiously. Groups stay together for at least 18 months and may stay together for up to 3 years or longer. The extended time together allows children to form strong ties to their primary teacher and to begin to form additional secondary relationships with other adults and children in the classroom (Cryer & Harms, 2000). This much time allows parents and teachers to get to know and understand each other's needs, expectations, and talents (Edwards, Gandini & Forman, 1998).

When children need changes in their environment, primary teachers make those changes in the familiar setting of the classroom instead of requiring children to move to a new location to have their needs met. Or, children move with their assigned teacher and their group of friends to a new classroom, changing only one of the components of continuous care at a time.

Facilitate Attachment Within Attachment Networks

Primary relationships create attachment security in infants and toddlers. The adults within these networks facilitate children's transitions from one attachment network member to another.

Myth or Misunderstanding
ONLY TIME WILL HELP CHILDREN ADJUST.

Pang is 12 months old and has been in 3 schools in the last 2 months. Last week he started school at Right Start. Pang is having difficulty adjusting. He cries when his mother leaves him and cries intermittently all day. He is especially upset when a teacher picks him up. His mother has started a new job and was separated from her husband (Pang's father) three months ago.

The misunderstanding here is that adjustment should be proceeding at all. Then, there is the misconception that only time will help. Given the amount of change and trauma in Pang's life, he is unable to cope with separation from his primary attachment figure, his mother. He is probably scared she will disappear like his father did, concerned about how to fit into the unfamiliar environment, and confused about who will meet his needs in the new school setting.

It is time for this school and Pang's teacher to go into action. There are many things they can do to help Pang make the adjustment. First of all, they can accept that Pang is going to need extra help for the next few weeks and come up with ways to make sure it is provided. They can work with Pang's mother to arrange for photos of both Mom and Dad to be added to Pang's classroom. He may even need a picture of Mom laminated and available to carry around. Above all, Pang needs someone to truly care that his emotional needs are met. He needs a primary teacher—one person who will be available to him, on his terms, ready to help with a smile, a cuddle, or just by being close enough to show she or he is there. Pang needs only one person to get to know, one person who will follow his lead and interact when he is ready. A conference with his mother might help the teacher understand his typical schedule, his preferences for routines, and his play interests at home. Adjustment takes time and can be facilitated by sensitive and caring teachers who get support for their efforts by managers and program administrators who understand the adjustment process.

What should happen next? How can Pang's teacher get support from her colleagues for helping Pang adjust? From her director or administrator?

Attachment Stage 1—Facilitating Indiscriminate Attachment

Stage 1 babies respond to most caring adults if their needs are met promptly. Crying normally persists for a moment even after babies get a response as their neurological system registers change. This stage usually lasts from birth to four or five months.

During this stage, members of the child's attachment network need to respond quickly to crying and work to differentiate what different cries mean. Then, by modifying responses to the needs of the child (offering a bottle when hungry or picking the child up when she needs closeness and comfort), adults enhance feelings of trust and security. Infants need to be held and cuddled and have adults who play with their fingers and toes. They benefit from adults who talk and sing to them while diapering, nursing or feeding them, and caring for them.

Babies show a definite preference for familiar people—the people who are in their attachment network. They smile, babble, coo, and respond more quickly to these familiar adults. Support progress during this stage by continuing to respond promptly to crying and calls for help, reinforcing that the world is a responsive, caring place.

Creating and perfecting a unique style of interacting with each infant is important for Stage 1 babies, as is taking individual schedule and temperament into consideration as interactions are implemented. In other words, attachment network members individualize their approach to each infant in response to the child's unique characteristics and cues.

Posting pictures of the family in the child's crib and in the family photo album facilitates Stage 1 attachment. It validates pictorially that parents and other familiar people in the child's world can still be close even if they aren't physically present.

Action/reaction games, rhymes, and fingerplays with surprises are one of the repeated behavioral sequences that form the content of social relationships (Cryer & Harms, 2000). Frequently repeated experiences with what might happen and what does happen should be an expected content of interactions from those in the attachment network.

Attachment Stage 2—Facilitating Discriminate Attachment

During Stage 2 of attachment, called discriminate attachment, infants spend a lot of their time beginning to differentiate between familiar and unfamiliar caregivers. This stage lasts from 5 or 6 months until about 11 or 12 months.

In Stage 2, babies smile, babble, coo, and respond more quickly to familiar adults. Babies show a definite preference for familiar faces and brighten considerably when a familiar face comes into view. Unlike babies in the first stage, where almost any sensitive caregiver would do, Stage 2 babies are quick to indicate with whom they would like to interact.

The following strategies will support infants in this stage of attachment:

▶ Continue to respond promptly to crying and calls for help as well as calls for interaction. This helps babies learn that they can really depend on the adults in their attachment networks.

▶ Describe what you are doing to the baby as you do it. Wait for a signal from the baby that indicates that she is ready to be picked up or to open her mouth. Look for an indication that the baby is aware of and ready for what is about to happen.

▶ Establish an arrival and departure routine. Routines can comfort children when they reach the next attachment stage.

▶ Encourage the use of security items or favorite toys as a support for transitions among and between adults in the attachment network. Consistent bridging and support cues such as these help children with transitions, even if that transition is to another adult in their attachment network. From these experiences, infants learn that they can bring their own resources to bear in managing and easing the transition.

▶ Play peek-a-boo games to help babies learn that you do re-appear. These games help infants learn that important adults always come back.

Attachment Stage 3—Facilitating Separation Anxiety

An amazing change begins to occur in infants as they approach the end of the first year. Smiling, cooing, responsive babies, who were friendly to almost every smiling face, begin to be wary of strangers and new situations. They begin to prefer one or two of the adults in their attachment network to other adults. Further, they begin to prefer those one or two people in their attachment network to others for comforting or for particular routines.

Characteristics like these indicate that infants are in the third stage of attachment. During this stage, which lasts from 11–12 months to 17–18 months, babies show a clearly defined preference for parents and other familiar adults. Friendliness toward strangers declines. Babies use parents as a secure base and hide their heads, hold on tight, and turn away from strangers or less well-known adults.

This behavior is good news! It means that the baby's emotional development is proceeding normally. The attachment network should take these changes in the baby's behavior into consideration when the child goes out into the broader social world. Some of the following strategies may help infants handle this stage of attachment.

- Accept cool response to unfamiliar adults. Don't push or encourage interaction until the baby seems ready to initiate it.
- Give the baby time to adjust to new people before the new people try to hold her or interact with her. Let infants stay close when a new person is around; use supportive, encouraging, non-verbal cues like eye contact or smiling and nodding your head to indicate that the new person is not a threat. If the infant decides to let the strangers interact, stay nearby to assure the child of your availability (or secure base) if it is needed.
- Allow infants to set their own pace—if they don't want to go to a new person, respect the decision.
- Explain what is going on to grandparents, friends, or relatives who do not see the baby often enough to be familiar to him or her. It is a developmental stage—not a rejection of their interest.

Myth or Misunderstanding
IT'S NOT FAIR TO THE OTHER CHILDREN TO GIVE SO MUCH ATTENTION TO A CHILD WHO IS GOING THROUGH SEPARATION ANXIETY OR STRANGER ANXIETY.

The addition of a new child to a group of children always presents dilemmas. Parents of children who are already enrolled may feel like the new child is getting attention that should be shared. They may also feel like the adjustment adds stress and strain to their child's day. For teachers, the addition of a new child, particularly at certain stages of attachment, may seem like a huge challenge—one that is not completely under the teacher's control and that is not guaranteed to succeed.

There are many times during a young child's life, particularly in the first three years, when she needs extra time and attention from the important adults in her life. Sometimes these events occur when other children in the group are on an even keel. Then, teachers feel able to devote extra time and energy to the child who needs it. Other times, a new child increases the stress levels in the classroom for everyone.

Myth or Misunderstanding—cont'd.

The misunderstanding here is that teachers must choose to meet the needs of the new child and her family or the children already in her group. In reality, they must do both. But, how? Organizational supports for transitioning children are important. Extra assistance from familiar support staff for the children who are already enrolled is a good beginning. Then, teachers need support from peers and mentors for doing the important work of establishing a relationship—investing in really getting to know the child and her family to be able to help the child adjust to the new setting. This work can be tiring and emotional for teachers as well as for the child. Providing mentors who understand the process and can validate, support, and encourage the teacher will enhance the likelihood of success. Newly enrolled parents also need help. Sometimes, enrolled parents can partner with new families to serve as a resource for transitioning.

When teachers are not prepared to help children adjust and aren't supported in the process by administrative staff, the result is usually an even more extended adjustment period—extending the stress for everyone. Investing in facilitating adjustment, particularly during separation or stranger anxiety, is a reciprocal and mutual process for the teacher and the child and her family. Each needs help to make it happen.

What should happen next? What steps should the teacher take with her or his currently enrolled parents before she or he starts a new child?
- *Give infants and toddlers many experience with action/reaction toys and games like peek-a-boo and find-the-doll-under-the-blanket. These activities give children opportunities to practice the emerging skill of understanding that objects have permanence and do not disappear simply because they are not visible. Ultimately, they will begin to understand the enduring nature of the attachment relationship and not be so upset with separation events.*
- *Spend long periods of time with infants and toddlers as they explore and discover the environment during floor time. Exploration is a marvelous distraction and can re-orient the child from being upset with separation to being interested in an activity.*
- *Help infants and toddlers say goodbye to members of their attachment network.*
- *Encourage a routine that includes hugs and kisses. Stay nearby to help when an important adult leaves.*
- *Always alert infants and toddlers to departures. They may object, but they will also learn that adults in their attachment network can be trusted to say goodbye before they leave.*

Stranger anxiety is a difficult time for children and their caregivers. Children are cautious and clingy and often resist or fear strangers. This stage usually lasts from 17 or 18 months until 24 or 25 months. To help children during this stage, consider the following:

- Limit the number of unfamiliar people that are in the child's space. Let visitors say hello from the door instead of entering the room. Support children through novel experiences with unknown adults. Experiences such as taking a portrait with a strange photographer, going into an unfamiliar environment, or entering a room full of new people will work better if you prepare the child for the experience and serve as the secure base—holding the child until she is ready to experience the new environment on her own.

- Then, stay close. Initial feelings of "I can do it" may be followed by equally as intense and valid feelings of "now I can't." If members of the attachment network are still close, these ambivalent feelings can be accepted and supported until the child is ready to try again.

- Always celebrate reunions! Make a big point of reuniting, so infants and toddlers clearly know an important person in their attachment network is back and very glad to see them!

Create Home-school Partnerships

Parents often feel insecure in their roles as their child's first and most important teachers. Some parents try to read everything possible on child rearing and development to try to overcome their feelings of uncertainty and inadequacy. Others ask many questions, seeking input from a wide variety of sources to aid parenting. Still others may try to defer parenting decisions to their child's teacher.

Teachers have the responsibility to become partners with parents. Sharing information is a great way to start. Respect for parents as their child's most important teachers will allow teachers to work together with parents to support young children as they grow and learn.

Parent/teacher partnerships are not the same as parent involvement or parent education. Partnerships are characterized by mutual respect, sensitivity to the perspective of the other, two-way communication, common goals that are clear and agreed on, equal distribution of power, recognition and valuing the strengths of each partner, and shared decision-making (Stonehouse, 1988).

Establish Two-way Communication with Parents

An important part of creating partnerships with parents is to perfect accurate and frequent communication between parents and teachers. These include written and verbal communication systems.

Using a written communication system is an important part of communication. Teachers need to keep a great deal of information to provide for the children in their groups. Information can be lost easily if parents and teachers depend just on their memories and their verbal interactions. Using a written system helps everyone keep up with information that needs to be exchanged and documents the progress of communicating.

Written communication systems support parents in giving information to teachers, and teachers in sharing how the day went at school with parents. Such systems usually begin with information about the child's time at home that might be helpful to the teacher. How long the child slept, when she last ate, information about elimination, and any special instructions for the teacher (See Appendix, page 355 for a sample).

This information is so important. It creates a platform from which the teacher is able to accurately anticipate and interpret children's needs. Likewise, parents need to know information about what happens each day at school. Activities like eating, sleeping, diaper changes, and so on should be recorded. Teachers also will record developmental notes and observations. Used this way, written communication systems help parents get a feel for how the day at school went.

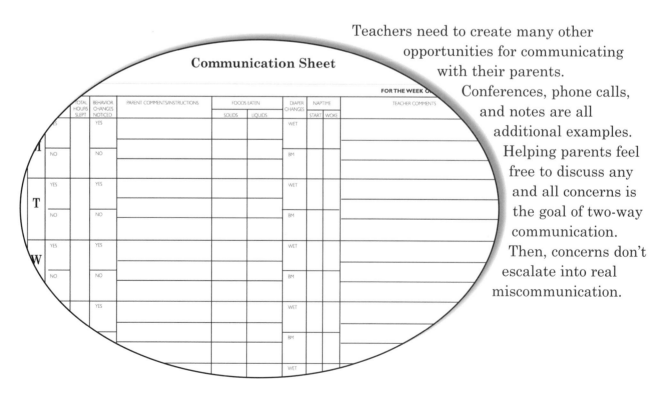

Teachers need to create many other opportunities for communicating with their parents. Conferences, phone calls, and notes are all additional examples. Helping parents feel free to discuss any and all concerns is the goal of two-way communication. Then, concerns don't escalate into real miscommunication.

Myth or Misunderstanding
PARENTS NEED TO KNOW WHAT HAPPENS AT SCHOOL, BUT TEACHERS WHO WANT TO KNOW WHAT HAPPENS AT HOME ARE BEING NOSEY.

Tom and Mary have just moved to Atlanta from their home in Texas. Before they moved, the couple had placed their children in a small church school in the basement of the church they attended. Tom and Mary knew all the teachers. When they talked with the teachers, they found out everything they needed to know.

At the new school, teachers use a written communication system to make sure that they communicate effectively with parents. Mary and John feel like everyone wants to be in the middle of their business—to know too much. They don't really know the teachers yet and certainly don't want to share details about their home life. Teachers keep asking questions, and are insisting that they fill out the communication forms when they bring their children to school.

This myth points to interesting questions. Whose job is it to help Tom and Mary understand the teacher's expectation? Is it the school director? The teacher? Does the parent handbook address this issue? Can other parents help? Was there a new parent orientation for Tom and Mary to help them understand the communication system? Did the school offer gradual enrollment to help Tom and Mary see the communication system in action? Does the school have a confidentiality policy that might help Mary and Tom understand that the information is kept confidential?

Tom and Mary don't realize how the teachers use the information that is provided by parents. Teachers want to know information about children's time at home so they can do the best job possible at school during the day. Information from parents creates a platform from which the teacher is able to accurately anticipate and interpret children's needs. Knowing that a child has eaten breakfast, did not get a good night's sleep, is teething, had an upset stomach, or is happy, will help the teacher know what to try and how to interact.

What should happen next? Make some suggestions to the teacher, to the parents, and to the school administrator about how to address this situation.

The better the communication is between home and school, the better the opportunity is for parents to feel comfortable with their child's school experience.

Employ Family-centered Practices

An important part of one's self-concept comes from being a part of a family group within a culture. Cultures have different characteristics, and families within cultures vary as well. Race, ethnicity, religion, gender, primary language, family size, family composition, and cultural values are all components of culture. How the school environment responds to children's cultural differences impacts self-concept.

Teachers have a marvelous opportunity to make sure that their classrooms are family centered as well as culturally inclusive. They can do this by creating family-centered practices that acknowledge, respect, and support all families. Three specific principles are suggested as core ideas about family-centered practices (McBride, 1999). The first principle is to establish the family as the focus, not the child. Focusing educational services on the family validates the influential role of the family on children's development.

The second principle is to support and respect the family as decision-makers—both by acknowledging them and by including them in all decisions made about their child. Learning to make decisions about educational issues is sometimes challenging for parents. Supported and shared decision-making helps make sure the child's educational needs will be met at school and supports parents in participating in, learning from, and guiding those decisions.

The third principle is to provide flexible, responsive, and comprehensive services to strengthen family functioning. In most educational systems, teachers come and go. The family provides the context for the child's ongoing development and growth. Teachers' support for families to meet their children's needs builds confidence and competence at being able to do so.

Other characteristics of family-centered programs include providing parents with choices that address family needs and concerns, helping families make informed decisions by fully disclosing information, and providing support in ways that empower parents and enhance parental competence (Shonkoff & Phillips, 2000).

Family-centered practices have particular characteristics. Some are under the direct control of the teacher. Teachers can begin by keeping the focus on the family rather than diverting the focus to the school. When families are validated as the primary educators of their children, teachers build bridges that will enable families to accomplish this goal.

Then, teachers can develop partnerships with families to enhance school experiences and validate home experiences. Helping families stay connected to schools requires that teachers both include them in making decisions about their child's early education and respect their ideas about how to do so. Partnerships require reciprocal communication, true two-way communication aimed at acknowledging family strengths. Having a partnership also requires teachers to make sure families can be a part of the classroom by creating many ways for parents and other family members to participate and be involved.

Use a Variety of Teaching Roles

The Teacher as Initiator

It is easy for teachers to take the lead—initiating actions that support the teaching role. For the tasks of connecting with school and teacher and making friends, initiation has a particular feel and timbre. Teachers take the lead with parents to get information about the child, her schedule, the parents' hopes and dreams, parenting strategies, and so forth. This information helps teachers see the school experience from the families' point of view and increases the likelihood that they are on the same page in their expectations.

Initiating connections with the child during transitions comes next. Sometimes, initiations can be direct, like inviting a child to join an activity.

At other times, the initiations may need to be more subtle, such as offering a play invitation through a non-verbal gesture such as a smile, through a toy, the parent, or another child.

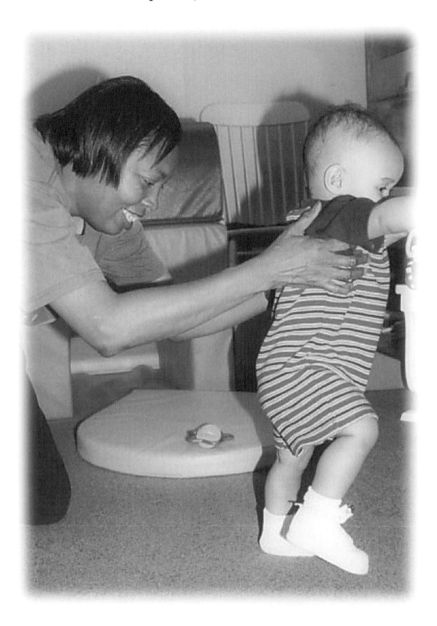

Making families feel welcome in the classroom can be initiated in many ways during the gradual enrollment process. More than any other role the teacher plays, this one can create a firm foundation for future collaboration and partnership. Families feel welcome when teachers accept their important role in the child's life and offer to support, validate, and strengthen it. Teachers may also need to initiate welcoming activities and experiences. They can make a place to "be" for the adults who are participating in gradual enrollment. Adult-size furniture, permission to sit on the floor with their child, a place to put things, and a nametag that helps others recognize and acknowledge their school participation are some ideas.

Offering to listen is a wonderful gift for new families, particularly families who are experiencing transitions for the first time. When teachers initiate conversations with open-ended questions that tell new parents that they are prepared to listen, connections and partnerships flourish. Some examples might be "How are you feeling about the transition?" or "Tell me how you felt about your child's experiences today," or "Should we make any changes in our plan for tomorrow?"

The Teacher as Investor

The role of teacher as an investor sounds so financial—so business-like. But this investor is looking for dividends beyond the monetary kind. Some parents "warm up" to teachers faster than others. Teachers may need to invest in contacts with cautious or uncomfortable parents, making the effort to open the door to create partnerships. Investing in collecting information that might be helpful in understanding each child's uniqueness gives parents an opportunity to fulfill their role as the experts on what their child needs from school.

She or he may need to invest extra time in sharing information about the school, insuring communication between school and home, and sharing with parents the new child's experiences during the school day. And, she or he will certainly need to invest in extra holding, cuddling, touching, talking, and interacting time with new children. As part of the gradual enrollment process, the teacher will need to invest in observing the child at school, the interactions between parents and children, and the child at play. Because observation gives teachers insight into the child's individuality, unique skills and abilities, and family relationships, it leads teachers to know what to do or try next.

Teaching Roles

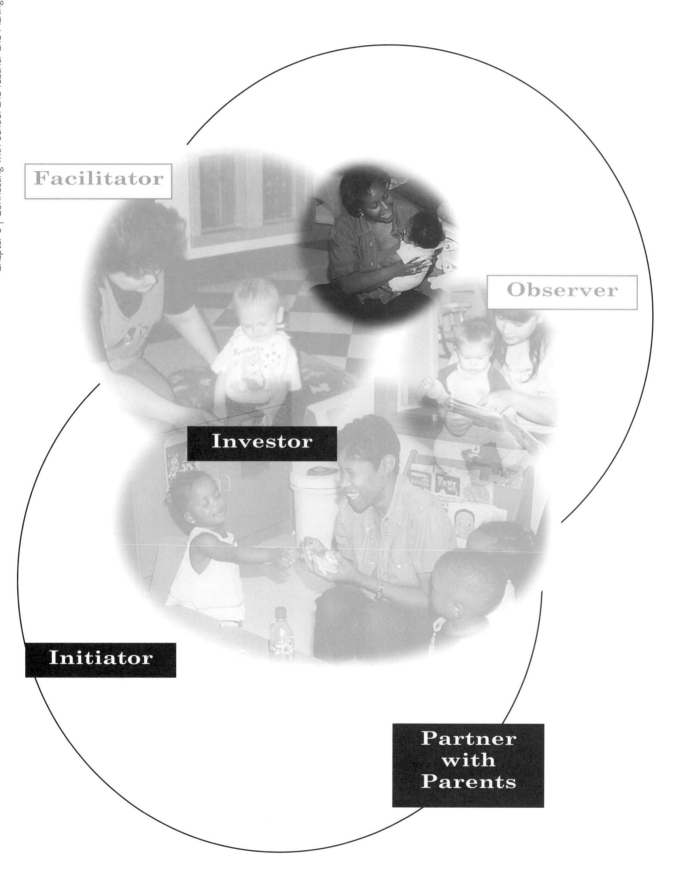

Facilitator

Observer

Investor

Initiator

Partner
with
Parents

The Teacher as Partner

Assuming the role of partner can begin early for teachers. Start by thoroughly explaining the purpose of gradual enrollment and providing sample schedules that have worked for others in the past. Then, work with the family to make a gradual enrollment plan that fits the family's situation and needs. Partnering with parents to make a gradual enrollment plan that works for everyone is an investment in the success of the adjustment process and says from the beginning that the teacher plans to work cooperatively with parents with the child's best interest as the goal.

Then, teachers partner with the new child to bridge interactions between peers in the classroom. For infants, this may mean positioning the child to observe others in the classroom. For toddlers, this may mean actively facilitating interactions so that initial ones go smoothly enough to give the child confidence to try on their own.

Facilitate Interactions Between Children

Infants and toddlers are fascinated by and interested in other children. This interest extends to children who are familiar to them and those who are not. Spectator sports—watching what other children are doing—are highly engaging and entertaining to infants and toddlers. But, children may not have the social skills needed to play successfully with other children because their egocentrism keeps them focused on their own needs and wants.

Most interactions between children need adult support. Because they are still learning to regulate their own emotions, children have more interest in playing than they have the skills to do so (Stonehouse, 1988). Adult support for interactions can support developing skills in children and help peer relationships to grow.

Children are working on developing social competence. Social competence is the ability to engage in satisfying interactions with adults and peers and, through such interactions, continue to grow socially (Katz & McClellan, 1997). Part of social competence is how children respond to and are responded to by peers. Are they accepted? Rejected? Included in play? Left out of play? Is the inclusion or exclusion mutual or one sided? Some researchers view negative early peer experiences as an early indicator of potential social/emotional and academic problems (Pellegrini & Glickman, 1990; Shonkoff & Phillips, 2000).

Children have many social difficulties. They have limited skills in controlling impulses, delaying gratification, using expressive language, entering play, reading social cues, and regulating emotions. These difficulties can show up in different ways in different children, but are most often seen in aggressive behavior that needs to be facilitated by adults.

Help Children Make Friends

Toddlers have a particular quality that can cause problems for them when they are in groups. They are egocentric—focused on themselves and not able to view situations and interactions from multiple points of view. They are not able, for example, to understand that biting someone's finger hurts someone else. Young children can't take the point of view of another, so they need adult support to understand that they are getting too close to, or need to be away from others to walk around the room.

At the same time, a wonderful new skill is emerging in toddlers. They are beginning to develop true friendships and learn about being a friend. Having someone to play with becomes a powerful drive that helps toddlers learn more social skills. Parents and teachers alike are often pleased to see children exhibiting sympathy (feeling sad when another child is sad), empathy (understanding how a hurt child feels without being hurt themselves), and altruism (concern about the welfare of others). These new skills increase the chance that children will get along better in groups.

In a classroom in which a number of children are sharing the same space, remember to look at them as a group of individual, unconnected children. Stay close and help them learn the process of interacting with others as their social skills grow. Children do not have the fully developed skills for social interactions, so they need the support of adults to help them function in a group setting.

Create Appropriate Environments

Create Environments that Welcome Families

Classrooms are the purview of teachers. Parents normally come in and out of them without really spending too much time. They may or may not feel comfortable being there. A good place to start is to create places for adults to comfortably "be" in the classroom. This may mean having an area that has adult-sized furniture, leaving a clear pathway from the door to the child's cubby area, or even providing a place to put purses, keys, or personal items while they are reconnecting with their children. Pair these kinds of accommodations with a stated and written "open door" policy. Clear explanations that parents are not visitors, but a part of the classroom, will go a long way to make parents feel welcome.

Post photos of parents, children, and families in the environment. Familiar faces and photos of children invite parents into the classroom. Make sure images of families posted in the classroom match the families enrolled in the classroom. If your picture file is inadequate, include parents in sharing magazines and photographs from their collections to enhance your own.

Applying Theory and Best Practices

A large part of professional practice in the field of care and early education is the synthesizing of knowledge, research, and best practices into teaching actions and strategies. A goal of *Innovations: Infant and Toddler Development* is to help teachers apply theory, research, and best practices to real-life situations and behaviors in the infant and toddler classroom. Let's take a look at a common behavior that is a part of most children's experience in care and early education settings to see if the knowledge we have gained, the research we have reviewed, and/or the best practices we have explored give any suggestions of how the behavior might be handled by teachers in the classroom.

Connecting with school and teacher and making friends are tasks that require children to adjust—adjust to new experiences, new people, and new settings. Sometimes connecting with school and teacher and making friends go smoothly and children are able to form relationships with new adults and begin to make friends, as well. Sometimes connecting with school and teacher or making friends can be difficult. So, let's begin exploring the integration of knowledge, research, and best practices by considering the implications of the topics covered in this chapter for children who are having adjustment difficulty.

Possibilities from Bronfenbrenner's Ecological Systems Theory for Adjustment Difficulty

Make a plan that works for each family—don't try to have a one-size-fits-all approach to gradual enrollment or parent relationships. Really work to individualize the plans you make with parents to fit their needs and resources.

Consider the characteristics of the microsystem and the mesosytem of the child and the family. Identify strengths and uniquenesses that each family has for supporting children in the adjustment process. When teachers look carefully at the systems of influence on the child and the family, they may discover similarities, differences, and even value conflicts between their culture, the culture of the school, and the culture of the child. When these differences are identified and out in the open, teachers and parents can recognize and acknowledge them, then work together to make sure the differences do not pose difficulties for the child in either the home or the school setting.

Possibilities from Erickson's Stages of Psycho-social Development for Adjustment Difficulty

Erickson's stages of psycho-social development inform teachers to go slowly, to give children and their parents time to adjust. When children resist or have difficulties in adjustment, think about the amount of time they have had to form new relationships and think of ways to support the connections between the child and the teachers. The dichotomies of Erickson's theory can serve as yardsticks to interactions—an indication of the way teachers are tilting the child's experiences at school. If they are generally positive, then adjustment should proceed. If they aren't, then teachers and parents need to work together to figure out why and modify the adjustment plan.

From Erickson's ideas, teachers can incorporate two specific types of activities and experiences for children who are connecting with school and teacher and making friends. Plan activities that celebrate and validate autonomy such as developmental banners that identify emerging skills for parents. When parents see children's growing and changing at school, they will be more comfortable with the school setting. Then, plan activities and experiences that validate and encourage attempts (successful or otherwise) at autonomy. Infants and toddlers need many positive experiences making things happen to objects, themselves, and to the environment. Celebrate successful attempts at calming oneself down, finding a toy to play with, and manipulating and influencing the environment.

Possibilities from Attachment Relationships for Adjustment Difficulty

These theories support teachers by providing information about where to start. Identify the child's stage of attachment for each child who is starting school. If you know, for example, that a child is in the age range for separation anxiety, go slowly—give the child time to look, smell, feel, touch, and interact with new people and new things with her parents' support before she has to do it on her own. If she is not yet experiencing separation anxiety, you may be able to interact more directly, responding to the child's attempts to connect socially with you as a mechanism for leading to emotional connections.

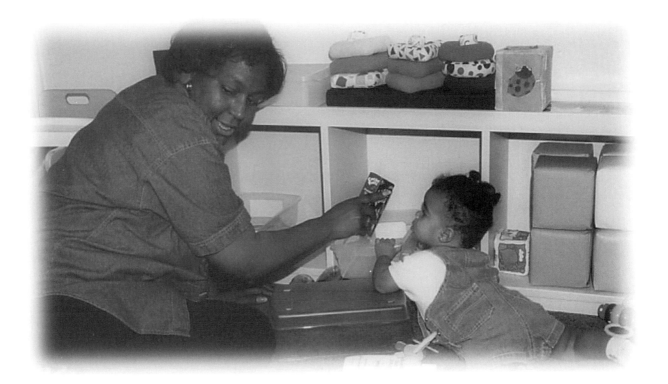

Be a secure base for children assigned to you. Stay in touch physically, visually, verbally, and emotionally. When teachers support secure base behaviors in children, they are facilitating attachment behaviors and communicating to children that it is worth getting to know the new people in their school environment.

Possibilities from Peer Relationships for Adjustment Difficulty

Because peer relationships are socially constructed—that is, they result from the interactive experiences that children have with one another—the teacher's role in supporting possibilities for connecting with school and teacher and making friends are clear. Children need teachers to create opportunities to have friends and to be friends. Situations and experiences that foster gathering information about, and experience in, social interaction can be planned. Then, children need help in successfully negotiating the planned experiences from close, facilitative adults. Finally, children need to know that teachers are there to help when conflicts arise so that play doesn't stop just because there is conflict.

Remember the need for regular and frequent experiences with peers. Children are more successful with familiar playmates, but it takes time for children to become familiar with each other. In the meantime, teachers can serve as playmates, including children in successful experiences as their comfort level and familiarity grows.

Integrating Theory and Best Practices into Curriculum

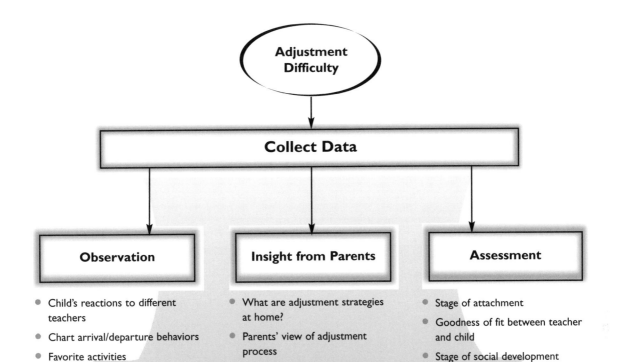

Adjustment Difficulty

Collect Data

Observation
- Child's reactions to different teachers
- Chart arrival/departure behaviors
- Favorite activities
- Difficult times of day

Insight from Parents
- What are adjustment strategies at home?
- Parents' view of adjustment process
- Parents' hello/good-bye rituals
- Security items used at home
- Parents' level of concern
- Willingness to extend/modify gradual enrollment

Assessment
- Stage of attachment
- Goodness of fit between teacher and child
- Stage of social development
- Favorite toy choices
- Favorite activities
- Desired level of stimulation

Increase Understanding

Theory/Research Knowledge
- Kovach-Da Ros (1998)
- McBride (1999)
- Brazelton (1992) (1990)
- Gradual enrollment
- Attachment stages
- Emotional development

Best Practices
- Good-bye/hello ritual
- Primary caregiving
- Extend/modify gradual enrollment
- Photos of parent to look at/hold at school
- Audiotape of parent reading a book
- Lots of holding time
- Try adjustment strategies

Cultural Context and Congruence
- Parents' view of child's adjustment difficulty
- Consistent support for transitions between home/school
- Shorten day
- Accommodation strategies to address context differences

Collaboration
- Ask other teachers for suggestions of things to try
- Conversations at staff meetings
- Identify expert to support teachers and parents

Possibilities

Parent Possibilities

Teacher-Initiated

Parent Participation

Written arrival/departure routines.

Individualize gradual enrollment plan.

Observations from home

Parent's view of adjustment process

Security items

Visit log of family member visits.

Innovations in Environments

Control overstimulation

Quiet place to be alone

Room broken into individual settings

Calm background colors w/ bright colors in the activities

Observation/Assessment Possibilities

Stage of attachment

Observe difference in transition w/ different family members, teachers

Temperament chart

Accurate read of information about unusual occurrences, accidents, or changes in child's behavior

Consistencies between microsystem and mesosystem of home and school, parents' and teachers' views

Interactive Experiences

Interact, rather than react to child

Anticipate needs and wants

Wait for cues that child is ready for something to take place

Sensitivity to over- and understimulation

Individualize schedule or pace of the day

Be a secure base

Create opportunities to have friends and be friends

Facilitate conflict

Serve as playmate

Work to read verbal/non-verbal cues

Respond quickly and affectionately

Plan

Web

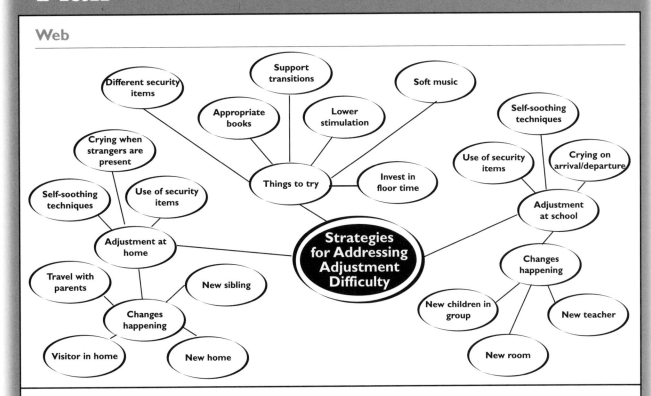

Dramatic Possibilities Key rattles, bags, purses, hats

Art/Sensory Possibilities Warm water or lotion experiences, tearing paper

Curiosity Possibilities Mirrors, keys and glitter in syrup in bottle

Music Possibilities Calm classical music, lullabies

Movement Possibilities Find Mommy's or Daddy's picture

Literacy Possibilities Add books (below)

Outdoor Possibilities Suitcases, bags outside

Project Possibilities Parents at work photo album

Books	Picture File Pictures/Vocabulary
You Go Away, by Dorothy Corey *Are You My Mother?*, by P.D. Eastman *When Mama Comes Home Tonight*, by Eileen Spinelli *Mama, Do You Love Me?*, by Barbara M. Joosse *Where's My Baby?*, by H.A. Rey *No Matter What*, by Debbie Gliori	Photos of family members Photos of teachers and children in classroom

Rhymes & Fingerplays	Music/Songs	Prop Boxes
"If You're Happy and You Know It" "Ten Little Friends"	Parent-recorded tape "The More We Get Together" "Where Is Thumbkin?"	Going Places prop box Mommy's or Daddy's Work prop box

Summary

The complement of separating from the comfort and familiarity of home is connecting to the world outside. Making friends becomes an important task once the connection with the social world is made. Everything that happens in children's lives takes place in the rich, complex, and changing cultural context.

The infant's connection to parents, teachers, and friends is facilitated by caring, involved parents, as well as responsive interactions from the other new people the child meets. Both adults and peer playmates become important as children widen their social experiences to include more than their attachment figures. Friendships begin to emerge as children integrate their experiences in the world of play.

Bronfenbrenner's ecological model of human development proposes that development occurs in the context of the systems that influence, impact, and direct development. The four systems of influence follow:

1. The microsystem is composed of the socio-cultural context of the family, including values, cultural practices, previous caregiving experiences, and relationships between the child and his frequent caregivers.
2. The mesosystem includes the educational context and the interface between cultural, religious, ethnic, family composition, racial, and socioeconomic backgrounds.
3. The exosystem is composed of the community and includes values and practices of schools, religious organizations, community agencies, and social groups.
4. The macrosystem is composed of the broader society including economic resource allocation, business practices employment, health and education priorities, government policies, demographic trends, and technological changes.

Erik Erickson's contribution to developmental theory is that development is cumulative, with each developmental step laying the foundation for the next and each future step forward being influenced by previous ones. Each stage is a crisis that must be resolved. Stages continue throughout a person's life. The stages that occur in children from birth to age three follow:

1. The first stage is the struggle to develop a sense of trust in the interactive, physical, social, and cultural world.
2. The second stage is related to feelings of autonomy vs. shame and doubt.

Feelings of security and trust emerge in infants and toddlers when they have intimate, reciprocal, continuing relationships with adults. Ainsworth proposed a stage theory of attachment with four discrete stages built upon one another. The stages are:

1. Indiscriminate Attachment (birth to five months)
2. Discriminate Attachment (5 months to 11 or 12 months)
3. Separation Anxiety (11–12 months to about 17–18 months)
4. Stranger Anxiety (17–18 months to 24–25 months)

It is the sequence of the pattern of behaviors that increases our understanding of emerging attachment, not the ages assigned to specific stages.

Children use attachment figures as a secure emotional base. When infants and toddlers are in familiar situations, they venture into the environment, explore it, and then return to touch base with important attachment figures. Children with attachment security and secure-base behavior have advantages that last throughout life.

Primary teaching focuses on the development of an intimate, sensitive, and reciprocal relationship between and the child and her most important caregiver. The *Innovations* model of primary teaching is more comprehensive and includes schools having the opportunity to develop close ties among parents, teachers, children, and between home and school. The three components of primary teaching are 1) the relationship between the parent and teacher, 2) the responsive relationship between the child and teacher, and 3) the balance between routines and interactions, and between stimulation and time alone.

Continuity of care is keeping all of the components of relationships intact over time. Because it takes time to develop close, reciprocal relationships, teachers and children need long periods of time together. Frequent moves of children to new classrooms with new teachers disrupt the relationship-building process, forcing everyone (child, parent, and teacher) to start over again and again.

Teachers have many opportunities to develop parent partnerships. Developing a close relationship with parents is the foundation of supporting children as they grow and learn.

Questions and Activities

1. When discussing emotional development, what is meant by the term "an organized sense of self"? How does this impact the teacher? What new cues and behaviors will a child demonstrate?
2. How is the teacher-child relationship based on reciprocity? Give specific examples of reciprocity.
3. Explain how and why primary caregiving facilitates children's emotional development.
4. Based on the four stages of attachment described by Ainsworth and her colleagues, when would be the best times for a child to enter care and early education setting? Why are these the best times? What additional considerations besides stage of attachment behavior should be included in the decision?
5. What is stranger anxiety? How would you protect children in your care from experiencing negative consequences from this developmental stage?
6. How does the role of the primary caregiver differ from caregivers in other settings? How does a teacher know to anticipate needs and read cues? In what ways does primary caregiving make the role of the teacher more manageable?

References

Ainsworth, M.D.S., M.C. Blehar, E. Waters & S. Wall. (1978). *Patterns of attachment: A psychological study of the strange situation.* Hillsdale, NJ: Erlbaum.

Albrecht, K., M. Banks, G. Calhoun, L. Dziadul, C. Gwinn, B. Harrington, B. Kerr, M. Mizukami, A. Morris, C. Peterson & R.R. Summers. (2000). The good, the bad, and the wonderful: Keeping children and teachers together. *Child Care Information Exchange,* 136, 24-28.

Albrecht, K., L. Dziadul, C. Gwinn, & B. Harrington. (2001). The good, the bad, and the wonderful: Keeping children and teachers together (part 2). *Child Care Information Exchange,* 137, 90-93.

Bernhardt, J.L. (2000). A primary caregiving system for infants and toddlers: Best for everyone involved. *Young Children,* 52(7), 12-15.

Bowlby, J. (1982). *Attachment and Loss: Attachment* (Vol. 1), New York: Basic Books.

Brazelton, T.B. (1992). *Touchpoints: The essential reference.* Reading, MA: Addison-Wesley.

Brazelton, T.B. & S.I. Greenspan. (2000). *The irreducible needs of children: What every child must have to grow, learn, and flourish.* Cambridge, MA: Perseus Publishing.

Bronfenbrenner, U. (1979). *The ecology of human development: Experiments by nature and design.* Cambridge, MA: Harvard University Press.

Cassidy J., S. Kirsh, K.L. Scolton & R.D. Parke. (1996). Attachment and representations of peer relationships. *Developmental Psychology*, 32, 892-904.

Cryer, D. & T. Harms. (2000). *Infants and toddlers in out of home care.* Baltimore, MD: Brookes Publishing.

Edwards, C., L. Gandini & G. Forman. (1998). *The one hundred languages of children: The Reggio Emilia approach to early childhood education – Advanced Reflections.* Norwood, NJ: Ablex.

Elkind, D. (2001). Thinking about children's play. *Child Care Information Exchange,* 139, 27-28.

Erickson, E.H. (1963). *Childhood and society.* New York: Norton.

Fein, G.G., A. Gariboldi, & R. Boni. (1993). The adjustment of infants and toddlers to group care: The first six months. *Early Childhood Research Quarterly,* 8, 1-14.

Gerber, M. & A. Johnson. (1997). *Your self-confident baby.* New York: Wiley.

Gordon, I. (1970). *Baby learning through baby play.* New York: St. Martin's.

Greenman, J. & A. Stonehouse. (1996). *Prime times: A handbook for excellence in infant and toddler programs.* St. Paul, MN: Redleaf Press.

Howes, C. (1988). Peer interaction of young children. *Monographs of the Society for Research in Child Development,* 53 (1).

Howes, C. (2000). Social development, family, and attachment relationships of infant and toddlers. In D. Cryer, & T. Harms, (Eds.), *Infants and toddlers in out of home care* (87-113). Baltimore, MD: Brookes Publishing.

Howes, C. & C.E. Hamilton. (1992). Children's relationships with caregivers: Mothers and child care teachers. *Child Development* 64, 859-866.

Howes, C., D.A. Phillips, & M. Whitebrook. (1992). Thresholds of quality: Implications for the social development of children in center-based care. *Child Development,* 63, 449-460.

Katz, L. & P. McClellan. (1997). *Fostering social competence: The teacher's role.* Washington DC: National Association for the Education of Young Children (NAEYC).

Kirsh, S.J. & J. Cassidy. (1997). Preschoolers' attention to and memory for attachment-relevant information. *Child Development,* 68: 1143-1153.

Kovach, B.A. & D.A. Da Ros. (1998). Respectful, individual, and responsive caregiving for infants: The key to successful care in group settings. *Young Children,* 53 (3), 61-64.

Laible, D.J. & R.A. Thompson. (1998). Attachment and emotional understanding in preschool children, *Developmental Psychology,* 34(5), 1038-1045.

Lally, J.R. (1995). The impact of child care policies and practices on infant/toddler identity formation. *Young Children,* 51 (1), 58-67.

Leavitt, R.L. (1994). *Power and emotion in infant-toddler day care.* Albany, NY: State University of New York Press.

McBride, S.L. (1999). Family centered practices. **Young Children,** 54 (4), 62-68.

McMullen, M.B. (1999). Achieving best practices in infant and toddler care and education. **Young Children,** 54 (4), 69-75.

Piaget, J. (1962). **Play, dreams, and imitation in childhood.** (C. Gattegno & F.M. Hodgson, Trans.) New York: Norton.

Pelligrini, A.S. & C.D. Glickman. (1990). Measuring kindergartners' social competence. **Young Children,** 45 (4), 40-44.

Post, J. & M. Hohmann. (2000). **Tender care and early learning.** Ypsilanti, MI: High/Scope Press.

Powell, D.R. (1998). Reweaving parents into the fabric of early childhood programs. **Young Children,** 53 (5), 60-67.

Raikes, H. (1996). A secure base for babies: Applying attachment concepts to the infant care setting. **Young Children,** 51 (5), 50-67.

Reisenberg, J. (1995). Reflections on quality infant care. **Young Children,** 50 (6), 23-25.

Rubin, Z. (1980). **Children's friendships.** Cambridge, MA: Harvard University Press.

Schweinhart, L., H. Barnes, D. Weikart, W.S. Barnett, & A.S. Epstein. (1993). Significant benefits: The High/Scope Perry Preschool study through age 27. **Monographs of the High/Scope Educational Research Foundation,** No. 10. Ypsilanti, MI: The High/Scope Press.

Shonkoff, J.P. & D.A. Phillips (Eds.). (2000). **From neurons to neighborhoods: The science of early childhood development.** Washington, DC: National Academy Press.

Shore, R. (1997). **Rethinking the brain: New insights into early development.** New York: Families and Work.

Sroufe, L.A., & J. Fleeson. (1986). Attachment and the construction of relationships. In W.W. Hartup & A. Rubin (Eds.) **Relationships and Development** (51-71). Hillsdale, N.J.: Erlbaum.

Stonehouse, A. (1988). **How does it feel?: Child care from a parent's perspective.** Redmond, WA: Exchange Press.

Vygotsky, L. (1978). **Mind in society: The development of higher psychological processes.** Cambridge, MA: Harvard University Press.

Glossary

Attachment Figures—The people with whom children have their most important and close relationships.

Attachment Network—The adult primary caregivers of infants and toddlers whose relationships are mutual, synchronous, abiding, and reciprocal.

Attachment Theory—A stage theory [developed by Ainsworth] with four discrete stages building upon one another characterized by behaviors that give clues to parents and others as to where infants and toddlers are in the development of attachment relationships.

Bronfenbrenner's Ecological Systems Theory—A theory that proposes that human development occurs in the context of complex, dynamic systems that influence, impact, and direct emerging development.

Discriminate Attachment—The second stage in Ainsworth's stage theory of attachment when babies begin to smile, babble, coo, and respond more quickly to the mother and other familiar adults.

Erickson's Theory of Psycho-social Development—A stage theory that views each stage as an identity crisis to be negotiated before moving on to the next stage.

Exosystem—One of the four systems of influence in Bronfenbrenner's ecological systems theory composed of the community and includes values and practices of schools, religious organizations, community agencies, and social groups.

Indiscriminate Attachment—The first stage in Ainsworth's stage theory of attachment when there is less difference in the way babies respond to adults. As long as they are fed when hungry and held when uncomfortable, infants allow a caring adult to meet their needs.

Macrosystem—One of the four systems of influence in Bronfenbrenner's ecological systems theory composed of the broader society including economic resource allocation, business practices, employment, health and education priorities, government policies, demographic trends, and technological changes.

Mesosystem—One of the four systems of influence in Bronfenbrenner's ecological systems theory composed of the educational context and the interface between cultural, religious, ethnic, family composition, racial, and socioeconomic backgrounds.

Microsystem—One of the four systems of influence in Bronfenbrenner' s ecological systems theory composed of the socio-cultural context of the family, including values, cultural practices, previous caregiving experiences, and relationships between the child and her frequent caregivers.

Motor Skills—Physical skills, such as feeding oneself, crawling, and walking.

Oppositional Behavior—Occurring during the second year of life, when toddlers begin to develop a view of themselves as separate and independent from their parents and teachers.

Primary Teaching—A system of teaching that focuses on the development of an intimate, sensitive, and reciprocal relationship between a child and her most frequent alternate caregiver.

Proximity-Seeking Behaviors—Types of behavior in which children seek the closeness of adults in their attachment networks.

Security Items—Items used by children to comfort themselves, especially during arrival and departure routines. Security items or favorite toys can be used as a support for transitions among and between adults in the attachment network.

Separation Anxiety—The third stage in Ainsworth's stage theory of attachment when children begin to show clearly defined preferences for mothers and fathers and the most familiar caregiver. Friendliness toward unfamiliar adults goes away.

Stranger Anxiety—The fourth stage of Ainsworth's stage theory of attachment when fear of strangers is present.

CHAPTER 4
Relating to Self and Others and Exploring Roles

Developmental Tasks: Relating to Self and Others and Exploring Roles

Relating to Self and Others

During infancy, babies go from being seemingly uninterested in the world that surrounds them to being intensely interested in the human world and their place in it. Relationships begin to develop seconds after birth as babies experience relating to their mothers from outside the comfort and security of the womb.

From the small circle of family, relationships widen to include extended family, neighbors, and friends, and then school and peers. As children become mobile, their view of the world broadens rapidly. Almost everything in the child's environment is stimulating and interesting. After they discover other people, it is the interaction with people that children seek most often and then enjoy with immense pleasure.

Exploring Roles

Toddlerhood is characterized by changes in the way children see the world. The focus on self broadens to include others—other adults, other children, and other settings. As the view of self stabilizes, children begin to see

themselves in relation to others. From this increasing ability to evaluate "self," children create a particular view of themselves. This view is commonly referred to as self-esteem or self-concept. Educators and parents know that self-concept has a great deal to do with how children continue to progress.

This view of self has lifelong implications. Children who develop views of themselves as able and competent are much more likely to turn negative experiences into positive ones—to learn from their interactions and self-reflection. Creating the environment to foster feelings of self-worth and self-concept is a crucial part of care and early education.

Chapter 4 focuses on the knowledge that teachers need to understand concerning the developmental tasks of relating to self and others and exploring roles. The best practices that emerge from this knowledge are then discussed. The chapter ends by applying this new understanding of theory and practice to a common behavioral challenge.

Knowledge

The Importance of Cultural Context

Human development is deeply and dramatically affected by the multiple contexts in which growth and learning occur. These contexts include the interactive emotional context of the family and the social context of the community, as well as the expectations of the society in which the family lives (Bredekamp & Copple, 1997; Bronfenbrenner, 1979; Shonkoff & Phillips, 2000). Children's growth, development, and learning are all influenced by the culture of their families.

"Culture is defined as the customary beliefs and patterns of and for behavior, both explicit and implicit, that are passed on to future generations by the society in which they live and/or by social, religious, or ethic groups within it" (Bredekamp and Copple 1997, p.12). It is within the context of culture that developmental and interactional theories merge with practice to facilitate each child's individual needs, competencies, abilities, and style of learning and growing.

An increased understanding of culture as a mediating and influential contributor to maturation, development, and learning is one of the major modifications of the developmental viewpoint during the last decade. Educators have grown to understand that a child's culture influences many things. Prenatal care, attachment, child-rearing practices, food preferences, sleeping arrangements, peer relations, self-esteem, emotional regulation and expression, and physical, social, emotional, cognitive, and language development are all influenced by culture. These influences are a part of the child's experience and development and cannot be excluded from the teacher's consideration.

Teachers' own experience with culture influences how they view the world and interpret those views in the teaching role. Adults are a product of the cultural context they experienced during their childhoods. Acknowledgment of this influence is necessary for teachers to allow them to consider multiple points of view in the teaching decision-making process (Bredekamp & Copple, 1997).

Implications of Cultural Context for Relating to Self and Others and Exploring Roles

Culture influences the behavior of children, parents, and teachers. Relational styles are embedded in the cultural contexts of the child and adult and may differ dramatically from the dominant culture and from the culture of the school or classroom.

Culture contributes to the lens through which children, parents, and teachers see the world. Points of view vary depending on the experiences of children and adults within their families and their cultures. These points of view come to school with both children and adults. Culture mediates and modifies experiences. The resulting cultural context of children and adults modifies the experiences they have at school and in the community.

Social Development

During the first three years, the social and the emotional domains of development weave together. It is hard to know where emotional development begins or ends and social development takes over. It is the connected nature of these two domains that makes focusing on both important. (See Chapter 7, page 307 for more information about emotional development.)

The reflexes with which a baby is born influence early social development. Crying, sucking, and other motor reflexes create connections with caregivers who are responsive to these early social attempts. Soon, though, interaction between children and their caregivers and interaction with the environment take over as the motivation for social and emotional development.

Learning socially acceptable behavior for interactions with others is what the socialization process is all about. Developing the ability to work and play cooperatively and productively with others is the goal. The socialization process includes all of the ways children incorporate the social rules, customs, and values of their culture into their views of themselves.

How Do Children Learn Social Skills?

Children learn social skills through three primary strategies. Although these strategies are also used to learn cognitive, language, and physical skills, it is in the social context that the results of these strategies are apparent.

The first strategy is imitation. Imitation is modeling or copying the behavior of another person. Imitation begins early in children's lives as they mimic the facial expressions of their caregivers. Then, children imitate actions with objects in the environment and with props.

Imitation is a powerful means of social learning because there are so many social interactions to observe and imitate. The interactive world that surrounds children is a rich source of material. Interactions between caregivers, between caregivers and the extended family, between caregivers and the neighborhood, all create opportunities for children to imitate.

To benefit from imitation, children must learn first to attend to what is going on around them. When children can attend, they are able to use their senses to gather data from the world around them. Being able to focus on the sensory information that is being gathered is important as a means of social learning. Observing—watching, listening to conversations, and picking up on subtle differences in the emotional messages that are included in actions— serves as a means of social learning.

Attachment, as discussed on pages 101-121 of Chapter 3, plays a role in emerging social development, creating a sense of trust that the world is a safe place to watch, listen to, and imitate. But more than any other developmental skill or behavior, play facilitates children's social development.

Theories of Play

The development of play overlaps all areas of development—physical, social, emotional, and intellectual, which includes cognitive and language development. In fact, we often determine where a child is on one or more developmental continua by watching him play. The developmental process guides play behavior from the simple to the complex, from concentrating on the self to interacting with others, and from concrete to abstract (Rogers & Sawyer, 1988).

Myth or Misunderstanding
CHILDREN ARE ONLY PLAYING—NOT LEARNING.

Abbey is an only child. Her parents, who have doctoral degrees, are in their late 40s and are professors at the local university. They are never pleased with the teacher's lesson plans. They are concerned that Abbey (30 months old) doesn't know her letters yet and are very worried that she will not be ready to take the entrance test for private school at four years of age. They gave Abbey a computer for her second birthday. Yesterday, Abbey's mother asked her teacher if they ever did anything at school but play.

The myth that children are not learning when they play has always dogged early childhood educators. We seem to have a limited ability to explain to parents and others the complex way that children construct their own knowledge of the world, using play as the medium. Elkind attributes this unfortunate legacy to misguided attempts to call play children's work. Work and play are not the same thing. "Play is an adaption of the world to the self while work is the adaption of self to the world" (Elkind, 2001, p.28).

Children's play has value. It is the venue for figuring things out—how to enter a group, what to do if the players say no, how to find acceptance, how to decide if there are enough seats for every player, and so on. Play helps children give meaning to their experiences. The challenge for Abbey's teacher is to help Abbey's parents see how she is using play to make sense of the world.

What should happen next? Make a plan to help Abbey's parents view play as an important part of her childhood experiences. Plan a parent participation activity to help other parents understand the value of play for their children's development.

The benefits of play for children are well documented. Because play is so integrated into the developmental context, it is helpful to look at the types of play behavior and to use this knowledge to understand the social development of very young children in school.

Piaget and Play

Piaget presented play as being divided into three types of play behavior—practice play, symbolic play, and play-with-rules (Piaget, 1962). Practice play is composed of repetitions of the same movements and actions both with and without objects. Children spend many hours repeating actions that interest them. Symbolic play involves the beginning of the traditional "dramatic play" where children recreate in play what they see happening in the real world. Play-with-rules is the last type of play behavior that develops during the late preschool years. During this type of play, children begin to impose rules on play to govern play or to manipulate interactions.

Infants are involved in plenty of practice play. Toddlers are beginning to exhibit symbolic play—the ability to play out the roles and activities they see in the larger world of family, school, and community. An emerging sense of self as independent from their primary caregivers entices toddlers to explore being just like these important people, as well as to explore being very different from these important adults in their lives.

Parten and Play

As children develop socially, they experience six increasingly complex types of peer play (Parten, 1932). The first type is unoccupied play in which children are not involved in social interaction. Then, onlooker play emerges in which children watch others play, seek to be near, and perhaps even respond to the play of others. Solitary independent play comes next. Children play alone with objects without interacting with others, regardless of how near.

Parallel activity emerges next with children playing alongside each other with similar toys—beside each other rather than with each other. In associative play, activities occur between children, but no specific roles are assigned or play goal identified. Cooperative play is the sixth form of play that finds children cooperating with others to create play situations. Group membership is defined and roles are played by group members. During infancy, play is predominately non-social: unoccupied, onlooker, and solitary. Toddlers may exhibit unoccupied play, solitary independent play, parallel activity, and may even participate in associative play occasionally.

Six Types of Peer Play

1. Unoccupied Play
2. Onlooker Play
3. Solitary Independent Play
4. Parallel Activity
5. Associative Play
6. Cooperative Play

Later appearing levels of play do not replace earlier ones. Instead, throughout the preschool years, children continue to exhibit all types of play (Howes & Mathesen, 1992). Understanding play behavior gives teachers cues as to what stage their children are in socially and emotionally. Information about such behaviors facilitates fine-tuning the interactive relationship.

Vygotsky and Play

While all of the theories mentioned in this chapter support play as the link between children and the larger society, Vygotsky's socio-cultural theory is based on the premise that children socially construct what they know in the context of their family and cultural experiences. Language is the primary strategy for communication and contact with others (Berk, 1994; Berk & Winsler, 1995). In other words, Piaget states that children construct knowledge by interacting with objects and perfecting errors. Vygotsky believes children construct knowledge through instructions of others and through social interactions.

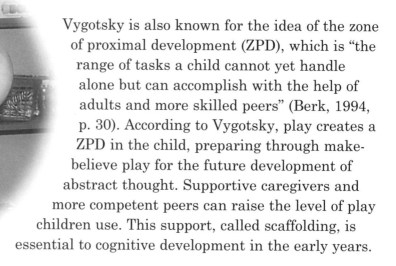

Vygotsky is also known for the idea of the zone of proximal development (ZPD), which is "the range of tasks a child cannot yet handle alone but can accomplish with the help of adults and more skilled peers" (Berk, 1994, p. 30). According to Vygotsky, play creates a ZPD in the child, preparing through make-believe play for the future development of abstract thought. Supportive caregivers and more competent peers can raise the level of play children use. This support, called scaffolding, is essential to cognitive development in the early years.

Myth or Misunderstanding
TEACHERS DON'T HAVE TIME TO PLAY WITH CHILDREN. THEY ARE TOO BUSY TEACHING.

Yesterday, when Mr. Zhongliang picked Lee up early in the afternoon, Pam, the teacher, looked up and smiled at Lee's father, welcoming him to the classroom. Then, she continued playing with the children at the water table. Mr. Zhongliang was upset that she did not immediately quit playing with the children to tell him about Lee's day at school. He commented to the director that the teacher should get her priorities straight—talking with parents is more important than playing with children.

The myth here is that teachers aren't teaching when they are playing with children. Playing with children (engaging in joint play, taking turns, suggesting imaginative play, choosing support that matches a child's abilities, scaffolding children's play) is a crucial teaching role in the classroom.

So is communicating with parents. The misunderstanding is tied to how parents and teachers differ in the ways they want to communicate. Pam felt she was "on the job," filling her role as teacher by participating in play. Mr. Zhongliang felt that it was the teacher's job to communicate with him about his child's day. What solutions do you see for this situation? Whose point of view is right? Could both points of view have merit?

Implications of Social Development and Play for Relating to Self and Others and Exploring Roles

To facilitate the developmental tasks of relating to self and others and exploring roles, teachers can provide opportunities for practice play with toys and materials. Because children construct their own knowledge of social interactions, it is experiences that are the best teachers. Repetition during the infant and toddler years, both with toys and of experiences, creates opportunities for knowledge construction about social relationships.

Teachers can create opportunities for symbolic play with props to encourage the exploration of roles. When props are readily available, children will often incorporate them into their play, widening and enriching the experience. For infants, teachers can provide plenty of sensory play. Manipulation of sensory materials engages children's senses and prepares the way for children to use props in their play.

Most of all, teachers can serve as good role models for socializing with others. Children watch and imitate the behaviors they see acted out in the school and home environments. When these behaviors are good models for interactions, children incorporate them into their own behavioral repertoire, usually with a great deal of success.

The Development of Positive Self-concept

From birth, children have feelings about themselves. If they feel they can make things happen, succeed in trying new things, surmount obstacles, and solve problems, they will likely develop positive feelings about themselves. Finding a thumb or finger to suck allows a baby to soothe himself, rather than just waiting for someone to do the soothing. Crying when he is hungry will alert teachers to give him a bottle, rather than just waiting until someone feeds him. Smiling and cooing at someone's face causes that person to smile and coo back at him. From these early attempts at independence comes a view of self that says, "I can!"

Success in achieving autonomy and independence throughout childhood has a profound impact on the way children mature. They are naturally motivated to make things happen. If their early attempts are successful and fulfilling, children will continue to develop competence. If their early efforts are unsuccessful and frustrating, children will carry this failure and the negative views of self with them into adulthood.

Children get feedback about attempts at independence from parents and other caregivers, and from peers. When teachers support emerging independence, they are expressing their confidence in the child's growing ability. Such expression creates the desire to increase independent behaviors and helps children feel successful, further enhancing self-esteem and self-confidence.

During toddlerhood, an increasing awareness of "self" leads children to view their actions, interactions, and their behavior as observers. This ability to "watch" one's own interaction and evaluate one's own "performance" is a crucial social skill that is uniquely human. It means that children can learn to anticipate the social responses and interactions of others before they occur and choose or modify their responses to match the situation. They get ideas about how to do so from their interactions and experiences with parents and extended family, the community, school, and peers.

This process is neither simple nor objective. Children's views of self are influenced by how they think others view them. If adults, the community, the school, and other children view them as competent, capable, and confident, and are clear in communicating this view, then children are likely to view themselves as competent, capable, and confident. If adults, the community, the school, and other children view them as incompetent, incapable, or lacking in confidence, then children may view themselves similarly. So, how we see (and therefore, interact and communicate with) children directly influences their self-concepts.

The creation of self-concept begins at birth and continues to be influenced throughout life. It is an emerging process to which children contribute actively, influencing their own development. The self-concept is constantly shaped and reshaped as children interact with the important people in their lives and experience the interactive environment (Curry & Johnson, 1990).

Erickson (1963) called this period of toddler development "autonomy vs. shame and doubt." The struggles for independence were viewed as creating a feeling of autonomy ("I can do it") or a feeling of shame and doubt ("Can I do it?" "Should I do it?"). These vivid word descriptions of the developmental challenge help illustrate the importance of this stage. The outcome obviously contributes to how development proceeds.

Greenspan (1999) noted the emergence of an organized sense of self during this period. This organization leads children to create and use emotional ideas, both with others and in their play. As they become more aware of themselves, children organize their own emotions and coordinate their behavior with the emotions.

Curry and Johnson (1990) present self-concept as the way individuals value themselves and others. Rejecting the view that self-concept is fixed or unresponsive to change, these authors conclude that love and acceptance, power and control, moral value, and competence are the lifelong issues that impact emerging self-esteem. Each of these issues requires consideration by teachers. Wardle (1995) expands on the issues that influence self-concept, describing themes that are present throughout life. Each theme is summarized in the following chart.

General Themes that Impact Self-esteem or Self-concept

Love and Acceptance	Feeling unique, special; feeling cared for and loved; feeling like a worthwhile individual.
Power and Control	Feeling in control of one's destiny; having control over some parts of one's experience.
Moral Value	A sense of belonging; feeling fairly treated; feeling like a worthy person.
Competence	Feeling like it is worth trying; feeling capable of accomplishing tasks and skills.

Notice the emphasis on "feeling." This emphasis is important because the way we "feel" about things is often different from the way things look or the way we respond. Creating feelings of acceptance, control, value, and competence is related to but different from planning activities that encourage acceptance, control, and so on. One is external to the child (plans, activities, questions, props); the other is internal (how the child evaluates and feels about those activities, plans, questions, props as he experiences them). It is this internal arena that is so important to the child's emerging sense of self.

Enhancing Self-esteem through Encouragement

Cautions about the rampant use of praise, stickers, and other examples of external motivation are included throughout the early childhood literature, particularly the literature about self-concept development. External motivation prevents children from placing their own evaluations on their experiences. This, in turn, can interfere with the emerging sense of self. For example, children often make a few marks on paper and then request another. When teachers praise children's work ("Good job!") and then ask the child to make more marks to prevent paper waste, children can be confused— if the marks were good, why are more needed? Maybe they weren't so good after all.

Some early childhood educators propose that teachers reconsider their use of praise to foster self-concept and to motivate children. Instead, they suggest that teachers use encouragement (Hitz & Driscoll, 1988). Encouragement acknowledges the effort or attributes of the work without evaluation or judgment. Encouragement has the advantage of being sincere and authentic, putting teachers in the role of honestly responding to children's experiences and efforts. These guidelines support the use of encouragement instead of praise.

Guidelines for Using Encouragement

Be specific.	"Your painting has lots of blue in it." "The paint covers all of the paper." "Your construction is built with lots of blocks." "You rode the tricycle all over the playground." "You chose the blue baby buggy."
Encourage individually and privately.	"You were able to find all the different pieces to the puzzle, Caitlin." "All of the star builders are in your construction!"
Focus on effort, improvement, and progress rather than products or outcomes.	"You made it all the way to the gate on the push trike." "You finished gluing two feathers." "You built with all of the Duplo blocks."
Be sincere and authentic.	"You worked hard on that." "You kept working until you finished everything."
Help children see their successes.	"Your tower is eight blocks tall." "Your baby doll is covered with a blanket and ready for bed." "You pulled your pants up all by yourself."
Help children appreciate their own achievements.	"Both feet left the ground when you hopped!" "You helped clean up the snack table."
Avoid comparisons and competition.	"You are ready to go outside." "You finished cleaning up."

Implications for Self-concept for Relating to Self and Others and Exploring Roles

Self-concept has implications for relating to self and others and exploring roles. As children play, they take on different roles they see being used in the broader social setting. Infants and toddlers observe roles like Mommy, Daddy, friend, teacher, firefighter, police officer, sister, brother, puppy, fast runner, tricycle pedaller, independent eater, leader, follower, helper, and many others. Then, through play, children get images of themselves as they attempt to play roles such as these. They evaluate these play experiences and use their evaluations to alter their views of themselves. If other children respond positively to their attempts at relating and role-playing, children evaluate themselves as successful in figuring out what to do and how to do it. The likely result is an enhancement of self-concept.

But children don't just have positive play experiences, particularly during the infant and toddler years. They often have disagreements over whether others can play, what they can play with, and the possible roles they can play. These disagreements increase during toddlerhood, peaking toward the end of the second year as children learn more effective skills for playing together (Shonkoff & Phillips, 2000).

How children handle negative experiences is just as important as how they handle positive ones and influences self-concept. If they are able to find another way to play (like being the puppy), join in the play as an onlooker (like being the time keeper on the railroad), find another place to play mommy (like in blocks rather than dramatic play), call to the teacher to help figure out how to play ("They won't let me play!"), and so on, the experience can still be self-concept enhancing. Children evaluate themselves as successful in finding a way to play. If, on the other hand, the child feels rejected and evaluates that rejection as a valid part of his view of himself, the experience can influence self-concept negatively.

Teachers have such an important role to play in supporting children's views of themselves and the evaluation of those views. First, they are responsible for setting up the environment to facilitate relating to others and exploring interesting and varied roles successfully. Second, teachers are responsible for creating interactive relationships with children that give them many messages about love, acceptance, control, value, and competence, the themes that influence self-concept throughout life. Third, teachers have to be observant enough to help children with limited views of self or negative evaluations of self. And, lastly, teachers have to make sure that their interactions support children who are bumping up against their own or others' negative views of self.

Throughout the **Innovations** series are repeated references to the importance of the interactive environment—the way adults and children interact with each other and the messages those interactions give children. Teachers begin to see the results of creating this warm, interactive environment and relationships as children approach exploring roles with confidence, competence, and capability.

Handling Biting in the Classroom

Without a doubt, biting is perceived as the most common behavior problem among children under the age of three. Dealing with biting behavior is not so difficult if the developmental reasons for biting are understood and dealt with appropriately.

Understanding why children bite is the first step in preventing biting. Noted psychologists Ilg and Ames point out that biting does not mean the child is "bad" or "cruel" (1976). Instead, it is a sign of the developmental age of the child. Children bite to explore, to get reactions, and because they lack language and social skills. They are not yet able to say, "Leave me alone," or "That's my toy." As soon as they learn to tell their peers to leave them alone, to move away from children who get too close, and to negotiate turns, the frequency of biting behavior will diminish.

Three Types of Biting

There are three types of biting generally observed in care and early education settings. The first type is investigative/exploratory biting. For children between early infancy and about 14 or 15 months, biting is often a part of the investigation and exploration that defines babies' play. They explore everything with their mouths and want to see what things taste and feel like.

The second type of biting is action/reaction biting. Children between the ages of 9 and 20 months are beginning to connect actions with reactions. They are exploring interesting combinations of actions to see what reactions they might discover. Other children provide a wide array of reactions to being bitten. When you bite down on the finger that is gingerly exploring your face, it gets a big, loud reaction from the other child and from the adults in the room.

The third type of biting is purposeful biting. This kind of biting attempts to get something or to change the outcome of a situation. Purposeful biting emerges about 18 months and usually disappears as children learn language and social problem-solving skills, declining dramatically as children near their third birthdays. To adults, this stage of biting often is the most difficult to handle.

Prevention—Prevention and anticipation of biting behavior are the best ways to deal with biting. The best prevention strategy is to create an environment that spreads children throughout the available space. Because children tend to be "groupie" in nature (they are wherever the teacher is), it is important to arrange the classroom to limit children's ability to see everyone and everything. If children are unable to see the toys other children are playing with, they will be less likely to want to play with those specific toys and, therefore, less likely to bite to get those toys.

The best environments for children are rooms full of "nooks and crannies," where children can play alone or with one or two playmates. Classrooms arranged in such a manner experience fewer biting episodes. Open, unbroken space only increases the tendency of children to group together and the chances that a child will use biting behavior to meet his needs.

Anticipation—Anticipation of biting is also an important part of coping with biting behavior. Careful observation of when, where, and with whom biting occurs provides the basis for anticipating biting episodes. Once the teacher has this information, she or he will be able to limit the development of situations in which biting occurs. Separating a regular biter from his most frequent target, anticipating tired or fussy times that will likely result in conflict, and rearranging play pairs are examples of anticipation strategies for preventing biting.

Substitution—Substitution is also a strategy for helping children learn to control biting. During some ages, sore gums that need rubbing can be the cause of biting behavior. The nearest available object to soothe sore gums just might be the arms or fingers of another child. When this is the case, keep cooled teething rings or soft rubber manipulative toys available to offer to teething children.

Supervising and Shadowing Biters—The next step is a preventive one designed to teach that biting doesn't get what the child may think it does. Children who are biting frequently (for example, three or more times a day for three or more consecutive days) may need increased supervision throughout the day. Shadowing the child or limiting his freedom within the classroom by having the child hold your hand as you move around the room for short periods of time will reinforce the idea that biting will be controlled in your classroom.

Finally, if biting persists, the last step is to get help. Often teachers are too close to the situation to be objective. Ask another teacher to observe. Sometimes an objective eye will pinpoint something you overlooked. If all efforts fail, reach out for additional assistance. Psychologists or early childhood specialists can offer insight into chronic biting and help remedy the situation.

Teaching Children Social Interaction Skills—Now is the time to teach social interaction skills to help children increasingly gain control over their own behavior. Because most conflict during this stage occurs over limited resources (toys, crayons, blocks, manipulatives, the teacher's lap), the first social interaction skill a child needs is the ability to wait just a moment. This is called delaying gratification, and it is a particularly difficult skill for a child to master.

Then, teach children to use their words. Start with "Mine!" As language grows, the words will get more specific ("I want the truck, please"). Then help children master the social problem-solving skills they have been practicing such as walking away from a problem or asking the other child to walk away. These skills make children feel powerful and capable of solving their own problems some of the time. Next comes asking for what is wanted instead of grabbing it. "Please put that in my hand" often works very well. The next step is trading a toy you don't want for a toy you do want. "Trade me a yellow car for the blue one," makes both children winners. Finally, help children accept no for the answer when all of these strategies don't work.

Taking turns (first me, then you) comes next, followed finally by actually sharing. Expect these skills to dramatically reduce biting specifically and aggression in general, as children master them.

When attempting to prevent action/reaction biting and to teach children social skills, remember these important points:

◗ Respond quickly when one child hurts another.

◗ Biting is a development phenomena that comes and goes.

◗ All children bite occasionally at various ages and stages.

◗ Quickly comfort hurt children who are bitten, hugging and cuddling them until they are calm.

◗ Discuss biting incidences with parents.

◗ Complete a written report.

◗ Biting disappears and is replaced by more mature skills as children grow.

◗ Don't let children bite without getting a negative reaction from you.

◗ Give older toddlers lots of attention and hugs for positive social behaviors with friends such as touching softly or taking turns.

◗ Talk about what children are doing and describe their actions and reactions and the actions and reactions of others as they happen.

◗ Model behaviors you want children to use such as talking softly, saying "please" and "thank you," and holding your hand in dangerous situations.

◗ Verbal children often identify the wrong child as the biter. Or, they may attribute every right and wrong in the classroom to one child. Check out the facts.

◗ Prevention, anticipation, and substitution take care of most biting incidences.

◗ Help children learn to wait for just a moment.

◗ Teach children to use words, walk away, trade, and take turns.

◗ Shadow children in new situations to prevent biting.

◗ Other teachers can be a resource to help in understanding biting.

◗ Who did the biting is not as important as the teacher's plan for handling it.

◗ Talk with parents about any concerns about children's behaviors.

◗ Bites rarely cause problems from a health perspective. Concerns about infection or contracting HIV are unfounded.

Dealing with Parents about Biting—The whole subject of biting is a very emotional one for parents. When they learn that their child has been bitten, parents often feel that the teacher failed to protect their child. What many parents do not realize is that most children bite at some time in their development and that the action of biting is developmental in nature. Children bite because they have not mastered skills necessary to do things in another way.

Teachers are very important to parents during this stage because they are able to offer the reassurance that many parents need. Although teachers may not want to deal with how parents are feeling about biting and other aggressive behaviors in children, it is crucial to do so in a way that keeps the lines of communication open.

Use the following approach to handling biting in your classroom. When a biting incident occurs, give your attention to the child who was bitten—not to the child who did the biting. Offer comfort and a cool washcloth or ice pack, if needed. Complete a written report (see page 356 in the Appendix), being very specific about what happened, but do not include children's names on each other's reports. Who did the biting is not as important as how you handled it and what you plan to do to prevent it in the future. Parents need to know that it is your responsibility—not theirs—to handle what happens in the classroom.

What you can do to reassure parents is to be calm and professional. Have a plan formulated and communicate that plan with parents. Emphasize that biting is a stage and that children will grow out of it as they mature and as you implement your plan.

Best Practices

Teach Children to Use Pro-social Behaviors

Pro-social behaviors are those that precede and lead to successful social interactions. When teachers are supporting social skill development, they are often modeling, teaching, validating, and supporting pro-social behaviors that will predict success in future social situations. Teachers serve as important role models. Their actions must coincide with the expectations they have for the children. For example, if teachers expect children to touch each other softly or to respect each other's personal space, then they must model these social behaviors for children by touching children softly and requesting permission to look into a child's cubby. Teachers have the opportunity to be an important role model for a whole range of social expectations in the classroom.

Teachers actively create the social climate of the classroom. They start by anticipating needs, so children don't have to cry or overreact to get their needs met. They continue by getting to know individual cues and by validating that communication sent through cries or nonverbal cues was received. Additionally, the teacher helps children solve social problems by learning new skills, including waiting a moment, trading, taking turns, and making plans.

The teacher's most important role in pro-social behavior is supporting interactions between children—by enabling them to interact successfully. Being close to where children are in the classroom helps facilitate social interaction. With the teacher nearby, children are able to try new experiences, such as looking at one another or exploring toys together on a blanket, exchanging toys, or playing together with blocks.

As children get older, words need the support of modeling and patterning. Teachers provide support as they pattern appropriate behaviors and model appropriate responses. When teachers support early attempts at social

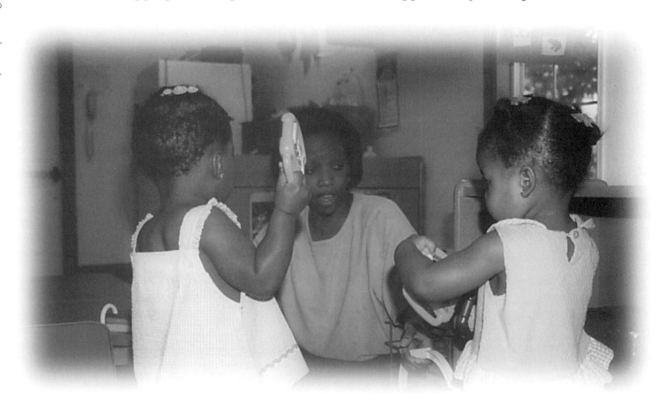

interaction, young children develop social skills that will stay with them throughout their lives.

Learning social expectations is a slow and gradual process that is tied very closely with emotional development. Social expectations for children should be grounded in their developmental context. Here are some appropriate expectations for teaching pro-social behaviors:

▶ Don't expect children to adjust quickly when they are left in a new situation unless there are familiar adults.

▶ Children are unable to share until well into the third year. Teachers and parents may help them take turns, share resources, or wait for a turn, so they will be prepared to share later.

▶ Manners are difficult for younger children. Eating with a utensil, staying at the table until finished, and not dawdling are complex expectations. Children will need support from teachers and parents to accomplish these tasks.

◆ Expectations like touching softly and keeping hands to yourself are also difficult. Stay close and help children learn these skills by modeling them and supporting children.

Teach Social Problem-solving

Patterning and Modeling—During the early years, children take much of their social learning directly from experiences. However, we often expect them to have more sophisticated skills than they do. What can teachers do to help children learn important social skills for social problem-solving?

Patterning and modeling are two excellent examples of teaching strategies that are appropriate for infant and toddler teachers to master. Patterning involves a hand-over-hand repeating of appropriate behaviors. Modeling involves showing a child what you want them to do by doing it.

Patterning is appropriate to use in showing children how to touch each other softly, how to pick up toys and materials after dumping them on the floor, or how to stand back when someone wants to come in or go out the door of the classroom.

Modeling is appropriate for demonstrating the appropriate use of toys and materials, demonstrating techniques like finger painting, brush painting, stacking blocks, pushing a ball back and forth, turning the pages of a book without tearing them, and so forth.

Calling for Help—The tendency to call for help emerges as children begin to interact with the environment and their friends—teachers and parents usually hear about problems as soon as they begin to arise. Quick response to cries when one child gets too close, crawls or walks on another child, or gets in the way, tells children that their communication was received. When teachers and parents validate such cries for help, children recognize that the world is responsive to their needs.

Myth or Misunderstanding
CHILDREN SHOULD SETTLE THEIR OWN PROBLEMS INSTEAD OF CALLING FOR THE TEACHER.

Oliver was a teacher in the after-school classroom while he was finishing his degree. After graduation, he wanted a full-time job, and a position was open in the toddler classroom. He has been in that classroom for two months. Sometimes toddler behaviors are irritating for Oliver. He becomes especially flustered when two children grab a toy and call for help. His usual reaction is to fuss at both children for fighting over the toy.

There are two myths at work here. One is that toddlers have the social problem-solving skills to work out their own problems. The other myth is that they don't need adult support to use the emerging skills toddlers do have.

Children depend on adults to help them play successfully. Because they are just developing social problem-solving skills, calling for help is a strategy young children can use in problem-solving. As teachers model and give them words to use, toddlers develop more sophisticated skills for solving difficulties with their peers.

But learning to solve your own problems is a process—one that develops over time from many repetitions of experiences. So, patience from adults is required as children try, but don't quite accomplish social problem-solving during the first three years.

What should happen next? Make some suggestions to Oliver to help him cope with his frustration. Suggest some strategies for keeping calm when he begins to get annoyed. How can Oliver's supervisor help him develop an understanding of how children learn self-control and social problem-solving? Make a professional development plan to reflect your ideas.

Children need to be reminded to call for help if the strategies they are using do not seem to be working. For example, when two children want the same toy, both will grab it and begin to scream for help. Teachers validate the call for help when they respond promptly. Then, they can help children begin to understand that while grabbing didn't work, some other ideas might work.

Trading—By the time children approach the end of the first year, guidance may need to be supported with appropriate discipline strategies. For children whose expressive language skills are not yet sophisticated enough to deal verbally with their peers, trading, taking turns, and walking away are good social problem-solving strategies to teach children (Albrecht & Ward, 1989). Then, older children need support in making plans with others to get what they want.

Myth or Misunderstanding
YOUNG CHILDREN CAN LEARN TO SHARE IF TEACHERS REALLY WORK AT IT.

Parents of children in the toddler room are amazed at how wonderful Marie, the teacher, is. She makes all the parents feel comfortable and appreciated and includes parents in activities of the classroom. Parents marvel at how she can get a group of toddlers to sleep at naptime! Sometimes, however, parents are impatient that their children are not yet able to "behave." They can't share and they fight with their siblings.

The misunderstanding here is that children can use the social problem-solving skills they have all the time and in various settings. Social problem-solving is a real challenge for young children. Social development is much like other areas of development. The stages build on each other. The steps—trading, taking turns, using words, and walking away—take time to perfect. By supporting children as they go through these stages, teachers and parents can help them prepare to share later, when they are ready.

Role-play how you would handle a conversation with a parent who is asking for suggestions on how to get her or his child to share.

The concept of sharing is too advanced for infants, although toddlers are beginning to understand that adults think they should share. However, trading something you have for something you want can be explained by sensitive adults who guide children to learn this new skill. In situations where children begin shrieking as another child grabs a favored toy, the adult hands the child who is grabbing the toy another one of equal interest to trade saying, "Ask him to trade with you." Or, "Give her the doll in exchange for the book." Regular assistance with the concept of trading (which exchanges something for something rather than something for nothing) facilitates socialization skills in children.

Taking Turns—After children learn to trade, the concept of turn-taking can be introduced. Turn-taking requires children to delay gratification for a little while and participate as onlookers until a child is ready to take a turn (or until another child is finished playing with toy). Again, sensitive adults need to help children learn this skill by explaining what is happening and providing the physical support and supervision to encourage children to take turns.

Using Words—An important part of learning social problem-solving is to be able to access and use language instead of responding physically. For infants, adults give children the language they need, putting into words the thoughts and ideas that are clear in interactions. For toddlers, adults remind them that words are an alternative to physical reactions and can be used to work things out. Both infants and toddlers need adults who model good language for social problem-solving and who support children in trying words first.

Walking Away—Walking away is a technique to help children begin to use words rather than actions to solve problems. Walking away can take two forms: I can tell you to walk away from me, or I can walk away from you if you are bothering me. Both techniques empower children to solve their own problems and to use words as problem-solving tools.

Walking away is an adult-supported activity. Just telling a child to walk away doesn't work. The child needs the teacher's gentle support to help him do so. Also, telling your friend to walk away is a supported activity. A sensitive teacher needs to be close and remind the child to talk to his friend who is too close and to provide the words and support the actions.

Plan-making—Finally, facilitated plan-making helps both children to get a turn. Plan-making requires adult support. Tell the children that you have an idea of how to solve the problem. Tell them that both children will get a turn. One child will get the toy for three minutes, and then the teacher will help the child give the toy to the other child for three minutes. While the second child is waiting, the teacher helps him choose another activity—even if that activity is sitting and waiting for three minutes with the teacher's help! Plan-making keeps teachers from feeling like referees. No one loses. One child has to delay gratification but gets the teacher's help to do so. Plan-making has another important benefit. It keeps teachers from saying "NO." Having a plan is very different from not being able to do something.

Social Problem-solving Skill Development— A Process Over Time

Step 1: Calling for Help

Step 2: Trading

Step 3: Taking Turns

Step 4: Using Words

Step 5: Walking Away

Step 6: Plan-making

Myth or Misunderstanding
THE BEST TOYS ARE BOUGHT TOYS.

Melanie is a teacher in the infant room, which contains bought toys. But she has also spent time collecting and creating toys. There are many teacher-made books, fill-and-dump toys, and rattle blocks and bottles, all made from recycled materials. Because she knows that very young children enjoy parallel play with duplicate toys, Melanie always makes and collects at least two toys. Recently, one of Melanie's parents cleaned out a toy closet and brought a bag full of used toys to Melanie so that she wouldn't have to use the homemade toys anymore.

The misunderstanding here is that children need "educational" toys to construct knowledge about their world. Most adults have experienced children's intense interest in discarded materials such as boxes, common household items including pots and pans, and interesting trash such as junk-mail brochures and envelopes.

Young children (especially infants and toddlers) enjoy a wide variety of play items including teacher-made, gathered, and bought toys. Teacher-made items are inexpensive and an easy way to provide variety and novelty and should be a part of every infant and toddler classroom.

What should happen next? Plan a parent meeting to help parents understand the value of found, gathered, and teacher-made toys. Discuss ways that teachers can involve parents in seeing the value of open-ended play materials. Make a list of gathered materials that are safe and easily available that could be used as open-ended toys by infants and toddlers.

Provide a Wealth of Appropriate Play Materials

Toys provide infants and toddlers wonderful opportunities to explore both familiar and new things. Toys (used here in a very broad sense) may be created by the teacher, gathered by the parent or teacher, or purchased.

Making toys for the classroom can be easy and inexpensive. Having a wealth of appropriate play materials will assure that young children have the chance to experience novelty, as well as to experience the security and pleasure of old favorites. The following are homemade toy ideas for teachers of infants and toddlers.

- *Shaker Bottles*—Put small, colored pieces of dry cereal or other objects inside any clear plastic bottle. Empty, clean plastic shampoo or dishwashing detergent bottles make great toys for infants and toddlers. Glue and tape the lids on tight.
- *Simple Hand Puppets*—Made from socks, or other simple materials, puppets are a good way for an adult to talk with a baby and are a good way to capture a young child's attention.
- *Boxes*—All shapes and sizes of boxes are appropriate for walking around or crawling into, sitting in, stacking, nesting, putting things in and dumping them out. A shoebox with a short length of twine attached makes a good pull toy.
- *Sorting Toys*—A cardboard egg carton or cupcake tin works well as a place to put objects (large spools or blocks). Check each object in a choke tester.
- *Dress-ups*—Infants and toddlers enjoy putting on hats and simple clothes. This is especially important for toddlers who are beginning to role-play.
- *Blocks*—Make blocks from simple materials like milk cartons, shoeboxes, and other small boxes.
- *Books*—Make simple books by mounting pictures or photographs on paper and joining the pieces together with large metal rings or short lengths of string or yarn. Covering pages with clear contact paper or placing pages in small, resealable plastic bags will make them more durable.
- *Hanging Toys*—Infants who are not yet mobile but who are reaching (around four to five months), enjoy trying to reach suspended objects (paper cups, large spools, toys).
- *Sorting Can*—Cut shapes in the plastic lid of a coffee can, so only certain shapes and sizes (blocks, for example) will fit through.

Gathered materials, such as lightweight pots and pans, plastic containers, paper tubes, old phone directories, and cloth bags with short handles add variety and interest to the classroom or the home. Boxes are always a hit, just be certain that staples and any rough edges are removed. Refresh the gathered toys and materials often, and check for safety.

Purchased toys have gotten more interesting and varied. Always check to be certain that toys fall in the age range provided on the packaging. The range is important both for interest level, as well as for safety. Toys that are too complex may frustrate young children. Toys for children under three years of age must be checked for small parts. All toys should be checked with a choke tube.

Provide Opportunities for Side-by-side Play

During most of infancy and toddlerhood, young children rarely play together cooperatively. Instead, they observe and copy each other. They play alongside each other in what is called parallel play, often imitating adult behaviors. Although there is little reciprocal interaction, parallel play is important in providing the basis for cooperative play.

Myth or Misunderstanding
CHILDREN LEARN NEGATIVE BEHAVIORS FROM OTHER CHILDREN.

This misunderstanding is a common one among parents and teachers of children in care and early education programs. As children learn new skills that parents don't like (like biting, hitting, or drawing on the walls), parents blame other children for teaching them inappropriate behaviors.

Imitation and modeling are powerful forms of learning for infants and toddlers. The ability to imitate others develops before the ability to learn from the consequences of observed behavior develops (Brunson, 2000). As they observe, then model or imitate what they see, children learn many new behaviors—both appropriate ones and inappropriate ones. In this case, adults are correct—their children did "learn" some inappropriate behaviors from modeling and imitating other children in the classroom.

Parents benefit from understanding that children learn from observing others, modeling, and imitation, and that they need supportive adults to help them figure out which behaviors are appropriate to model and imitate and which ones aren't. Parents also benefit from having teachers identify all of the appropriate behaviors that children have learned from one another, rather than just focusing on the negative ones children have learned from each other.

Then, children need to learn from their parents and teachers how to limit inappropriate behaviors. The same skills that were used to learn the inappropriate skills (watching, modeling, and imitating) help children learn that biting doesn't work as a solution to getting what you want, that hitting doesn't result in accomplishing the goal you intended, and that coloring on the walls will not be tolerated.

Watching, listening, and imitating are good learning strategies. Just as children can use them to learn both appropriate and inappropriate behaviors, they can also use them to learn which behaviors to continue to use and which ones just won't work to accomplish their desired goals.

What should happen next? How can the teacher help parents understand their role in limiting the use of inappropriate behaviors that are learned in the classroom through watching, listening, and imitating? Make two lists. One list should have on it all of the "appropriate behaviors that children learn from one another through imitation and modeling." The other list should have all of the "inappropriate behaviors" children learn through imitation and modeling. Which one is longer? How could you use this list to help parents see that both appropriate and inappropriate behaviors are learned through imitation and modeling?

Adults are often in a hurry to get young children to share, even though they are not ready developmentally to do so. Parallel play works well for children because they do not have to be involved with the same materials. Each child has his own toy or play prop.

When the child wants someone else's toy, provide a similar or duplicate item. If this is not possible or acceptable, give the child the words to ask for the toy after the other child is finished with it. "Shania, ask Timothy to give you the truck after he is finished. I will help him remember." The abilities to negotiate, to wait, and to take turns are all important steps on the road to children later being able to share.

Use a Variety of Play Cues and Play Props

The props and play cues that are part of the environment invite children to play. When classrooms are full of props and play cues that lead to appropriate, exploratory play, children are able to look at an activity, area, or planned experience and figure out what to do and where to get started.

Carefully plan the classroom to take maximum advantage of children's natural desire to explore and learn. Choose simple, safe toys and ordinary objects for them to explore and manipulate. Provide uninterrupted time, so children can begin, explore, and elaborate without being distracted.

Creating an environment that stimulates play is one of the teacher's most important roles. She or he is the stage manager, costume designer, orchestra conductor, and set designer. When all of these elements of the environment are planned, children can find varied and interesting places to play, both alone and with their friends.

Both over-stimulation and under-stimulation are important issues in the school setting. Over-stimulation can occur from too much noise, light, color, and activity, under-stimulation from too little interactive experiences, physical isolation of children, or too few toys and materials in the environment.

Play cues or invitations can come from many sources. The first and best source of play cues is you. When the teacher picks up a toy and plays with it, the toy becomes very interesting to children. Called triangulation, this strategy for inviting play and interactions is an excellent way to initiate interactions and to interest children in new materials or props.

The second source of play cues or stimulation is color. Graphics, photographs, and pictures from the picture file/vocabulary list and colorful toys all interest infants and toddlers. But, color also can be overwhelming. Children benefit from color in the toys they play with and colors worn by the children and adults in the environment. They need soothing neutral colors to serve as the backdrop. Avoid adding color in bold swatches to the walls and floors of children's classrooms. This will help insure that the stimulation comes from child-directed and child-initiated activity and not from the background (Cherry, 1976).

The third source of play cues is the way toys are displayed. Make toys available where children are in the classroom, on low shelves, in clear plastic containers, in baskets, and in tubs. Provide duplicate and similar toys, so children are not forced to share popular items and so toys can be removed for disinfecting after they are used. Separate toys on shelves, so children can consider each specific toy. How toys are displayed can invite children to move around the room and choose interesting things for play.

Children are developing their ability to explore roles as they play. They actually become the mommy or daddy or the bear as they make use of appropriate play props provided in the dramatic play area. Toys that are real items from the child's world (purses, wallets, pots, pans, clothes, shoes, hats) are interesting and important support for beginning role-play efforts. Continue to provide duplicate items, so children can play side by side without taking the toys away from each other.

The teacher's role is to support role-playing efforts, first by providing an appropriate environment. Observe children as they begin playing roles. Limit interruptions as children explore their ideas. After the play is established, extend the experience through verbal exchanges or through adding more items to the area. Open-ended questions such as, "Where are you taking the baby for a walk?" and "How will you build the house?" Give children opportunities to add to and elaborate on the experiences they are having.

When children lose interest in the props and play cues in an area, they will let you know. Children won't go there to play. This indicates that it is time to change materials to add interest, change the roles that are being explored, or supplement the area with additional props and play cues.

Add Mirrors to the Environment

Unbreakable mirrors are a source of interest and interaction. More than any other image, young children are drawn to the images of their own faces (Edwards, Gandini, & Forman, 1998; Shore, 1997). The perfect interactive experience involves discovering and exploring one's own face and the faces of others in the mirror.

Mirrors attract children's attention and allow them visually to orient themselves to others within the classroom. With large mirrors, children can keep their visual connection with teachers and other children even if they are out of physical reach of them.

Place small, unbreakable mirrors in boxes and containers for children to discover. Imagine the delight when a child looks in a box and sees his own face. Small mirrors with adhesive on the backs can be placed throughout the room, so toddlers can discover and explore their own image again and again. Mirrors underneath tables, on low shelves, on the walls at various heights, on doors and windowsills, and even attached to walls hidden behind curtains will provide stimulating discoveries.

Place larger mirrors over the diaper-changing table, on walls where children can see themselves eating, and in other areas of the room where children can see their entire images. If possible, cover one entire wall with a mirrored surface. This will brighten the classroom, as well as help children keep an eye on their teacher and each other.

Use a Variety of Teaching Roles

The Teacher as Play Partner

Vygotsky's socio-cultural theory validates the importance of adults as play partners for children (Berk & Winsler, 1995). The teacher is in a unique position to partner with children as they play.

Teachers are the most interesting element in any classroom. No matter where the teacher is physically in the classroom it is usually the most popular place to be. Children choose teachers as play partners. Teachers are able to enhance play by providing props and ideas, extending play, and scaffolding play ideas that would be too difficult for the child without support from adults.

Infants and toddlers often need ideas about what to play and how to play. Teachers can provide play cues that open up possibilities for children, giving them ideas that they might not have thought of or offering play themes and props that stretch children's socio-dramatic play.

The Teacher as Model

Children learn from watching, modeling, and imitating others. From this initial play, more complex play can often emerge. Teachers show children how to use complex social skills such as entering a playgroup or getting a desired toy and support attempts to try out the new skills. On their own, these skills might be too difficult for children. With the teacher's help, they might be possible.

Do what you want children to do—if you want children to sit on the floor or in chairs instead of on tables or furniture, sit on chairs and the floor. If you want children to keep their belongings in their cubbies, always put your belongings in your cubby. Being a good role model is an important teaching role.

Children are intensely interested in the behaviors of adults. As children observe how teachers play and interact, they see behaviors they can try themselves. Because children are learning from teachers all the time, teachers must be careful to model appropriate behaviors in the classroom.

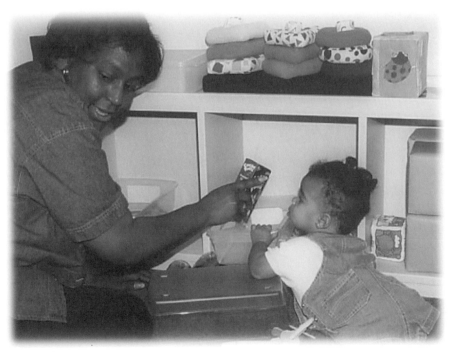

Teaching Roles

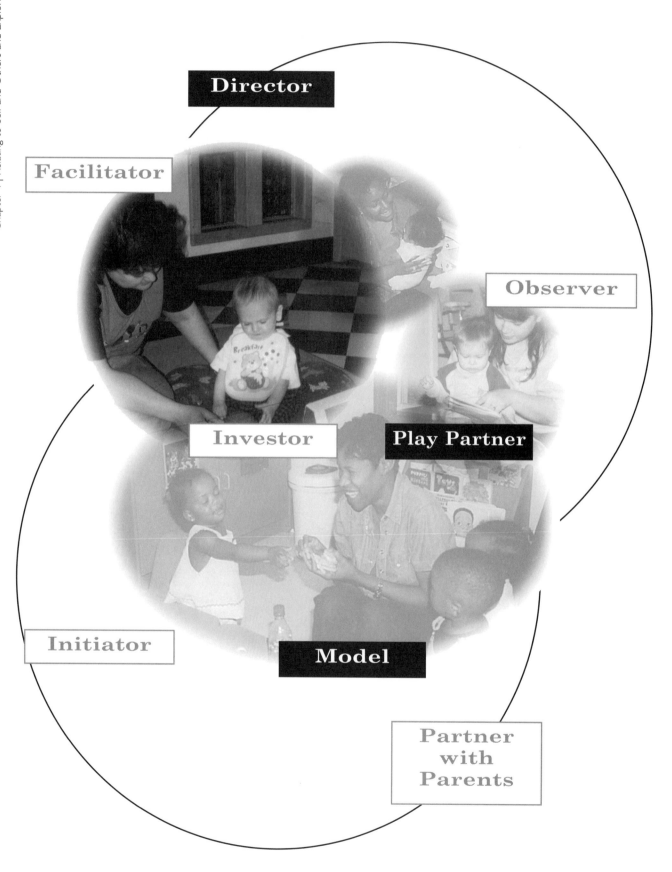

Director

Facilitator

Observer

Investor

Play Partner

Initiator

Model

Partner
with
Parents

The Teacher as Director

Teachers direct a large amount of a young child's life. But the type of direction meant here is that of play director. Teachers create stages for play—providing props, play cues, and materials that children incorporate into their play. Sometimes these props are tied to play themes that children enjoy revisiting often in play, such as mommy, daddy, or baby. Sometimes they are tied to emerging interests in things (for example, trucks or dirt). Other times they are tied to new experiences such as going to get a haircut or watching a play at the children's theatre.

Teachers also direct children to fill roles that are challenging and rewarding. Encouraging children to try to be the cashier at the grocery store or the shoe salesperson at the shoe store are examples.

As teachers help children explore roles, they are responsible for creating the environment to support children's explorations. Adding materials, especially props, to the classroom can create interest and variety for children's early role-playing experiences. Not only does the teacher create the setting, but also the teacher changes materials to refresh the classroom setting.

Teachers in the play-director role must be cautious to support but not to dominate the child's play. Scaffolding play, adding to children's ideas, asking interesting and thought-provoking questions, and playing roles assigned by children are appropriate. Telling children what to play or how to play isn't.

Create Opportunities to Explore Roles

Dramatic play is the area that is most conducive to supporting the exploration of roles. Dramatic play themes usually start close to home with the roles children see their significant others filling. The roles of mommy, daddy, and baby, sister, or brother are endlessly popular as children explore the things these significant people do.

Children often move on to the roles that interest them in the wider world, frequently based on their experiences. Going grocery shopping, to the shoe store, to the doctor or hospital, and to Mommy or Daddy's work setting provide children with rich opportunities to explore roles. These interests are usually followed by preferences for types of materials, types of play, or types of roles. Truck driver, hairstylist, construction worker, farmer, police officer, and dance teacher all become interesting as children are exposed or introduced to these people in the course of experience.

Creating and using prop boxes gives teachers the play props children need and the ability to change the dramatic play areas to create a wide variety of roles for children to explore. When boxes are prepared and available, they can be pulled out to enhance, support, and scaffold children's play as needed.

Support Children's Role Exploration

Relationships form the core of curriculum in the infant and toddler years. Teachers enhance children's self-concept by maintaining close connections to them as they begin to evaluate themselves and their actions.

Central to this connection is an understanding of children's uniqueness and individuality. It is not the aim of the infant or toddler teacher to treat every child the same. Rather, the teacher bases interactions and teaching on her or his understanding of each child's developmental age and stage as well as on the child's uniqueness. Some children need the teacher very close to try new roles while others can pick up a prop and explore a role without much more than a smile from the teacher. Figuring out these differences is part of the observation/assessment job of the teacher. Then the teacher can modify her or his teaching to support the children who need it and smile at the ones that don't!

Teachers may want to look at their curriculum plans for chances to provide children with messages about love, acceptance, control, value, and competence, the themes that influence self-concept throughout life. Exposing and validating these messages is an important teaching skill. For example, when one child asks another if he wants to play, a sensitive teacher might point out the acceptance that the invitation to play held. "He wants you to play with him" is an example of teacher talk that labels and validates the child's acceptance.

Observe to Support Exploring Roles

Observation emerges once again as a crucial teaching skill. In this case, teachers are observing to see when they might need to help children with self-evaluations that are challenging the child's view of self. When a child has a limited view of the roles he can play or negatively evaluates a role-playing experience, observant teachers step in. Their goal is to help the child understand what is happening and learn from the experience.

For example, finding play partners or entering a playgroup is often difficult for toddlers. Some children stand back and watch until others notice them and invite them in. Other children jump in the middle and try to take over. Another child might find a similar toy and begin to play beside the other players. Still another child might begin to cry and wail, "They won't let me play." Each of these responses offers teachers an opportunity to help children learn.

The observant teacher might help the watchers to use words to ask if they can play and support them if the answer is no. The teacher might help the "jumpers" see how others feel about their intrusion into their play and explore other ways to join in. She or he might help the parallel player offer an additional toy to the players as a way to join in. The teacher might stay close to the crying child to help him see that crying isn't working but words might be worth a try. All of these examples show how dynamic the role of the teacher is in supporting children's exploration of roles and emerging self-concepts.

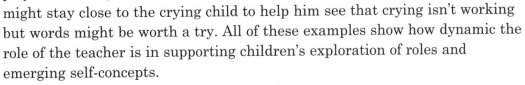

Teachers have to make sure that their interactions support children who are bumping up against their own or others' negative views of self. Because children are learning to modify their behavior to fit the situation and to understand the impact of their behavior on the feelings of others, they need help when things don't work out. When you don't get to play, when you're not first, when someone else chooses the tricycle you wanted to ride—each of these examples creates opportunities for teachers to help children learn new social skills. In the process of social problem-solving, teachers help children convert an experience that could be evaluated as negative into one that recognizes a new skill is being tried out or learned.

Myth or Misunderstanding
CHILDREN'S SELF-CONCEPTS ARE DAMAGED WHEN THEY HAVE CONFLICTS WITH OTHER CHILDREN.

This misunderstanding has different roots for parents and for teachers. Parents often fear that conflicts among children won't turn out fairly—that one child or the other will be the victim. No parent wants their child to be victimized by other children. For teachers, conflicts are time consuming—diverting the teacher's attention to the classroom management role, away from more enjoyable roles like play partner and facilitator.

Classroom management strategies for infants and toddlers are often aimed at preventing conflicts between children. Parents and teachers might think that less conflict is better. But that may not be true. Establishing relationships with other children is a major childhood task. Children's success at friendship matters because it is usually the context in which children evaluate their self-worth, competence, and view of the world as welcoming or hostile—all of which influence self-concept.

Playmate familiarity and compatibility are two important components of peer relations. Children who know each other and who are compatible have an easier time playing together (Howes, 1988). And, children who are friends are more likely to try to work out conflicts so that they can continue to play together (Shonkoff & Phillips, 2000).

This information leads to an understanding that conflicts between children are opportunities for children to learn and for teachers and parents to teach. Children learn to persist in trying to negotiate and compromise while teachers and parents can help children learn social problem-solving skills that enable children to stay and play.

What should happen next? Videotape a group of children at play in the school setting. Watch the tape with your colleagues. Discuss the conflicts that occurred and how the teachers handled them. Would you handle the conflict the same way or differently?

Applying Theory and Best Practices

A large part of professional practice in the field of care and early education is the synthesizing of knowledge, research, and best practices into teaching actions and strategies. A goal of **Innovations: Infant and Toddler Development** is to help teachers apply theory, research, and best practices to real-life situations and behaviors in the infant and toddler classroom. Let's take a look at a common behavior that is a part of most children's experience in care and early education settings to see if the knowledge we have gained, the research we have reviewed, and/or the best practices we have explored give any suggestions of how the behavior might be handled by teachers in the classroom.

Relating to self and others and exploring roles are tasks that require children to interact—with other adults and peers. So, let's begin exploring the integration of knowledge, research, and best practices by considering the implications of the topics covered in this chapter for handling a common classroom behavior—biting.

Possibilities from Understanding Cultural Context for Biting

An understanding of the influences of cultural context gives teachers several different directions to explore before determining specifically how biting will be addressed in the classroom. An understanding of the cultural context of the child, the family, the teacher, and the school will all lead to a clearer picture of how to proceed. The issue of congruence—how closely these different contexts view the behavior of biting—becomes an issue. If the family, the teacher, and the school all view biting the same way and agree on how to handle it, addressing the biting behavior will be rather straight-forward. A more likely scenario is that each will view biting differently.

So, the first possibility is to determine the points of view of each of the constituents. How does the family view biting? How do they handle it at home? How does the teacher view biting in the classroom? How does she or he plan to handle it? What are the school policies about biting behavior? What supports are in place to help families and teachers deal with this behavior? The answers to each of these questions will shape the approach used to replace the inappropriate response of biting with more socially acceptable strategies.

Teachers will be able to use the information gathered about this behavioral issue to increase individualization to meet the needs of the child. For example, if the child is encouraged at home to bite back and told at school to use words to solve biting problems, the teacher will need to approach handling biting differently. She or he will need to help children see that, while biting a child back may be acceptable at home, it is not acceptable at school. Then, the teacher will need to share her or his solutions for school with the parents, recognizing that the two approaches differ and explaining that the child can learn different responses for school and home. While the teacher may prefer for the parents to handle biting at home as she or he does at school, recognizing that parents may have different points of view, exploring why they have them, and providing them with information to broaden their view of how biting might be handled differently may all be possibilities that emerge from a better understanding of the child's cultural context.

Possibilities from Social Development and Play for Biting

The teacher may want to begin here by assessing levels of social problem-solving for both the child who is biting and the child who is bitten to find out where to begin helping both learn new skills. The bitten child may need to learn to call for help when he is having problems with other children. Or, the biter may need to learn to use language to tell others to stay away from his toys and play materials. Or, it may be time to help a child learn to divide the available resources so that both children can stay and play. Knowing how each child is responding socially is the place to begin.

Then, teachers can plan to use playmates and play themes as scaffolds for learning new social problem-solving skills. When children are interested in continuing to play together, but biting (or other forms of aggression) gets in the way, it is always a possibility for the teacher to stay close and bridge or scaffold the children's play. When she or he is there to help children wait a minute to get what they want, ask for what they want, or come up with another problem-solving solution, children can solve problems in a more sophisticated way than they might be able to do without her or his support.

Often, biting behavior happens when children are frustrated socially—they want to play, get a turn, use a toy, or do exactly what another child is doing. Creating a zone of proximal development (ZPD) for the child to try out ideas through play may be just what is needed to bridge the gap between social needs and social problem-solving ability.

Possibilities from Theories of Self-concept for Biting

From theories of self-concept, it is easy to see how biting might relate to themes of power and control, love and acceptance, moral value, and competence. In fact, most biting incidences are probably related to experiences around these themes that impact self-esteem. These theories suggest that teachers should make sure that children get many messages about these ideas from the classroom, the teachers, and other children. Planning positive experiences with power and control, like making choices in play and exerting autonomy over decisions, allow children to practice using personal power without hurting others and controlling situations within their purview. Providing many experiences that communicate love and acceptance to children, such as warm and welcoming responses upon arrival and sensitive responsiveness when children are hurt or afraid, prepare and insulate children from threats to their emerging self-esteems.

Teachers are in a wonderful position to provide many and varied experiences with competence. By planning within children's ZPD, children are challenged but not overwhelmed, creating in them feelings of competence and confidence. When children do get overwhelmed by inadequate feelings, teachers can help them see that they will be able to try again another day, a powerful message in maintaining confidence and self-esteem. Teachers can encourage feelings of being worthy, addressing the theme of moral value, by their investment in relationships—really trying to know and understand each child and furthering the emotional attachment and social relationships with them at the same time.

Another possibility from theories of self-concept relates to how and when teachers provide reinforcement and encouragement to children. When teachers use encouragement (rather than praise or reinforcement) to let a child place his own value on his behavior, the child learns the important lesson that what he thinks about his behavior is much more important than what others think. Believing in your own images of self is the foundation of learning from regular and frequent social interactions with others.

Finally, theories of self-concept lead teachers to see the development of the sense of self as a process—a cumulative one that can be influenced by the way adults support children's conflicts, including biting. When teachers who are committed to helping children learn more appropriate ways to respond approach biting as a normal part of growing up, the biting behavior becomes similar to other inappropriate behaviors that have come and gone rather than being the inappropriate behavior that upsets the direction of self-concept development.

Integrating Theory and Best Practices into Curriculum

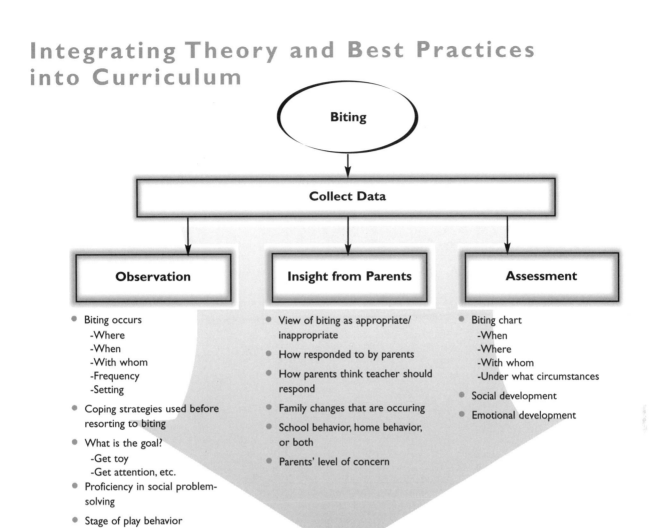

Biting

Collect Data

Observation

- Biting occurs
  - Where
  - When
  - With whom
  - Frequency
  - Setting
- Coping strategies used before resorting to biting
- What is the goal?
  - Get toy
  - Get attention, etc.
- Proficiency in social problem-solving
- Stage of play behavior

Insight from Parents

- View of biting as appropriate/inappropriate
- How responded to by parents
- How parents think teacher should respond
- Family changes that are occuring
- School behavior, home behavior, or both
- Parents' level of concern

Assessment

- Biting chart
  - When
  - Where
  - With whom
  - Under what circumstances
- Social development
- Emotional development

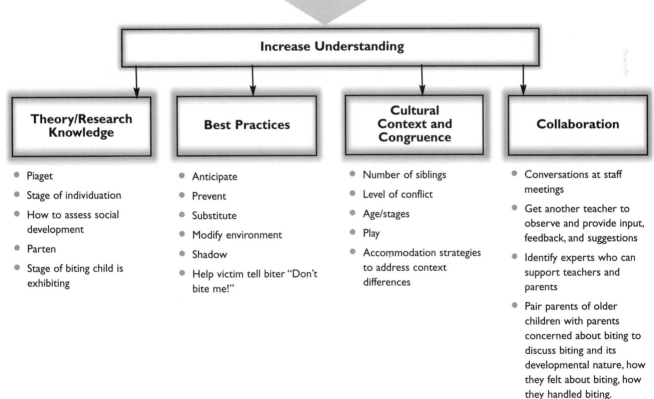

Increase Understanding

Theory/Research Knowledge

- Piaget
- Stage of individuation
- How to assess social development
- Parten
- Stage of biting child is exhibiting

Best Practices

- Anticipate
- Prevent
- Substitute
- Modify environment
- Shadow
- Help victim tell biter "Don't bite me!"

Cultural Context and Congruence

- Number of siblings
- Level of conflict
- Age/stages
- Play
- Accommodation strategies to address context differences

Collaboration

- Conversations at staff meetings
- Get another teacher to observe and provide input, feedback, and suggestions
- Identify experts who can support teachers and parents
- Pair parents of older children with parents concerned about biting to discuss biting and its developmental nature, how they felt about biting, how they handled biting.

Possibilities

Parent Possibilities

Teacher-Initiated

Share frequency chart w/ parents of biter to put biting in perspective.
Use parent postcard w/ parents before biting stage emerges.

Parent Participation

Share plan w/ parents
Parent discussion group w/ parents of older kids who have outgrown biting.
Discuss biting w/ parents to uncover similarities and differences in handling biting.

Innovations in Environments

Duplicate toys
Add teethers to classroom
Duplicate popular centers—make two block centers or two dramatic play areas

Observation/Assessment Possibilities

Where, when, why, with whom, frequency, setting chart
Observe for goal of biting—to get toy, to get attention, to express frustration, to be noticed, etc.
Which children have learned what social problem-solving skills

Interactive Experiences

Provide additional reminders about upcoming transitions.
Engage in extra floor time with children who bite and those who are bitten.
Serve as a play partner.
Label feelings and their expressions
Provide many experiences related to self-concept theme
Plan play experiences w/in child's ZPD
Use encouragement

Plan

Web

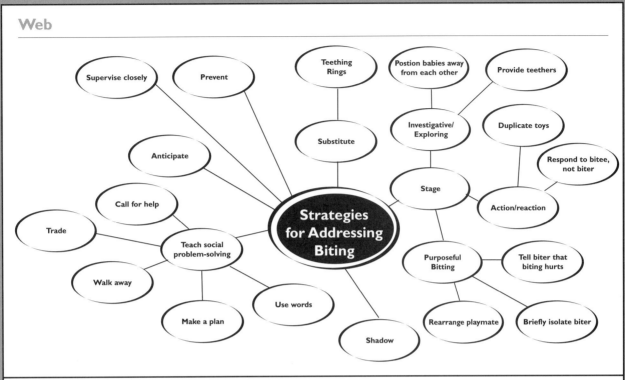

Dramatic Possibilities Biting prop box, put bite marks on baby doll's arms w/ washable markers

Art/Sensory Possibilities Gelatin gigglers, fill and pour experiences

Curiosity Possibilities Mirrors to explore mouth and teeth, add animals with teeth, dinosaurs with teeth

Music Possibilities "Mommy Loves You"

Movement Possibilities Tongue exercises with mirror

Literacy Possibilities Paper plate emotions in book

Outdoor Possibilities Big box play

Project Possibilities Picture book of appropriate places to make teeth marks—on a piece of cheese, toast, cracker, apples, on a teether, spoon of ice cream, cold wash cloth, cookies, etc.

Books	Picture File Pictures/Vocabulary
Two Bullies, by Junko Morimoto How Do I Feel?, by Norma Simon Mine!, by Miriam Cohen	Teeth, tongue Emotions (anger, happiness, frustrations, boredom)

Rhymes & Fingerplays	Music/Songs	Prop Boxes
"Row, Row, Row Your Boat" (w/ friend as partner) London Bridge (for turn taking)	"Johnny Works with One Hammer" "Put Your Finger in the Air"	Biting prop box w/ Band-Aids, teethers, cold packs, cotton balls, babies with bite marks, teeth (dental impressions)

Summary

During infancy, babies go from seeming to be virtually uninterested in the world that surrounds them to being intensely interested in the human world and their place in it. Toddlerhood is characterized by changes in the way children see the world. The focus on self broadens to include others—other adults, other children, and other settings.

As the view of self stabilizes, children begin to see themselves in relation to others. From this increasing ability to evaluate "self," children create a particular view of themselves. Educators and parents know that self-concept has a great deal to do with how children continue to progress. The way children explore their views of themselves is through play, which provides a vehicle for exploring roles, practicing outcomes, and considering alternatives.

Human development is deeply and dramatically affected by the multiple contexts in which growth and learning occur. It is within the context of culture that developmental and interactional theories merge with practice to facilitate each child's individual needs, competencies, abilities, and style of learning and growing.

The development of play overlaps all areas of development–physical, social, emotional, and intellectual (which includes cognitive and language development). Piaget presented play as being divided into three types of play behavior–practice play, symbolic play, and play-with-rules (Piaget, 1962). Parten presented play as social development with six increasingly complex types of peer play – 1) unoccupied play, 2) onlooker play, 3) solitary independent play, 4) parallel activity, 5) associative play, and 6) cooperative play (Parten, 1932). Vygotsky believed that children construct knowledge through

instructions of others and through social interactions. Adult support for interactions can increase skills in children and help peer relationships to emerge (Berk & Winsler, 1995).

Success in achieving autonomy and independence throughout childhood has a profound impact on the way children mature. If their early attempts are successful and fulfilling, children will continue to develop competence. The creation of self-concept begins at birth and continues to be influenced throughout life.

Through play children get images of themselves as they attempt to play roles. Even negative experiences, depending on how they are handled, can be self-concept enhancing. Teachers play an important role in narrating and interpreting experiences. Additionally, teachers help children develop prosocial behaviors. In developing children's problem-solving skills, the teacher can support children as they go through the following steps: 1) calling for help, 2) trading, 3) taking turns, 4) using words, 5) walking away, and 6) plan-making.

When children are in the classroom environment, props and play cues support them as they explore. Mirrors are especially important as a source of interest and interaction. Relationships form the core of curriculum in the toddler years. Teachers enhance children's self-concept by maintaining close connections to toddlers as they begin to evaluate themselves and their actions.

Questions and Activities

1. What is the developmental sequence of play behavior?
2. Why is it unrealistic to expect infants and toddlers to share? What prosocial behaviors can teachers support to make sharing a possibility for later?
3. What would you do if a 24-month-old with limited language started biting every day while involved in dramatic play?
4. Give an example and explain how a negative experience can enhance a child's self-concept.
5. Create a prop box for your classroom. How will you decide what kind of prop box to create? How will you introduce the items?
6. Plan a parent activity or event that will communicate to parents the importance of play.

References

Albrecht, K.M. & M. Ward. (1989). Growing pains. **Pre-K Today**, 36, 54-55.

Berk, L.E. (1994). Vygotsky's theory: The importance of make-believe play. **Young Children**, 50 (1), 30-39.

Berk, L.E. & A. Winsler. (1995). **Scaffolding children's learning.** Washington. DC: National Association for the Education of Young Children (NAEYC).

Bredekamp, C. & C. Copple (1997). **Developmentally appropriate practice in early childhood programs, Revised edition.** Washington, DC: National Association for the Education of Young Children (NAEYC).

Bronfenbrenner, U. (1979). **The ecology of human development: Experiments by nature and design.** Cambridge, MA: Harvard University Press.

Brunson, M.B. (2000). Recognizing and supporting the development of self-regulation in young children. **Young Children,** 55(2), 32-37.

Cherry, C. (1976). **Creative play for the developing child: Early childhood education through play.** Belmont, CA: Fearon.

Curry, N.E. & C.N. Johnson. (1990). **Beyond self-esteem: Developing a genuine sense of human value.** Washington, DC: National Association for the Education of Young Children (NAEYC).

Edwards, C., L. Gandini, & G. Forman. (1998). **The one hundred languages of children: The Reggio Emilia approach to early childhood education – Advanced Reflections.** Norwood, NJ: Ablex.

Elkind, D. (2001). Thinking about children's play. **Child Care Information Exchange,** 139, 27-28.

Erickson, E.H. (1963). **Childhood and society.** New York: Workman.

Greenspan, S.I. (1999). **The six experiences that create intelligence and emotional growth in babies and young children.** Reading, MA: Perseus Books.

Hitz, R. & A. Driscoll. (1988). Praise or encouragement? New insights and implications for early childhood teachers. **Young Children,** 43(5), 6-13.

Howes, C. (1988). Peer interaction of young children. **Monographs of the Society for Research in Child Development,** 53 (1).

Howes, C. & C.C. Mathesen. (1992). Sequences of the development of competent play with peers: Social and pretend play. **Developmental Psychology,** 28: 961-974.

Ilg, L. B. & F. L. Ames. (1976). **Your two year old.** New York: Delacorte Press.

Katz, L. & P. McClellan. (1997). **Fostering social competence: The teacher's role.** Washington, DC: National Association for the Education of Young Children (NAEYC).

Parten, M.P. (1932). Social participation among preschool children. **Journal of Abnormal Psychology,** 27, 243-269.

Piaget, J. (1962). **Play, dreams and imitation in childhood** (C. Gattegno & F.M. Hodgson, Trans.) New York: Norton.

Rogers, C.S., & J.K. Sawyer (1988). **Play in the lives of children.** Washington, DC: National Association for the Education of Young Children (NAEYC).

Shonkoff, J.P. & D.A. Phillips (Eds.) (2000). *From neurons to neighborhoods: The science of early childhood development.* Washington, DC: National Academy Press.

Shore, R. (1997). *Rethinking the Brain: New insights into early development.* New York: Families and Work Institute.

Wardle, F. (1995). How young children build images of themselves. *Child Care Information Exchange,* 104, 44-47.

Glossary

Action/Reaction Biting—Biting in which the child is exploring actions and the reactions that occur as a result.

Associative Play—Activities that occur between children in which no specific roles are assigned or play goal identified.

Autonomy vs. Shame or Doubt—In this period of psycho-social development, children's struggle for independence is viewed as creating a feeling of autonomy ("I can do it") or a feeling of shame and doubt ("Can I do it?" "Should I do it?").

Calling for Help—A social problem-solving skill that involves alerting an adult to help with a problem.

Cooperative Play—A form of play in which children cooperate with others to create play situations.

Culture—Customary beliefs and patterns of and for behavior that are passed on to future generations by the society in which they live and/or by social, religious, or ethnic groups.

Developmental Theories—A view of how children grow and learn through relatively predictable stages in each domain of development.

Imitation—Modeling or copying the behavior of another person.

Interactional Theories—A view of how children grow and learn from among and between interactions with others, the environment, and children's biological predispositions.

Investigative/Exploratory Biting—Biting that occurs as a result of exploration of the environment with the senses.

Modeling—Imitation of behaviors of other people after observing their behavior.

Onlooker Play—A type of play where children watch others play, and seek to be near, perhaps even responding to the play of others.

Organized Sense of Self—An awareness of one's separateness from parents and other primary caregivers.

Parallel Activity—A form of play in which children play with similar toys alongside each other, rather than with each other.

Parten—A play theorist who presented play as six increasingly complex types of peer play.

Patterning—Physical support for appropriate behaviors.

Piaget—A play theorist who characterized peer play in six categories.

Plan-making—Helping children solve problems by making a plan with an adult's support.

Play Cues—Ideas provided by the environment, the things in the environment, adults, or other children about how to get started playing.

Play Props—Materials that children use to support or initiate play.

Play-With-Rules—A type of play behavior that emerges during the late preschool years.

Practice Play—Composed of repetitions of the same movements and actions both with and without objects.

Prop Boxes—Consist of materials that support a particular play theme and give teachers the play props children need to create a wide variety of roles for children to explore.

Prosocial Behaviors—Those behaviors that precede and lead to successful social interactions.

Purposeful Biting—Biting that is aimed at getting something or changing the outcome of a situation.

Self-concept—A child's view of himself or herself, also called self-esteem.

Social Problem-solving—Social learning taken directly from interactive experiences.

Solitary Independent Play—A type of play where children play alone with objects without interacting with others, regardless of how near.

Symbolic Play—A type of play that involves the beginning of the traditional "dramatic play."

Taking Turns—A social problem-solving skill that gives children sequential turns and provides adult support while waiting.

Trading—A social problem-solving strategy that involves giving something a child has for something the child wants.

Triangulation—Strategy for interacting with a child through a toy or another person.

Unoccupied Play—A type of play in which children watch others at play.

Using Words—A social problem-solving skill that supports children in beginning to use words rather than actions to solve problems.

Vygotsky—A theorist who suggested a socio-cultural theory based on the premise that children socially construct what they know in the context of their family and cultural experiences.

Walking Away—A social problem-solving technique used to help children remove themselves from situations that are becoming difficult, either by moving away themselves or by asking the other child to move away.

Zone of Proximal Development (ZPD)—The range of tasks a child cannot yet handle alone but can accomplish with the help of adults and more skilled peers.

CHAPTER 5

Communicating with Parents, Teachers, and Friends

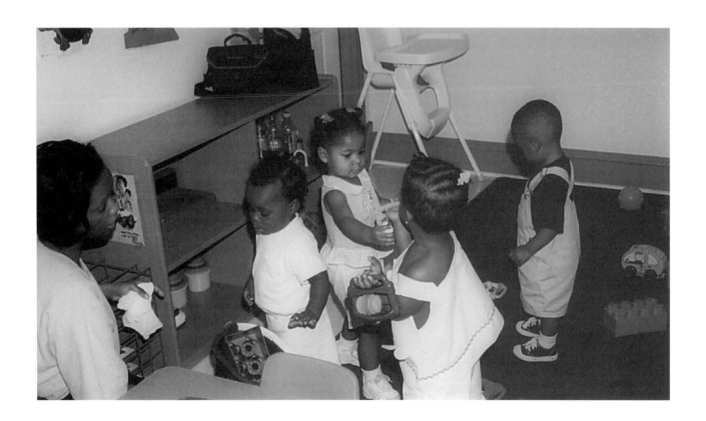

Developmental Tasks: Communicating with Parents, Teachers, and Friends

Infants

Newborns arrive able to communicate with others primarily through gestural language such as facial expressions and crying. During infancy, though, this changes as babies transition from having almost no understanding of spoken language, to understanding spoken words, and then to expressing their knowledge of language with their own words.

Infancy is thought to be a sensitive period for the acquisition of language. The window for optimally learning language opens at birth and begins to

close around 18 to 24 months. From gestural cues to spoken language, infants acquire skills as responsive adults use language during routine and stimulation activities and experiences. After this period, language still can be acquired, but it is a more difficult process.

Stimulating language is a crucial task for infant teachers. Unless children understand how language functions, they have little success in learning to use it. Communicating is not an isolated skill. It is a reciprocal task—communicating with someone who responds in kind. Creating this interactive dialogue is the first step down the road of learning to communicate.

As infants increase their ability to communicate with others, future thinking skills are being developed. Sensory exploration of the environment and everything in it gives infants considerable information about how the world works. Cognitive understanding expands as infants begin to put word labels with objects, activities, and experiences from the environment and then begin the process of communicating their ideas through gestures, facial expression, and then with words.

Toddlers

Toddlerhood marks the beginning of an exciting and challenging period in the lives of young children. Toddlers emerge from infancy with a considerable range of skills and abilities. They have perfected the motor skills of getting around and eating and drinking without assistance. Toddlers have learned to understand a rather large number of words and are beginning to communicate their needs and wants with an ever-growing spoken vocabulary. And, they are inquisitive about everything—wanting to interact, discover, manipulate, and explore everything in sight.

Intellectual development has also progressed. Evidence of learning is clearly seen in the curiosity of toddlers—they are interested in everything—from minute details to the "whys" of the big picture—and are trying to put together their understanding of the world in which they live.

Knowledge

Theories of Language Development

During infancy and toddlerhood, children go from being non-verbal to communicating effectively with words. To the casual observer, this rapid growth may seem like magic. Several different theories propose different ideas about how language is learned.

Some view language development as an innate biological system—something with which children are born. Noam Chomsky (1957) proposes that children are born with a biologically innate system that primes them to learn language. This view of an inborn ability to talk and communicate is used to explain why children all over the world follow roughly the same language acquisition process.

Behaviorists propose that operant conditioning and imitation are the primary mechanisms for learning language. Parents reinforce and respond to sounds that match their native languages, helping children learn language. In this form of learning, children interact with the environment, getting reactions that increase the chances that the child will repeat the original action. So, when Mom and Dad are delighted with ooohs or ahhhs, or experimentation with da da da, their reactions of excitement and enthusiasm increase the infant's desire to repeat the verbal expressions. If no one responds to these early attempts at language, or if hearing loss prevents the baby from getting auditory feedback, which makes her want to continue to make sounds and communicate, language development does not continue.

Behaviorists also suggest that children use imitation to learn language. As adults talk to infants, they model adults who talk and interact with them. As adults and other children reinforce children's language efforts, language acquisition is promoted.

Others view language as a much more complex process, one that depends on innate predispositions as well as responsive, interactive environments. The interactional perspective considers both innate capacities and environmental influences as important. As infants experience language, innate abilities are stimulated (nature viewpoint) and supported by observation, participation, and exploration (nurture viewpoint). These experiences combine to support children's construction of understanding of form, content, similarities, and differences of language (interactional viewpoint).

Children's innate ability is stimulated by early gestural and vocal communications from adults and others, while emerging relationships stimulate the desire to continue the non-verbal dialogue and learn a verbal one (Bloom, 1998). Relationships create a context for acquisition of language. Then, reciprocal language, starting with gestures and facial expressions, creates shared meaning between children and adults in their attachment networks, intensifying and facilitating the mutuality of relationships (Stern, 1985).

Greenspan (1997) suggests that the innate ability to use language requires an emotional foundation. Language acquires purpose and function with emotional meaning. If children don't feel emotions as they experiment and learn language, they are less likely to be able to access and use developing skills. Without reciprocal, enduring, developing, supportive relationships to add emotional meaning to language, innate language functions don't respond to experiences and stimulation from parents and the environment.

Adults who are part of children's attachment networks help them learn language when these adults spontaneously talk to children, stimulating and creating the context for the acquisition of language. Language competence is fostered and unfolds when children and adults have frequent, reciprocal conversations. From these conversations, children learn to pay attention to each other, to take turns, expand vocabulary, and develop an interest in talking with peers and significant adults (Katz & Snow, 2000).

During the first three years of life, children typically go from babbling to using grammatically correct sentences. As magical as this rapid growth seems, language follows predictable growth patterns that we can identify and follow. In general, the sequence of acquisition of speech sounds follows these developmental principles:

1. Motorically simple to motorically complex; for example, (m) as in mama to (kw) as in queen
2. Acoustically simple to acoustically complex; for example, (p) as in pie to (thr) as in throw
3. Visible (simple) to less visible (complex); for example, (b) as in boy to (r) as in red

The sequence of sound articulation is also predictable. During the first four years, a child will typically master the following groups of sounds:

(b), (p), (d), (t), (g), (k), (f), (m), (n), (ng), (w), (h), (y)

Other sounds are mastered after the fourth year.

Children's language behaviors also follow a fairly predictable developmental pattern. The following language behaviors can be expected to emerge within a few months following chronological ages:

Normal Ranges of Language Behaviors

Age	Language Behaviors
(birth–6 months)	• Responds to familiar voices. • Changes type of cry with different emotional state. • Turns eyes and head toward the source of sound. • Is aware of the sounds she makes. • Makes soft vowel sounds: uh, ah.
7–10 months	• Turns head and shoulders toward soft, familiar sounds. • Imitates intonational patterns of familiar phrases using some vowel and consonant patterns. • Practices a variety of intonational and inflectional patterns. • Understands simple phrases such as bye-bye, no-no, and her own name. • Directs vocalizations toward people and familiar objects in the environment.
11–16 months	• Says first words, "da-da," "ma-ma," "muk" (milk), and so on. • Uses several words correctly and consistently. • Points or looks to familiar objects when asked to do so. • Imitates and jabbers in response to human voice. • Frowns when scolded. • Imitates sounds she hears: "moo," "baa baa," and so on. • Expresses bodily needs with non-verbal and verbal responses.
18 months	• Begins to identify body parts; is able to point to eyes and nose. • Uses several meaningful words that may not be articulated correctly such as "ba-ba" for bottle, "muk" for milk. • May use one word to represent several things, including "wa-wa" for "I want water," "look at the water," and "I spilled the water."
18–24 months	• Follows simple commands without visual clues. • Enjoys books; likes being read to if book is familiar; will ask to have the same book read again and again. • Points to familiar pictures in books or magazines. • Develops a sense of "me" and "mine." • Uses a variety of common words consistently heard in the classroom or at home (usually between 10–20 words). • Refers to self by name. • Puts familiar words together to make simple sentences like "Daddy work" or "Mommy bye-bye" and "All gone." • Talks mainly about self. • Imitates animal or object sounds. • Expresses refusal by saying "no."
24–30 months	• Likes listening to music or singing. • Sings short songs or says short fingerplays. • Imitates 3–4 word sentences. • Reacts to sound by telling what is heard, or running to look at the source of the sound. • Continues to express refusal by saying "no." • Objects to help from others; wants to do it all by herself.
30–36 months	• Understands and uses simple verbs, pronouns, prepositions, adverbs, and adjectives such as "in, me, big, go, more." • Uses plurals. • Understands contrasts such as yes/no, come/go, run/stop, hot/cold. • Uses complete sentences frequently. • Answers simple questions from familiar people. • Uses "I" and "me."

As these skills emerge, children's language becomes more intelligible. Expect about 20%–25% of an 18- to 28-month-old's language to be understandable to strangers. This percentage goes up to 60%–65% for a 30- to 36-month-old, and 75%–90% for a 3- to 4-year-old.

It is interesting to note that almost all children follow this relatively predictable path, regardless of culture. This is not to say that the cultural context doesn't influence language—it does. But the influence of culture seems independent of the developmental process of acquiring language (Shonkoff & Phillips, 2000).

Myth or Misunderstanding
CHILDREN OUTGROW MOST SPEECH AND LANGUAGE DISORDERS.

During the language acquisition process, parents and teachers are often concerned about mispronunciations, lisps, lack of initial sounds, substitutions of one sound for another, limited talking, limited vocabulary, tongue thrusts, pacifier use, and other language and articulation problems. Sometimes this concern leads parents and concerned educators to enlist the support of pediatricians and speech and language pathologists to evaluate whether the problem should be causing concern. At other times, parents and teachers assume that children will just outgrow speech and language problems.

There is support for pursuing both of these options. Some types of speech and language problems are indeed the result of maturation and will go away as children mature. Others are not and need intervention to remediate the problem in order for speech and language development to continue.

To determine if a child's speech and language skills are within normal ranges, assess her skill level using the speech sound acquisition chart and the language behavior chart on pages 199 and 200. If the child is not exhibiting behaviors within normal ranges on these assessment tools, an appropriate next step is to talk with the child's parents about concerns and suggest a referral to the child's pediatrician or an appropriate certified speech and language therapist. For more information, contact the American Speech and Hearing Association at www.asha.org, or the American Academy of Pediatrics at www.aap.org. The influences of culture are usually seen in children's language learning styles (Berk, 1999). Some children view language learning as a mechanism to label and identify objects while others view language learning as a way to get their needs met and express their feelings. These style differences originate in the interactive style of the adults and others in the cultural context of the child.

Expressive and Receptive Language

Children have two kinds of language skills. One kind is children's expressive language skills, meaning the production of language, those things the child can say, the size of the spoken vocabulary, and the grammar and syntax of language. The other kind is receptive language, which refers to children's comprehension of language, regardless of their expressive ability. Very young children learn the meaning of language, such as "no" or "go bye-bye," before they are able to say those words themselves.

Implications of Language Theories for Communicating with Parents, Teachers, and Friends

Teachers get clear direction about what to do to stimulate language from each theory of language development. Behaviorists remind teachers to be good language models for children. Modeling includes not only using language with children but also modeling the way sounds are formed (with facial expressions) and the way language is used (by slowing it down and simplifying the language you use with children).

Interactional theories provide many ideas about how teachers can further language development. Talking to and with children often is a good starting point. Encouraging experimentation with language with fingerplays, songs, and rhymes can create a fascination and interest in language. Point out similarities and differences in words, expressions, and language, making it easy for children to see how language works. And, most importantly, work on relationships. When teachers are mutually involved in relationships with children, they create a foundation for language to grow and expand.

Including children in the functional use of language is important. Use language stimulation techniques described in the Best Practices section of this chapter, pages 221-223. Including children in language as it is used in the adult world helps children see its function—what language can do, what language can make happen, and how language works within relationships in the real world.

Greenspan (1997) suggests that teachers help children connect emotional meaning to language. When language is used in the context of warm and responsive relationships, positive emotional meaning is likely to be attached to experiences. This increases the chances that the cataloging and referencing that makes language purposeful and functional occurs in the neural networks of the brain. But, don't forget to have fun. Children love having fun with language—saying rhymes, singing songs, and acting out fingerplays. What better way to connect positive emotional meaning to language than to have it be interesting, fun, participatory, repetitive, and, sometimes, a little silly!

Intellectual Development

The intellectual development of infants and toddlers is stimulated by virtually everything parents and teachers do with children. In fact, during the first three years of life, intellectual and language development is stimulated naturally as children explore and interact with the environment, exploring their place in it.

Piaget's Cognitive-development Theory

According to Jean Piaget, the most noted scholar of cognitive development in very young children, children learn cognitive skills by making mistakes, by actively experimenting with the real world, and by trying to understand how things work (Piaget, 1977). Piaget viewed active experimentation, experiences with real things, concrete objects, and the environment as the best ways to stimulate intellectual development.

Piaget's Cognitive-development Theory is a stage theory. It proposes four periods of development. The first two of Piaget's stages occur during early childhood. During the first stage, the sensori-motor stage, children use information gathered through their senses and through motor movement to construct an understanding of the world. Beginning with reflexes, then with motor movement, and finally, through manipulation of objects, infants discover and explore the environment.

Two complementary cognitive processes are responsible for construction of knowledge in infants and toddlers, according to Piaget. The first, called assimilation, is the process of interpreting new information or learning into existing ideas or thought—transforming the world to meet personal needs (Elkind, 2001). When infants convert everything they pick up into something to mouth and explore orally, they are assimilating.

The second, called accommodation, is the creation of new ideas or the adaptation of old ones when new information is received from exploration and manipulation of objects—or transforming the self to meet the demands of the external world (Elkind, 2001). An example of accommodation is learning to use a toilet instead of a diaper. These processes are repeated over and over as children explore their physical and social environments, and were viewed by Piaget as the primary mechanism for cognitive learning.

Object permanence is the concept that objects are there whether you can see them or not. Piaget stated that children develop this thinking skill during the sensori-motor period. Prior to learning that objects have permanence, children interact and think about only those things and people in view. The acquisition of the concept of object permanence indicates a major accommodation of thought processes. Once an object can be held in the child's mind, thinking skills advance and become more complex. The following chart summarizes the characteristics of Piaget's sensorimotor stage of cognitive development.

Piaget's Stages of Cognitive Development

Overview of the Sensorimotor stage	Birth-2 years	• Adaptaion (through assimilation and accommodation) to environment does not include the use of symbols or oral language. • Child develops schema (cognitive pictures).
Simple Reflex	Birth-1 month	• Reflex actions are practiced to become more efficient; child begins to exercise reflexes. • Lacks object permanence; if object can be seen, it exists. If not seen, it does not exist.
Primary Circular Reactions	1-4 months	• Child repeats reflexive behavior as well as other pleasant behavior (for example, sucking). • Object permanence advances—child perceives object as having its own separate existence. • Continues to *gaze* at spot where object was, as if expecting it to return.
Secondary Circular Reactions	4-10 months	• Behaviors discovered by chance are repeated to produce interesting results. Child is beginning to understand that something happens as a result of his actions. • Object permanence advances—child *looks* for removed object where it was last seen.
Coordination of Secondary Schemata	10-12 months	• Beginning to see what Piaget calls "intelligent behavior." Behavior is intentional—it has a goal. • Object permanence advances—object has own existence. Child *searches* for object in the last place seen. • Imitation of models increases.
Tertiary Circular Reactions	12-18 months	• Actively experiments with environment: varies responses to obtain interesting results. • Uses trial-and-error techniques. • Object permanence advances—child *follows* visual sequential displacement of objects.
Imagery Stage	18 months-2 ½ years	• Begins transition to symbolic thought. Vocabulary grows rapidly. Uses formed mental images to solve problems. Thought processes relate to concrete experiences and objects. • Object permanence advances—child searches for objects when displacement is visible.

The second stage of Piaget's theory is the pre-operational stage. During the pre-operational stage, Piaget believes that children's cognitive skills are very different from adult skills. Children's cognitive development is dominated by the formation of cognitive images that are based on direct, interactive experiences. Many mistakes in thinking occur in this period. These mistakes fascinated Piaget and led to his ideas about how children generalize learning from one experience to another.

Thinking errors that children make during the pre-operational period include reasoning errors and misunderstandings of causal relationships. These errors explain so well what every adult understands about children this age—that they are much more interested in figuring things out for themselves than they are in having adults tell them how things work (Mooney, 2000).

The following chart summarizes the characteristics of Piaget's pre-operational stage of cognitive development.

Piaget's Stages of Cognitive Development

Overview of the Pre-operational Stage	2–7 years	• Characterized by the beginning of symbolic thought and the use of mental images and words. • Have flaws in thinking: egocentrism, centration, irreversibility, transductive or illogical reasoning. • Beliefs of causal relationships: animism, artificialism, participation.
Pre-conceptual Stage	2–5 years	• Develops ability to classify objects: child will group similar objects together but will not appear to have an overall plan to complete task. • Develops the ability to serialize objects: child will serialize sporadically without plan or goal. • Cannot conserve quantity, substance, or volume.
Intuitive Stage	4–7 years	• Classification of objects can be done by classes and sub-classes. • Serialization develops to constructing an ordinal arrangement with some difficulty.

Recent consideration of Piaget's ideas reveals limitations in his observations about cognitive development, particularly in light of the advances in brain theory and research, and in our understanding of the role of emotion and social relationships on cognitive development (Cryer & Harms, 2000; Mooney, 2000). Nevertheless, Piaget's basic ideas are still useful in understanding how children construct their own knowledge as well as how to create challenging experiences for young children.

Implications of Piaget's Theory for Communicating with Parents, Teachers, and Friends

Piaget's theory has implications for teachers as they support the developmental task of communicating with parents, teachers, and friends. An understanding of the way children assimilate and accommodate through sensory exploration means that teachers need to provide long periods of uninterrupted time for exploration of the environment, following the child's lead rather than focusing on the teacher's direction or teaching. The idea of time alone to interact and experience is also one of the premises of primary teaching (see pages 110-114 in Chapter 3). It gives children time to integrate and understand their experiences. Piaget's theory suggests that teachers resist the urge to provide unending stimulation. In fact, this theory supports allowing children to design and modify their own stimulation, with the interesting things they discover in their environment and children's individually novel ways of exploration.

Another Piagetian idea is the careful, planned preparation of the environment. If children manipulate and construct knowledge through sensory investigation of the environment, environments with a variety of objects, toys, and materials make the best platform for this exploration. Within this well-planned environment, children need many opportunities for trial and error. The opportunity to try again, change the way you try, and experiment with outcomes based on what you try, are important Piagetian experiences.

Peek-a-boo and hide-and-seek games play an important role in supporting Piaget's ideas about emerging object permanence. Experiences with disappearing and reappearing objects and people support children's construction of knowledge about permanency and exploration of causal relationships.

Vygotsky's Socio-cultural Theory

Vygotsky (1978) shared many of Piaget's ideas, but felt that the child's social and cognitive worlds are much closer together than Piaget did. This theory placed increased emphasis on family and where the child lived and experienced learning. Vygotsky viewed social interactions between children, supportive adults, or more competent peers as a significant part of the learning process.

Language, particularly language used in play, is the primary mechanism for advancing children's construction of knowledge. As children participate in play, their conversations, discussions, conflicts, and negotiations extend and enhance cognitive skills and abilities.

Vygotsky validates the importance of the teacher as a keen observer of children. The goal of observation is to allow teachers to understand each child's zone of proximal development (ZPD). The ZPD is the range of tasks children cannot handle on their own but can manage with the help of a supportive teacher or more competent peers. To be able to challenge children cognitively, Vygotsky believes that teachers have to be aware of children's socio-cultural contexts and their zones of proximal development. From this understanding, teachers create and develop challenging experiences.

Encouraging conversations, interactions, and play experiences in small groups is the optimal way for children to learn. Within small groups, scaffolding of children's learning by peers is most likely to occur. Vygotsky also considered the teacher's role in supporting learning as a challenging one. Knowing when to intervene with which teaching strategy is a crucial teaching skill. When to ask a questions, which question to ask, what idea to offer, which suggestion to make, and when to let children proceed on their own are delicate considerations—considerations that can disrupt the flow of children's learning or scaffold it to an even higher level.

Implications of Vygotsky's Socio-cultural Theory for Communicating with Parents, Teachers, and Friends

Implications from Vygotsky's theory include gaining a clear understanding of the similarities and differences between the socio-cultural context of the family and the school. When there is congruence between the two cultures, children will be able to move between the two without conflict or miscommunication. This understanding guides teachers' use of language with children in ways that are compatible with the social and cultural uses of language in the child's context. Understanding how parents and significant others use language and what their language styles are allows teachers to be able to match language usage and styles while children are learning to understand and interpret teachers' unique style of language.

Vygotsky's theory also encourages teachers to allow lots of time for peer play—even with very young children, and to facilitate such play. The idea of the ZPD is clear to most infant and toddler teachers. Very young children are often in need of scaffolding to be able to play together successfully. Supported, children are more successful in playing together than they are without support. Vygotsky suggests that teachers become careful observers so they know children's ZPDs—the place where support could increase a child's ability to interact successfully with others or accomplish a task. Knowledge gained from observation cues teachers to when and where support for interactions and learning is needed. Finally, Vygotsky tells teachers to support conversations by listening carefully, learning to read non-verbal cues and gestures, by initiating and participating in conversations with children, and supporting conversations among children.

Gardner's Theory of Multiple Intelligences

Gardner's Theory of Multiple Intelligences proposes that children have several kinds of intelligence that operate at the same time in complementary ways (Gardner, 1983). Many of the intelligences, like logico-mathematical and spatial intelligence, seem to apply to older children, not to infants and toddlers. Are these ideas applicable to younger children?

Gardner's Multiple Intelligences

Intelligence	Description
Linguistic	Sensitivity to the meaning and order of words
Logico-mathematical	Ability to handle chains of reasoning and recognize patterns and order
Musical	Sensitivity to pitch, melody, rhythm, and tone
Bodily-kinesthetic	Ability to use the body skillfully and handle objects adroitly
Spatial	Ability to perceive the world accurately and to recreate or transform aspects of that world
Naturalist	Ability to recognize and classify the numerous species of an environment
Interpersonal	Ability to understand people and relationships
Intrapersonal (also called emotional intelligence by Goleman)	Access to one's emotional life as a means to understand oneself and others

Gardner's theory supports the idea that children have many different types of intelligence, not just one or two types. Theorists and researchers who think children have multiple intelligences believe that there are many ways for children to learn and for teachers to teach.

This theory proposes that all of the multiple intelligences are present at birth. Early indicators of different intelligences can be seen in infants and toddlers. For example, some children are watchers—they like to watch others try new things. Others are doers—they have to be in the middle of any experience embracing it all. Still others listen carefully to what goes on around them before they begin to interact. These differences emerge from the individual's unique collection of intelligences and are part of what makes each of us different from one another.

Myth or Misunderstanding
THE ONLY SKILLS THAT MATTER ARE ACADEMIC SKILLS.

At a parent-teacher conference with Rene, Timmy's mother, Mary, asked about her son's progress. She indicated that she doesn't think Timmy is very smart. Rene is surprised by Timmy's mother's concerns. Her observations are that Timmy is operating developmentally within normal ranges and participates successfully in the wide range of activities offered in the classroom without difficulty. She reviews with Mary her observations and assessment of how Timmy is doing, focusing on all of the domains of development. When she is finished, Mary asks Rene how Timmy is coming along in learning to read and do math problems. Rene is astounded. In her mind, she has just gone over how Timmy is doing in all areas of development, including the intellectual area, and is amazed that Mary can't make the connection between the developmental information she has shared and his future preparation for school.

This myth seems to permeate our society. Because reading, writing, and mathematics skills are highly observable—either you can do them or you can't—many adults use them as the measure of a child's potential and success. So, early reading, early writing, and early mathematics skills are viewed as important. Equally problematic is the view that acquiring these skills earlier is possible and desirable.

McCall and Plemons (2001) conclude from their review of the importance of early and intensive stimulation that it "is not always beneficial and can be harmful" (page 276), particularly if the stimulation is forced or aversive to the child. These authors suggest that at every stage, stimulation appropriate to the age and stage of the child is most beneficial.

Rene has two things to work on with Timmy's mother. First, Rene can help Mary understand that she is teaching important academic skills to Timmy by reading to him every day, offering him many manipulatives to play with, encouraging his scribbling, and including Timmy in functional writing experiences as they occur naturally in the classroom. She can help Mary see that Timmy has other intelligences—not just his academic intelligence—so Mary can view her son as capable and competent in many ways. Then, she can partner with Timmy's mother to help her feel she is also contributing to Timmy's future literacy by what she does with Timmy

Myth or Misunderstanding—cont'd.

at home. Most importantly, she can read to Timmy each day and include him in functional experiences that support academic skill acquisition like sorting laundry to find his socks and finding all of the spoons in the dishwasher silverware basket to put away in the drawer. When Timmy's mother views preparing him for school as her job, in partnership with Rene, Timmy will undoubtedly be well prepared for formal schooling when the time comes.

Rene has another job. Because she understands the integrated nature of development and shares her observations with Mary, she assumes that Mary understands the implications of the information. Teachers are challenged to help parents understand the developmental context and explain how children learn in ways that make sense to parents. Until this understanding is a shared one, parents and teachers will never be on the same page.

What should happen next? Think of ways that Rene can help parents gain a better understanding of the integrated and sequential nature of development. It might be helpful to develop a parent reading list.

One type of intelligence—intrapersonal intelligence—is considered a crucial type of intelligence to support during the early years. Also called emotional intelligence, it includes self-awareness, managing emotions, emotional self-control, recognizing emotions in others, and handling relationships (Goleman, 1998). Goleman believes that every interaction between children and their parents and teachers carries emotional messages that can influence emotional intelligence. If messages are positive and responsive, children learn that the world is a supportive and caring place. If children receive curt, insensitive responses, or worse, abusive or cruel responses, these emotional encounters will negatively mold children's views of relationships. Both of these experiences affect functioning in all realms of life, for better or worse.

Another tenet of Gardner's theory is that interaction is cumulative—each one matters. The actions and reactions of adults, the teaching plans, and school schedules tell children if and how much we care for them.

This theory validates what every parent and teacher knows—every child is unique. Such ideas help us to understand individual children better and modify our programs to fit each child, rather than requiring children to fit into our programs. Further, the theory of multiple intelligences helps us support parents in viewing their child's unique skills rather than comparing their child to other children—a wonderful way to guarantee that cumulative interactions of important caregivers positively affect children's potential.

Myth or Misunderstanding
EARLY DEVELOPMENT MEANS A BRIGHT CHILD.

Bert is 10 months old and he just started walking. His mother is thrilled. Because Bert is walking early, she expects that he will do everything early. She is even talking about private school where he can start kindergarten at age four. This mom is responding to the myth in American society that earlier is better.

Bert's teacher, Masami, wants to tell Bert's mom to put his walking in context with other developmental areas so that she understands how young children grow and develop. He also wants her to see Bert's competence in other areas of development.

Masami discusses his concerns at the next parent-teacher conference as he shares with Bert's mom the progress Bert has made developmentally. Masami shows her observations, photographs of Bert at play in the classroom, and examples of Bert's experiences with projects. During their conversation, Bert's mom sees that her son is growing and developing well. By talking about all the different areas of development (physical, intellectual, emotional, and social), Masami is able to give Bert's mom the big picture, helping her understand Bert's developmental progress at school and how she and his teachers could continue his care and early education together.

What should happen next? What should Masami do to continue the connection he made with Bert's mom during the conference? Make a parent participation, involvement, and education plan for Bert's mom for the next three months.

Implications of Gardner's Theory for Communicating with Parents, Teachers, and Friends

Gardner's Theory of Multiple Intelligences offers teachers of infants and toddlers a wonderful framework for interacting with and teaching children. It is very freeing for teachers to know that it is acceptable, even desirable, to treat children differently—when the treatment matches the child's learning style and combination of intelligences. This theory cautions teachers to remember the cumulative nature of relationships by watching the tone and timbre of their voices and actions.

Gardner's theory guides teachers to build relationships, observe for different intelligences, and include stimulation for all kinds of intelligences as they plan environments and experiences for children in their classrooms.

Literacy Development

The Development of Literacy

Reading and writing is a concern for parents and teachers. As children's oral language grows to the point they can express what they know with words and ask about what they are interested in knowing, many adults think it is time to start "formal" instruction in reading and writing.

The foundations of reading and writing are formed during infancy when parents and significant adults read and respond to non-verbal cues—an important precursor skill that leads to an understanding that communication has meaning. Without meaningful relationships with others in the context of children's daily interactions, the ability to read, write, and spell cannot develop.

Critical literacy skills then develop as children learn symbolic awareness, and the ability to think before doing— to solve problems mentally or symbolically (McMullen, 1998). Symbolic awareness is the awareness that something stands for something else—the association of a symbol with the object or person to which it refers. When children pick up a telephone receiver and say hello, they are indicating their symbolic awareness—the telephone symbolizes a connection for talking to another.

The ability to think before doing is observed when children increase the amount of time between their thoughts and action. When the time lengthens, it means that children have learned not only to represent the idea in their minds, but also to hold on to the idea and work with it while they plan their response or actions. When children pause in their play with manipulatives, then return to successfully complete an action (like fitting a puzzle piece into a puzzle or figuring out how to make the roof on a block house), they are demonstrating symbolic problem-solving. By no longer relying on the trial-and-error method, children move from the sensori-motor stage of cognitive development to the pre-operational stage of cognitive development, according to Piaget. In addition, they are practicing an important literacy skill of thinking before acting.

On this foundation, children construct their own understanding of how the world of letters and words work through many informal experiences. Adults can contribute to children's emerging literacy by developing positive, nurturing relationships with children, engaging them in frequent interactions, talking to children, and using language to describe and explain what is happening in the world around them.

Myth or Misunderstanding
THE EARLIER CHILDREN START PHONICS DRILLS, THE SOONER THEY WILL BEGIN READING.

This myth is spread by the extensive availability of educational materials that claim to teach phonics and are marketed as appropriate for very young children. Learning to read is a much more complex process than just learning letter/sound association. Children benefit from a wide variety of literacy experiences in the context of their relationships with important others like parents and teachers. Rarely, if-ever, will teaching one discrete reading skill in isolation advance children's reading and writing skills during the preschool years.

The National Association for the Education of Young Children and the American Reading Association's joint position paper, "Learning to Read and Write: Developmentally Appropriate Practices for Young Children," describes the beginning of the continuum of learning to read during the infant, toddler, and preschool years as one of awareness and exploration (1998). Appropriate reading activities for very young children include listening to and discussing storybooks, understanding that print carries a message, engaging in reading and writing

> ### *Myth or Misunderstanding—cont'd.*
>
> *attempts, identifying signs and labels in the environment, participating in rhyming games, making letter/sound associations, and having many experiences with scribbling and drawing. Classrooms and homes with these experiences are encouraging and supporting early literacy development.*
>
> *Because this is such an important issue to a child's future success, create a parent/teacher early literacy program to implement in the classroom. What would your program look like?*

Teachers provide props like large and small paper, crayons, markers, tempera paint, and other artistic media for children to use to support and expand children's play and to facilitate the expression of ideas and thoughts. Then, they demonstrate the usefulness of representing words and ideas in a wide variety of ways, always connecting reading and writing to activities and experiences. For example, when teachers routinely record information, children see them writing over time. It isn't long before they will ask to "write" notes, also. This connection between the writing and communicating with parents is a perfect example of a functional literacy experience for children.

Providing print-rich environments is also suggested by research (Neuman, Copple, & Bredekamp, 2000). Labeling cubbies with photographs and names, putting pictures on containers to help find where things go, using photographs, using pictures to check into school and out to home, reading real books and literature on your own or with an adult, and the availability of printed materials from the environment like logos, advertisements, cereal boxes, T-shirts, store and traffic signs, are all examples of ways to include the connection between reading and writing in children's experiences.

Reading in the First Three Years

It doesn't take long for children who have been exposed to books to love them. They like to look at them by themselves and have adults read books to them.

Children begin the process of attaching meaning to the symbols of the written or pictorial word by connecting sounds of language to symbolic representations. Then they begin to explore their own scribbles as they experiment with making marks on paper to simulate the writing process, often "reading" or assigning meaning to these early scribbles.

Many literacy skills are already present by the time a child reaches the age of 18 months. For example, most toddlers position books appropriately when they pick them up—turning them upright and starting at the beginning. They are usually adept at turning pages, although the coordination to prevent crimping and tearing the pages may be intermittent. They can usually "read" the pictures, looking, pointing, identifying and labeling concepts, ideas, and events depicted in the illustrations. And, they have developed preferences for types of books and topics that appeal to them. They ask adults to read favorite books again and again.

Many more skills will develop over the next 18 months. These skills are called "emergent literacy" skills because the process of becoming literate—able to read and write—grows and changes during the toddler years (Neuman, Copple, & Bredekamp, 2000). Literacy includes oral language, reading, and writing.

But these are not discrete areas of literacy. Children develop literacy skills in an integrated way, with skill acquisition in one area creating learning in other areas. Children develop literacy skills by using oral language, interpreting written language, and connecting writing to what they say and what the written word says in practical and useful ways. The process of becoming literate is an interactive one—children learn as they interact and explore the functions and applications of oral language and written language.

Writing in the First Three Years

Children are excellent scribblers. They enjoy making marks just about anytime and anywhere. Parents and teachers who are so anxious to see emerging intellectual skills are less excited about scribbles on the walls, floors, and tabletops! But it is precisely this intense interest in making marks that indicates that children's literacy is growing and that children are ready for many scribbling experiences. The transition to the next stage—making marks that have circles, angles, and shapes in them—emerges after many experiences with scribbles.

Myth or Misunderstanding
WE NEED TO START LETTER FORMATION EARLY.
PRACTICE MAKES PERFECT.

Although her son, Billy, is only two years old, Mrs. Ballard asks Billy's teacher at least once a week why she isn't working on letter formation. Her husband expects Billy to practice his letters at the kitchen table as they cook dinner. Dad is usually very disappointed because the more letters Billy makes, the less they look like letters.

When Billy's mom asks about letter formation, Billy's teacher explains the connection between fine motor development and letter formation. She talks about the stages of emergent writing, beginning with scribbles as young children develop their gross motor skills and continuing with circles, squiggles, images, and then letters as children develop their fine motor skills. Then, she helps Billy's mother come up with some more appropriate ideas for encouraging Billy's fine motor skills like playing with Duplos®, making puzzles, and experimenting with different writing mediums such as pencils, water colors, brush painting, and markers.

Then, the teacher takes Billy's mom to the classroom to see that the curriculum plans that she makes include literacy, fine motor development, creative art, manipulatives, and many other activities that will support Billy in developing his fine motor skills and lead to making letters when he is a bit older. Together, the teacher and Billy's mom decide to invite Billy's dad to visit the classroom and have a similar discussion with Billy's teacher so that he can understand more appropriate ways to help Billy learn to write.

What should the teacher do to prepare for the visit from Billy's father? How can she figure out the best way to approach the issue of appropriate writing experiences for Billy while still validating the interest being shown by Billy's father?

As in other areas of development, there are stages to emerging writing. First, children scribble, using the large muscles of the arm to make marks. Then, these marks begin to make shapes, starting usually with circles and then moving on to squiggles, angles, and other shapes. Finally, children begin to represent what they know in ways that are recognizable to adults, usually beginning with common images from the child's world, the face, the body, and

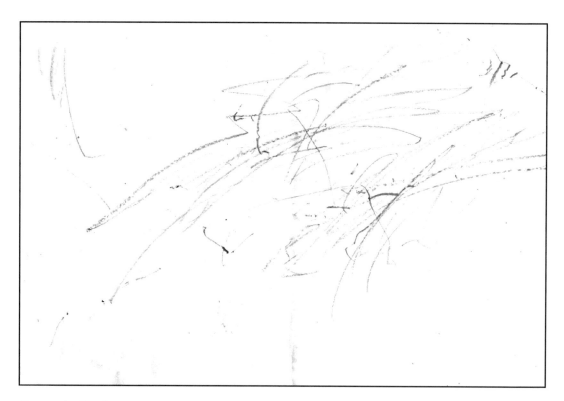

Drawing 1—The first tentative strokes; light pressure on the page; single color.

Drawing 2—A month later; bold strokes; multiple colors.

Drawing 3—A month later; circular strokes dominate; straight lines, angles, and up-and-down marks indicate the beginning of left-to-right symbolic writing.

the immediate world around them, and progressing to marks that are letter-like. Children remain in the first stage of writing until well into the third year, increasingly labeling their letter-like marks.

The remaining stages of literacy usually emerge in the preschool years. They include understanding stories, understanding that printed words have meaning, and understanding the clear association of letters with the sounds that they make.

Getting Ready to Spell

The recognition of letters also begins to develop during the toddler years. Rarely do children associate a letter name to the written letter, but instead, they associate the patterns that letters make with the written letters. For example, children can usually find the pattern of their names on piece of artwork well before they can tell you the letters of their names. They are beginning to recognize the pattern that the letters of their names form—how many lines, how it begins and ends, how long or short it is, and how the middle goes up and down.

This is the foundation for spelling and later recognition that /b/ faces to the right and /d/ faces to the left. Many experiences with patterns are the very best preparation for good spelling. Puzzles, manipulatives, and blocks create many exciting patterns with lots of different compositions. These are great activities for teaching the skills children will need to spell when they are older.

Implications of Literacy Development for Communicating with Parents, Teachers, and Friends

The first implication of literacy development theory for teachers is to work on accurately reading and interpreting the non-verbal and verbal cues that children use. Communication requires reciprocity. When adults are good at understanding and interpreting children's cues, a sense that communication works develops in the child. It is on this foundation that future skills can build.

Read to children every day. The importance of book reading is confirmed by research that shows a close correlation between being read to and becoming a good reader (Center for the Study of Reading, 1985). Infant teachers should begin with about 5–10 minutes of book reading a day and work up to 20 minutes by the time children reach toddlerhood. Toddler teachers should aim for at least 30 minutes of book reading every day.

Providing opportunities for infants and toddlers to have many different kinds of writing experiences such as scribbling is also suggested to enhance communicating skills. Crayons, brush painting with tempera and watercolors using different sizes of paintbrushes, and experimenting with pencils, markers, and chalk are all examples. Finally, encourage children to look for and find patterns in their environment. Signs in the neighborhood, familiar logos of popular restaurants and products, and the pattern of a child's written name are all examples.

Best Practices

Talk to Children Often Using Language Stimulation Techniques

The field of speech and language development offers several indirect language stimulation techniques that adults will find extremely useful. These techniques, called description, parallel talk, self-talk, expansion, and expansion plus, direct the adult's language behaviors and encourage the continuation of language acquisition.

Description—Description is a technique in which the parent or teacher narrates or describes what is going on in the child's world by putting word labels on things. For example, if a child looks toward the door as a parent enters the room, the adult might say, "That's Jenny's mother. She must be here to pick up Jenny." Description is also helpful in communicating mutual respect. When a teacher tells a child what will happen to her before it happens and waits for the child to indicate that she is ready for the action or activity, the teacher is showing mutual respect for the child (Gerber, 1979). A teacher might say, "In five minutes, it will be time to wash hands so we can eat lunch," as a description of what will happen to the child and when it will happen. Then, a respectful teacher waits before continuing, so the child can finish what she is doing and indicate she is ready. The teacher then describes each step as it occurs, "Up go your sleeves. Now put your hands under the water. Here's the soap, so you can scrub the front, back, and in between. Now rinse your hands and dry them."

Parallel Talk—Parallel talk is a short phrase that focuses on the child's action. Parallel talk usually begins with "you." For example, "You're playing with the cars and the trucks," is parallel talk. Other examples might be, "You're putting the Duplos in the bucket," "You've got the baby doll," or "You pulled off your shoe." Focusing on the action helps the child put word labels on behavior and more importantly, connect the word labels into a sentence describing the action.

Self-Talk—Self-talk focuses on adult behavior, labeling and describing what the adult is doing. Adults who use self-talk usually start their utterances with "I." For example, a teacher might say to a child who is getting fussy, "I'll help you put these toys back on the shelf," or "I think it is time for Maureen to take a nap." Self-talk is particularly helpful in preparing children for transitions. When they announce and remind children about transitions with self-talk, adults are preparing children for the transition, a very important guidance technique. To use self-talk this way, say things like "I think it is almost time to put up the blocks." Or, "In ten more minutes, I will get the mats down to get ready for naptime," or "In five more minutes I'll be ready for you to park the riding toys to go inside." Because the amount of language children receive and the responsiveness of adults to children's language supports overall language development, this technique is an important teaching skill.

Expansion and Expansion Plus—Expansion and expansion plus are extremely useful techniques to use with children when their vocabularies begin to grow. These techniques take what the child says and expand on it (expansion) or add to what the child says (expansion plus). For example, when a child says, "cracker," the teacher might say, "You want another cracker," or "Jason would like another cracker, please," to expand what the child says into a complete sentence. If the child says, "Outside," the teacher might say, "You'd like to go outside." For expansion plus, the teacher adds a little more to the sentence a child uses. An example might expand, "Go bye-bye," uttered by the child, to "It's time to get your things and go bye-bye." Expansion and expansion plus restate what the child says in complete and sometimes expanded sentence form. Vocabulary development correlates strongly with later literacy development and these differences in vocabulary development seem to show up during the preschool years (Katz & Snow, 2000). Adults can support vocabulary development significantly with this technique.

Notice that these techniques require nothing of the child. The child is not asked to repeat the larger sentence, to repeat the label of an object identified by description, or to respond further to the teacher. These techniques are teaching techniques that add information to the child's language skills and foster language development. The techniques are not designed as drills or exercises for very young children.

robin

Build Vocabulary

Children's expressive vocabulary increases from about 200–400 words to over 2,000 words during toddlerhood. Adults who help children learn new vocabulary fuel this growth. Teachers and parents help children develop vocabulary when they use the following techniques:

➧ Provide word labels for things in the environment, increasing the sophistication of the labels as children age. For example, when you are on a walk, start by pointing out birds, clouds, trees, and so on. Then, add descriptive characteristics as you label the birds. "That's a blue bird; that one is called a mockingbird; that one's a crow."
➧ Use pictures to enhance and expand vocabulary. Continuing with the bird example, post pictures from your picture file of different species of birds along with their written names so that you can point out and use

expanded vocabulary words. Exposing children to words, whether they use them expressively or not, is a great literacy activity.

▶ Play word games with children. Toddlers love to be silly with language—playing nonsense games with words. Encourage and expand on this interest by enjoying word games, too. Change the initial letter of a child's name (Baitlin instead of Caitlin or Mavid instead of David). Or, use sequential initial sounds like Aitlin, Baitlin, Caitlin, Daitlin, Eaitlin, Faitlin, Gaitlin, etc. to explore initial sounds.

▶ Add vocabulary words to your curriculum plan to focus your attention on new words and to remind parents that you have identified new words for vocabulary development.

Support Linguistic and Cultural Diversity

English is not the primary language of a growing population of children who are in school settings (Tabors, 1998). This creates the need for increased understanding of linguistic and cultural diversity. Teachers also need strategies for supporting emerging oral language and literacy skills while accepting and validating the child's home language.

Young children are capable of learning more than one language at a time—particularly if the adults in their lives support the process of language learning (Shonkoff & Phillips, 2000). Children learn language by having caring, responsive adults use language with them long before they begin to use language themselves. When children are exposed to second languages during the first three years, each language develops as a primary language, without slowing overall language development.

There are components of language that are not specific to the language spoken. For example, non-verbal communication develops in young children as they are developing verbal communication. Facial expressions, crying, whimpering, wiggling, running away or toward something or someone all communicate without words.

Myth or Misunderstanding
CHILDREN NEED SECURITY IN A FIRST LANGUAGE
BEFORE THEY CAN LEARN A SECOND ONE.

As the diversity of children has increased, educators and parents have often been at odds on the issue of English as a second language. Some feel that children need a firm foundation in the language of the dominant culture from the beginning of school while others feel children need to have their home languages validated in order to give children confidence to pursue understanding the language of the dominant culture.

It turns out that brain research is leading the way in clarifying this controversial issue. An understanding of the way the brain learns and processes language has led child development scientists to conclude that learning more than one language at a time poses no problem for children who are developing normally (Shonkoff & Phillips, 2000). A summary of these new insights reveals that children's brains are readily capable of learning multiple languages during the early childhood years. Fears about slowing down language development or of confusing children appear to be unfounded for most children. There is an apparent delay in articulation acquisition and vocabulary for preschool children, only because they are learning simultaneous articulation skills, vocabulary, grammar, and syntax. This delay happens because they are learning the structure and function of more than one language, not because they are experiencing any developmental or maturational delay.

Further, it appears that there are some sensitive or critical periods for the acquisition of the structure of language that make early exposure to more than one language an advantage from the point of view of brain development.

So, concerns about children learning more than one language, simultaneously or sequentially, appear to be unfounded. As our world becomes increasingly multi-lingual, it appears that the brain is poised and prepared to help us continue to communicate with each other.

Discuss ways to offer appropriate early second language experiences to young children. How can teachers help? How can parents be involved? Is there a role for the community to play? How should the second language be determined?

Children whose primary language is not English need support bridging the two language worlds. They need validation of their home language and time to begin the process of acquiring receptive and expressive language skills in two (or more) languages at the same time. Try some of the following suggestions to support families and children for whom English is not the primary language.

- Collaborate with parents to support the home language. Ask parents to help you learn a few words of the child's home language, particularly needs-meeting words such as "more," "Mother," "Daddy," the words used to express hunger, sleepiness, and fear. Specifically, learn to say "hello" and "goodbye" and how to communicate changes in routine in the child's home language.

- Use both English and the child's home language when you use these familiar words. Use the home language first and then repeat the word in English. This helps children begin to understand that the two languages they are hearing are different.

- Ask parents to help you translate fingerplays and rhymes into the home language, and to provide fingerplays and rhymes from the home language for you to use in the classroom. Encourage them to record lullabies, songs, and other oral language traditions in the home language for you to use at school.

- Expand your children's book collection to include some books in the home language of children in your group.

- Maintain eye contact and physical proximity during transitions so you can provide non-verbal cues as well as verbal ones to children whose home language is not English.

- Create predictable routines—particularly those cued by oral language. For example, if you sing the clean-up song when it is time to clean up and go outside, non-English speaking children can pick up on other cues besides the words, in this case, the action and the tune. Think about transitions and try to support them with other cues besides just oral language.

Provide Cognitively Stimulating Environments

Current understanding of the importance of adult and peer relationships has implications for environments. As teachers focus on cognitive learning, it must be in the context of supportive relationships. Then, the environment needs plenty of sources of physical stimulation—the kind of physical stimulation that Piaget says helps children construct their own knowledge as they interact.

Cognitive development proceeds in environments that are characterized by plenty of opportunities for children to be the source of their own discoveries and knowledge. Self-directed exploration with toys and materials that hold children's interest and allow for many different outcomes is the right kind of stimulation.

Environments support children as they grow and learn by providing predictability and predictable responses. Children need to know that they will be able to count on a stable surrounding, one that offers the same furniture in the same place with the same or similar materials. They also need to be able to count on the responses from important adults in their lives. Thus, the same adults need to be present, and they need to offer predictability.

In balance with predictability young children need environments with novelty. They need new things to explore and manipulate. Children need a variety of challenges from which to choose. All of the items do not need to be novel. Instead, offer a few novel items in the context of predictability.

Create Environments that Value Multiple Intelligences

What does a classroom that understands multiple intelligences look like? Infant and toddler classrooms are characterized by individual, intimate interactions between teachers and children. Children are allowed to follow their own schedules for eating, sleeping, and playing, rather than following a superimposed schedule. These routines are conducted intimately, for example, one or two infants are eating while another one or two are playing on the floor, and another baby is taking a nap. Rarely, if ever, are children under the age of three required to do the same thing at the same time in the same way as all of the other children in the group.

Teachers who understand multiple intelligences recognize that different children like different types of stimulation. For example, a child with highly complementary spatial and body kinesthetic intelligence might love exploring tight spaces like the inside of boxes, underneath table, and behind furniture.

Another child, who has complementary spatial and logico-mathematical intelligence, might prefer to mouth and manipulate items in an open space. These examples illustrate the individual nature and variety of multiple intelligences.

Support Emerging Literacy

What teachers do in their classrooms with children is so important in supporting emerging literacy. Try some of the following strategies in your classroom.

- Label your classroom with pictures and words. Both are important. Children learn to read pictures easily, and connecting the picture to the word emphasizes the pattern of the word as well as its letter components. Don't go overboard. Label the important things, starting with 6–8 word/picture labels and building up to 12–15 over time.

- Label storage containers with pictures of what goes inside them. Label cubbies with pictures and names. Make copies of children's pictures and use them for labels, charts, and so on. Label coat hooks with pictures and names. And don't forget to label routinely used items like the bleach water squirt bottle (always stored safely out of reach) or the bathroom door.

- Develop patterning skills by coding shelves indicating where thing go, particularly the blocks in your classroom. Returning blocks to the shelves by following a picture pattern of the blocks is an excellent literacy experience as well as an appropriate mathematical experience.

- Make and use signs in your classroom. When you leave your classroom to go to the playground, put a simple sign on the door that says so. When you close an area of the classroom, put a closed sign on it to cue children that the time to play in that area is over. When a child finds something special on the playground or on a nature walk, post a sign that tells everyone about the discovery.

- Fill your classroom with real reading materials—cookbooks, newspapers, magazines, instruction manuals for toys and materials, appropriate junk mail advertisements, and so on. These are functional reading materials, not ones just for children. They will enjoy the novelty and have an opportunity to perfect page turning skills in the process. And, they will see that reading materials are functional—useful for getting needed information.

- Read to children. Read to individual children, to children in small groups of three or four, and occasionally, to the whole group. Frequent book reading should be a mainstay of the infant and toddler classroom.

- Add books and writing materials to every area of the classroom. When you consider adding or changing an area of the classroom, also consider what kinds of reading and writing materials will go along with the change.

- Write down children's ideas, words, and stories. When ideas, words, and stories are written down, they take on a special meaning for children (Cooper, 1993; Paley, 1981). Children can learn to dictate the words they want you to add to their work. Offer to do so often. Make your offer open-ended, "Would you like to tell me some words to write down?"

- Connect functional writing to children's behavior. For example, when a child does (or doesn't) like something at snack or lunch, you might ask the child if she would like to write the note to Mom or Dad to let them know about the preference or an idea the child had at school. If she says yes, provide a piece of clean paper and a marker or crayon for her to do so. Then, make sure you tell the parent about the importance of the written note by including additional information for the parents. Or, if a child wants the toy another child is using, help her write a note to the child to remind him who to give the toy to when he is finished. Put the note near the child who has the toy and tell him what it says. If the child forgets, point to the note and read it to him.

- Explore initial sounds—particularly initial sounds of names, words, and toys, objects, and materials. Note the word *explore*. Drills and direct instruction about initial sounds are still inappropriate. But, songs, chants, poems, fingerplays, and action rhymes are excellent ways to explore initial sounds. For example, when you call a child by name, say "Rodney, it's your turn to paint with the red paint. Red, Rodney, those words start with the same sound." Or, "Caitlin has carrots for lunch. Caitlin and carrots start with the sound /k/." Or, "Thomas is reading a *Thomas the Tank* book. The name of the book and the name of the boy are the same!" Or, use fingerplays, rhymes, and songs to reinforce the connection between sounds. "Rosy the Little Red Car," for example, is a great song for practicing the initial sound /r/.

- Use narration to connect initial sounds to their word labels. This exploration is teacher's work—not children's work. Teachers point out the obvious connections between sounds and letters as they use them in daily experiences. Repeated experiences with adults connecting letters and sounds facilitate phonemic awareness in children that will prepare them for individual letter/sound association when they are older.

Use Multi-age Grouping

If Vygotsky is right, children need frequent opportunities to learn from more competent peers as well as to scaffold learning in younger children. Multi-age grouping is the way to insure that children have role models to watch, peers who need help, and peers who can help. Widening the age range of children in primary caregiving groups is the first step in providing multi-age experiences.

In our society, children have fewer opportunities to relate to children of different ages because of smaller family size, extended time in care and early education settings, and isolation from extended family members. Children glean both social and intellectual benefits from being in mixed age groups (Katz, 1998; Katz, Evangelou & Hartman, 1990). Older children benefit from being the experts and being able to model for younger children. Younger children benefit from having older children for interactions. All children benefit from decreased pressure to be like other children the same age. Teachers also benefit from not having all the children involved with similar developmental issues at the same time.

Teachers can create opportunities for younger children to have interactions and experiences with older children. These can be formal, like visits to each other's classrooms, or informal, like being on the playground at the same time.

Use a Variety of Teaching Roles

The Teacher as Instructor

One of the traditional roles of a teacher is instructor. Although less frequently used by infant and toddler teachers, there are times when instruction is appropriate. Often, instruction occurs around safety matters—where teachers instruct children about behavior that will keep them safe or prevent injury.

Vygotsky's socio-cultural theory supports the idea of the teacher as different kind of instructor. He believed that children learn best when they are assisted in learning. Vygotsky's instructor role includes explaining, demonstrating, prompting, interpreting, analyzing, probing, illustrating with examples, clarifying, summarizing, questioning, and supporting peer collaboration and cooperation along the way. These teaching tasks are used when the child is near her ZPD, so that learning can be scaffolded to the next level.

Knowing when instruction will support children's learning is based on observation and knowledge of each child's ZPD. This view of instruction as embedded in intimate knowledge of individuals, not applied to everyone at the same time, differentiates the instructor's role from the traditional view.

The Teacher as Documenter

In this role, teachers observe, record, reflect on, and synthesize into documentation what is happening to children in their classrooms. The goal of documentation is to communicate—communicate children's ideas, competence, and knowledge construction while engaging teachers in co-constructing their own knowledge about children, their interests, and their competencies. Stimulated by dialogue with the teachers of Reggio Emilia in northern Italy, documentation is receiving additional attention from teachers who have discovered its rich benefits.

Documentation is a cycle of inquiry that proceeds in fits and starts (Gandini & Goldhaber, 2001). It begins with framing the questions to focus thinking on the types of appropriate experiences for children. Then, teachers begin the process of collecting evidence of children's experiences. The techniques of collection can be quite varied, including written notes, photographs, samples of children's work, videotapes, or audio recording.

The Documentation Process as a Cycle of Inquiry

organizing observations and artifacts

analyzing/interpreting observations and artifacts; building theories

observing, recording, and collecting artifacts

(reframing questions)

framing questions

planning (projecting) and responding

Reprinted by permission of the publisher from Lella Gandini and Carolyn Pope Edwards. *Bambini.* New York: Teachers College Press @ 2000 by Teachers College, Columbia University. All rights reserved. p. 136.

Organizing, analyzing, and interpreting the results of the observation process is the next step. This synthesis step often leads right back to reconsidering the questions that were framed in the beginning of the process. Then, teachers use the results of the organizing process to guide what to do next with children. It is at this stage that documentation becomes "public," resulting in an opportunity to share children's competence with others, as it was observed and recorded during the process of documentation.

This brief introduction to the documentation process is only a beginning. Teachers who are interested in expanding their teaching roles to include documentation will need to explore these ideas further. Several books, including *Bambini: The Italian approach to infant/toddler care* (2001), *The Hundred Languages of Children* (1998), and *Windows on Learning: Documenting Children's Work* (1997), are available to support teachers in further understanding and experimenting with these ideas.

Teaching Roles

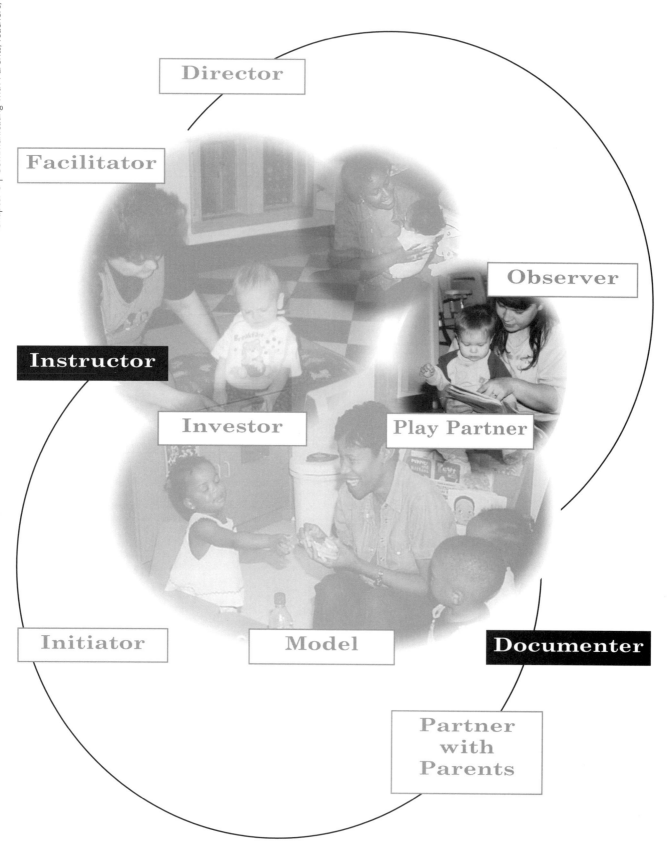

Director

Facilitator

Observer

Instructor

Investor

Play Partner

Initiator

Model

Documenter

Partner with Parents

Identify Developmental Challenges

Teachers have many opportunities to observe children as they grow and learn. Occasionally, these observations raise questions concerning how children are developing. When a teacher notices that a child is outside of the age range for accomplishing a task or skill, she or he should remember that differences in development are normal. The teacher can continue careful observations and data collection. She or he is probably observing the differences in the individual pace of development. If the trend continues and the child is still not demonstrating widely held expectations for tasks and skills within her chronological age range, the teacher can talk to the child's parents about her or his observations. Suggest that the parents discuss those observations first with their pediatrician and then (if needed) with a developmental specialist such as a developmental psychologist, or another type of specialist, such as a speech pathologist, a physical therapist, or an occupational therapist.

Children who are six months or more behind their chronological age need to be evaluated further to determine if the delay observed is related to maturational factors, developmental uniqueness, or alternative developmental pathways. Early identification of developmental delays is an important role for teachers. They are not diagnosticians, but they are excellent observers. Often early intervention can completely remediate problems. Careful observations by teachers can support parents in making sure that their child's needs are met.

Brazelton & Greenspan (2000) are even more explicit about the conditions under which a child should be referred for further evaluation to identify challenges or disorders in development. These authors suggest that a full evaluation is in order for any of the following developmental signs:

- By two months of age, if there are no signs of looking or listening
- By four to five months, if there are no signs of relating to caregivers with joyful smiles, and sounds
- By eight to nine months, if there are no signs of back and forth communication (e.g., reaching for a rattle in Dad's hand or initiating and reciprocating different emotional expressions and sounds)
- By 12 months, if there are no signs of multiple circles of communication in a row (e.g., back and forth exchange of emotional gestures sounds and even a word or two)
- By 16 months, if there are no signs of complex problem-solving interactions (e.g., taking caregiver by the hand to help get toy or food)
- By 24 months, if there are no signs of beginning pretend play (hugging a doll) or understanding or using words to get needs met (e.g., "give juice")

> By 36–48 months, if there are no signs of the logical use of ideas with caregivers and peers (e.g., answering where, when, why, what questions as part of conversation lasting at least a few minutes)

> At any time, if there are signs of serious family or emotional difficulties in Mom or Dad or other family members (Brazelton and Greenspan, 2000, p. 75)

Applying Theory and Best Practices

A large part of professional practice in the field of care and early education is the synthesizing of knowledge, research, and best practices into teaching actions and strategies. A goal of *Innovations: Infant and Toddler Development* is to help teachers apply theory, research, and best practices to real-life situations and behaviors in the infant and toddler classroom. Let's take a look at a developmental milestone that is a part of most children's experience in care and early education settings to see if the knowledge we have gained, the research we have reviewed, and/or the best practices we have explored give any suggestions of how the developmental milestone might be handled by teachers in the classroom.

So, let's begin exploring the integration of knowledge, research, and best practices by considering the implications of the topics covered in this chapter for helping a child who is not talking.

Possibilities from Theories of Language Development for a Child Who Is Not Talking

Language development theories are clear in their guidance for teachers. As with many areas of development, language is best stimulated from the firm foundation of a strong, reciprocal relationship where gestural and non-verbal cues are accurately read and responded to with consistency and predictability. These theories suggest that teachers encourage language development by being good language role models, using language to get needs met and to make things happen. Filling the important role of stimulating language by talking and using appropriate language stimulation techniques fosters an interest in and motivation to communicate and increases the likelihood that children will try to communicate reciprocally. Finally, theories of language development support the importance of reciprocity to reinforce language development. Unless children feel that their communication is received and believed, their language skills will not expand and grow.

Possibilities from Piaget's Cognitive-development Theory for a Child Who Is Not Talking

Piaget's theory directs teachers to provide children with long periods of uninterrupted time to explore, process, and manipulate the environment. During the sensori-motor period, self-directed, rather than teacher-directed exploration is compatible with Piaget's ideas of assimilating and accommodating cognitive thinking. As children explore, they compare, contrast, classify, catalog, and add word labels to motor and sensory experiences, forming the system by which children will organize thought as they mature.

Because children are using their senses to discover and interact with the environment, Piaget also encourages teachers to think of the possibilities of the environment. Providing multi-sensory stimulation of all of the senses; creating opportunities to touch, taste, smell, hear, and see; and varying the environments in which sensory stimulation takes place are all ways to encourage cognitive growth and development.

Possibilities from Vygotsky's Socio-cultural Theory for a Child Who Is Not Talking

Possibilities from Vygotsky's theory start with a thorough understanding of the context of the family. Knowing how the school environment and the home environment are similar and different is baseline information for modifying programs to fit children. The home language, cultural features of the home environment, parenting styles, cultural point of view, customs, and family celebrations all socialize the child in a particular way. For teachers, an understanding of this culture is a crucial building block of providing programs that stimulate and challenge children's individual abilities.

Vygotsky suggests that teachers consider the possibilities of peer support for emerging skills. Providing opportunities for peers to play together increases the chances that they will scaffold each other's play to higher levels. Finding ways for older and younger children to share time and space, setting up frequent play opportunities between children who are slightly more skilled than their peers (particularly those who are more verbal), and participating in children's play all increase the chances that scaffolding can occur.

Another possibility suggested by Vygotsky's work is the careful assessment of where children are in language development. Then, support for using language—both non-verbal, gestural language, and verbal expressive language—can be integrated into routines, rituals, and stimulation activities. Vygotsky's theory provides teachers with a strong rationale for using language with children regardless of their level of expressive skills. Labeling, describing, narrating, using language functionally, and expanding children's expressive language attempts all fit with this theory.

Possibilities from Gardner's Theory of Multiple Intelligences for a Child Who Is Not Talking

Gardner's ideas remind teachers that there is so much we don't really know. It makes sense that children have differing abilities in different areas and that teachers are better at stimulating some kinds of intelligences than others. This theory suggests that teachers consider the wide range of intelligences as they plan, implement, and evaluate activities, experiences, and interactions with children. To insure that all of the intelligences are stimulated, the variety of activities and experiences becomes an important consideration for teachers. This may be particularly challenging for teachers who feel their own multiple intelligences don't include some of those described by Gardner. If this is the case, then teachers must work even harder to assure that intelligences are not overlooked in the planning process.

Another possibility is to observe intently to discover children's unique repertoire of intelligences. Then, teachers can share their observations with parents, increasing the chances for parents to observe and validate multiple intelligences in their own children.

Possibilities from Literacy Development for a Child Who Is Not Talking

Ideas from literacy development remind us that development is a process—one that unfolds rather than occurs. For teachers, this means having a good idea of where they are going with literacy and making sure that the appropriate stimulation is readily available for children. Print-rich environments, reading to children often, providing images along with the written language that they suggest, offering many experiences with books and reading materials, using language to create word labels for things in the child's immediate environment, and connecting the written word to the spoken word are all important possibilities for teachers to provide.

Literacy development theories also guide teachers to focus on what children can do instead of what they can't do. Validating skills and abilities, rather than focusing on what children can't do or don't do motivates children to continue their pursuits. Creating motivation to keep exploring, learning, and developing is important when skill acquisition is so focused on outcomes, such as "Is the child reading?"

Integrating Theory and Best Practices into Curriculum

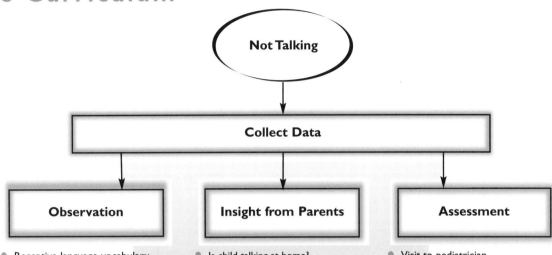

Not Talking

↓

Collect Data

Observation

- Receptive language vocabulary
- Expressive language vocabulary
- Typical language milestones

Insight from Parents

- Is child talking at home?
- Is parent reading with child at home?
- Parents' level of concern about delay
- Feedback from last pediatric visit
- Labor and delivery experience
- Make word list
- Family history of language onset

Assessment

- Visit to pediatrician
- Session with speech therapist (if suggested by pediatrician)
- Schedule speech and language screening by trained personnel
- Language skills checklist
- Language development

Increase Understanding

Theory/Research Knowledge

- Brain development (Shore, 1997)
- Language acquisition process
- Language stimulation techniques
- Typical language development

Best Practices

- Encourage vocalizations
- Repeat word attempts back to child
- Use language stimulation techniques
- Description
- Parallel talk
- Self talk
- Expansion
- Stress single words in speech
- Add non-verbal cues to verbal ones (e.g. song to transition outside)

Cultural Context and Congruence

- Family history of language onset
- Number of other children in environment
- Birth order
- Amount of language used
- Form of language used
- Explore accommodation strategies to address context differences

Collaboration

- Talk with other teachers to get ideas
- Training session with speech/language therapist
- Teacher conversations at staff meetings
- Schedule speech and language screening
- Ask speech therapist to observe teacher's language style and provide feedback

Possibilities

Parent Possibilities

Teacher-Initiated   Labor and delivery information   Family history
Discuss cultural similarities and differences

Parent Participation   Visit to pediatrician, screening by language specialist (if referred by Dr.)

Innovations in Environments

Lots of books
Vocabulary/picture file
Mirrors throughout
Create language-rich environment with fingerplays, rhymes, and songs

Observation/Assessment Possibilities

Skills checklist
Expressive language vocabulary—make list
Receptive language vocabulary—make list

Interactive Experiences

Repeat word attempts back to child   Use language stimulation techniques
Stress single words in speech   —description
Read favorite books over and over   —parallel talk
Explore other intelligences   —expansion
Be a good role model   —expansion plus
   —slow down language   Connect emotions to words
   —exaggerate facial expressions   Provide word labels for pictures from file
   —simplify grammar
Match style of communicating at home and school

Plan

Web

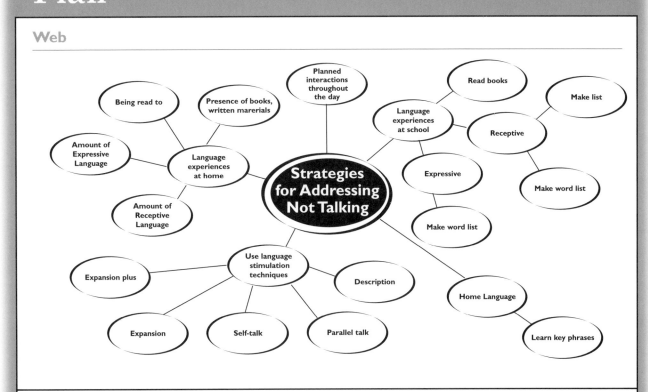

Dramatic Possibilities Play telephone

Art/Sensory Possibilities Blow bubbles, teacher description

Curiosity Possibilities Hidden mirrors

Music Possibilities Songs with simple words

Movement Possibilities Texture walk

Literacy Possibilities Favorite books, sounds books, such as Who Says Quack? by Jerry Smith

Outdoor Possibilities Read books outside

Project Possibilities Make book of images of understood words and expressed words, I Can! cans

Books	Picture File Pictures/Vocabulary
You Go Away, by Dorothy Corey Good Night Moon, by Margaret Wise Brown Brown Bear, Brown Bear, What Do You See by Eric Carle and Bill Martin Jr. No! No! No! by Anne Rockwell	Familiar things in child's environment Pictures from file with different initial sounds

Rhymes & Fingerplays	Music/Songs	Prop Boxes
"Where is Thumbkin?" "Eye Winker, Tom Tinker" "Head, Shoulders, Knees and Toes"	"Old MacDonald Had a Farm" "Row, Row, Row Your Boat"	Face/head items Hats prop box Sounds prop box

Summary

Newborns arrive in this world able to communicate with others primarily through gestural language such as facial expression and crying. Although the changes that occur during this period in brain development may not be as visible to parents and teachers as skill acquisition in the emotional, physical, and language domains, the future of thinking skills is being developed.

Toddlerhood marks the beginning of an exciting and challenging period in the lives of young children. Along with curiosity comes an emerging interest in the larger physical and social world. Children want to interact, get to know, and play with someone rather than just with objects and toys.

Children's innate ability is stimulated by early gestural and vocal communications from adults and others, and emerging relationships stimulate the desire to continue the non-verbal dialogue and learn a verbal one. During the first three years of life, children typically go from babbling to using grammatically correct sentences. The development of language follows a predictable growth pattern.

Children have two domains of language skills. One domain is children's expressive language skills, meaning those things the child can say. The other domain is receptive language skills, meaning language that the child can understand, regardless of her expressive ability.

According to Piaget, children learn cognitive skills by making mistakes, by actively experimenting with the real world and by trying to understand how things work. Experiences with real things, with concrete objects, and with the environment are the best ways to stimulate development. Vygotsky shared many of Piaget's ideas, but felt that the child's social and cognitive worlds were much closer together. Language, particularly language used in play, was viewed as the primary mechanism for advancing children's construction of knowledge.

Gardner's theory of multiple intelligences proposes that children have several kinds of intelligence that operate at the same time and in complementary ways. Multiple intelligences begin at birth (or even before). According to the theory of multiple intelligences, there are many ways for children to learn and for teachers to teach. Gardner's theory also proposes that interaction is cumulative.

The foundations of reading and writing are formed during infancy when parents and significant adults read and respond to non-verbal cues—an important precursor skill that leads to an understanding that communication has meaning. Children construct their own understanding of how the world of letters and words works through many informal experiences. Children begin the process of attaching meaning to the symbols of the written or pictorial word by connecting sounds of language to symbolic representations.

Children develop literacy skills in an integrated way, with skill acquisition in one area creating learning in other areas. As in other areas of development, there are stages (starting with scribbling) to emerging writing. During the first three years, many experiences with patterns are the very best preparation for good spelling.

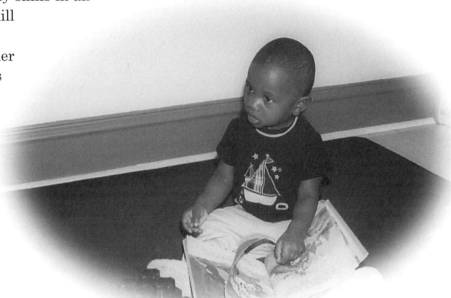

Several indirect language stimulation techniques are useful for speech and language development. These techniques include description, parallel talk, self-talk, expansion, and expansion plus. Use these teaching techniques to add information to the child's language skills and to foster language development.

Children whose primary language is not English need support bridging the two language worlds. They need validation of their home language and time to begin the process of acquiring receptive and expressive language skills in two (or more) languages at the same time.

Teachers can support emerging literacy by using literacy techniques in the classroom. A print-rich environment will have labels with pictures and words, signs, reading materials, books, and writing materials. Teachers will also support emerging literacy by reading to children and modeling writing.

Questions and Activities

1. How can teachers support language development during routine times?
2. Evaluate your classroom environment. What evidence of over- or under-stimulation did you find? What evidence did you find of balance between predictability and novelty? What can you do to correct problems?

3. Describe where a particular child is as far as intellectual development. Use the theories of Piaget, Vygotsky, and Gardner to further explain the child's development.

4. Explain specific techniques you can use for language stimulation in your classroom.

References

Berk, L.E. (1999). *Infants and Children.* Boston: Allyn and Bacon.

Berk, L.E. & A. Winsler (1995). *Scaffolding children's learning.* Washington, DC: National Association for the Education of Young Children (NAEYC).

Bloom, L. (1998). Language acquisition in the context of development. In W. Damon, D. Kuhn, & R. Sigler (Vol. Eds.), *Handbook of child psychology: Cognition, perception, and language.* 5, 309-370. New York: John Wiley.

Brazelton, T.B. & S.I. Greenspan. (2000). *The irreducible needs of children: What every child must have to grow, learn, and flourish.* Cambridge, MA: Perseus Publishing.

Center for the Study of Reading. (1985). *Becoming a Nation of Readers: The Report of the Commission on Reading.* Champaign, IL: University of Illinois.

Chomsky, N. (1957). *Syntactic structures.* The Hague: Mouton.

Cooper, P. (1993). *When stories come to school: Telling, writing, and performing stories in the early childhood classroom.* New York: Teachers and Writers.

Cryer, D. & T. Harms. (2000). *Infants and toddlers in out of home care.* Baltimore, MD: Brookes Publishing.

Edwards, C., L. Gandini, & G. Forman. (1998). *The hundred languages of children: The Reggio Emilia approach to early childhood education – Advanced Reflections.* Norwood, NJ: Ablex.

Elkind, D. (2001). Thinking about children's play. *Child Care Information Exchange,* 139, 27-28.

Gandini, L. & C.P. Edwards. (2001). *Bambini: The Italian approach to infant/toddler care.* New York: Teacher's College Press.

Gandini, L & J. Goldhaber. (2001). Two reflections about documentation, In L. Gandini, & C.P. Edwards (Eds.), *Bambini: The Italian approach to infant/toddler care.* 121-145. New York: Teacher's College Press.

Gardner, H. (1983). *Frames of mind: The theory of multiple intelligences.* New York: Basic Books.

Gerber, M. (1979). *Resources for infant educarers: A manual for parents and professionals.* Los Angeles: Resources for Infant Educarers.

Goleman, D. (1995). *Emotional intelligence.* New York: Bantam Doubleday Dell.

Goleman, D. (1998). *Working with emotional intelligence.* New York: Bantam Doubleday Dell.

Greenspan, S. (1997). *Growth of the mind and the endangered origins of intelligence.* Cambridge, MA: Perseus Books

Helms, J.H., S. Beneke, & K. Steinheimer. (1997). *Windows on learning: Documenting children's work.* New York: Teacher's College Press.

Katz, L.G. (1998). The benefits of the mix. *Child Care Information Exchange,* 124, 46-49.

Katz, LG., D. Evangelou, & J.A. Hartman. (1990). *The case for mixed-age grouping in early education.* Washington, DC: National Association for the Education of Young Children (NAEYC).

Katz, J.R. & C.E. Snow. (2000). Language development in early childhood. In

McCall, R.B. & B.W. Plemons. (2001). The concept of critical periods and their implications for early childhood services. In Bailey, D.B., J.T. Bruer, F.J. Symons, and J.W. Lichtman (Eds.), *Critical thinking about critical periods.* (267-287). Baltimore, MD: Brookes Publishing.

McMullen, M.B. (1998). Thinking before doing: A great step on the road to literacy. *Young Children,* 53(3), 65-69.

Mooney, C.G. (2000). *Theories of childhood.* St. Paul, MN: Redleaf Press.

National Association for the Education of Young Children. (1998). Learning to read and write: Developmentally appropriate practices for young children. *Young Children,* 53(4), 30-36.

Neuman, S., C. Copple & S. Bredekamp. (2000). *Learning to Read and Write: Developmentally Appropriate Practices for Young Children.* Washington, DC: National Association for the Education of Young Children (NAEYC).

Paley, V.G. (1981). *Wally's stories.* Cambridge, MA: Harvard University Press.

Piaget, J. (1962). *Play, dreams, and imitation in childhood.* (C. Gattegno & F.M. Hodgson, Trans.) New York: Norton.

Piaget, J. (1977). *The origins of intelligence in children.* New York: International Universities Press.

Shonkoff, J.P. & D.A. Phillips (Eds.). (2000). From neurons to neighborhoods: *The science of early childhood development.* Washington, DC: National Academy Press.

Stern, D. (1985). *The interpersonal world of the infant: A view from psychoanalysis and developmental psychology.* New York: Basic Books.

Tabors, P.O. (1998). What early childhood educators need to know: Developing programs for linguistically and culturally diverse children and families. *Young Children,* 53(6), 20-26.

Vygotsky, L. (1978). *Mind in society: The development of higher psychological processes.* Cambridge, MA: Harvard University Press.

Glossary

Accommodation—One of two underlying strategies for constructing knowledge in infants and toddlers. Accommodation is the creation of new ideas or the adaptation of old ones when new information is received through exploration and manipulation of objects. These processes are repeated as children explore their physical and social environments and were viewed by Piaget as the primary mechanism for cognitive learning.

Assimilation—One of two underlying strategies for constructing knowledge in infants and toddlers. Assimilation is the process of interpreting new information or learning into existing ideas or thought.

Chronological Age—Age related to time since birth.

Cognitive-developmental Theory—A stage theory of cognitive development proposed by Jean Piaget.

Constructivism—Cognitive theory whereby children actually construct their own knowledge based on their own experiences.

Description—A language stimulation technique in which the parent or teacher narrates or describes what is going on in the child's world by putting word labels on things.

Emergent Literacy—Skills children acquire in the process of becoming literate—able to read and write. Literacy includes oral language, reading, and writing. But these are not discrete areas of literacy.

Expansion—A language stimulation technique to use with children when their vocabularies begin to grow. This technique takes what the child says and expands on it.

Expansion Plus—A language stimulation technique to use with children when their vocabularies begin to grow. This technique takes what the child says and adds to it.

Expressive Language—Spoken language, language that children both understand and speak.

Intrapersonal Intelligence—One of Gardner's multiple intelligences, also called emotional intelligence, which includes self-awareness, managing emotions, emotional self-control, recognizing emotions in others, and handling relationships.

Language Stimulation Techniques—Techniques that are useful in supporting language development.

Multiple Intelligences—A theory that children have several kinds of intelligence that operate at the same time in complementary ways.

Nonverbal Communication—Components of language that are not specific to the language spoken.

Object Permanence—The concept that objects are there whether you can see them or not—children were thought to operate cognitively with only those things and people who were in view.

Parallel Talk—A language stimulation technique that focuses on the child's action, connecting word labels into a sentence describing the action. Parallel talk usually begins with the word "you."

Receptive Language—Language that children understand, but may not be able to speak.

Scaffolding—Supporting children in operating within their zone of proximal development by more capable peers or adults.

Schema—Cognitive pictures created by sensory and motor exploration of the environment and by associating words with the ideas they represent.

Self-talk—A language stimulation technique that focuses on adult behavior, labeling and describing what the adult is doing. Adults who use self-talk usually start their utterances with "I."

Sensori-motor Stage—The first stage of Piaget's cognitive-developmental theory in which children gather information with their senses and motor movements to construct an understanding of the world.

Verbal Communication—Spoken language, also called expressive language.

CHAPTER 6:
Moving Around and Problem-solving

Developmental Tasks: Moving Around and Problem-solving

Moving Around

There are many ways to describe the infant and toddler brain—amazing, flexible, capable, adapting, vulnerable, complex, changeable, plastic, a work in progress, a construction site, or even a rough draft awaiting editing and rewriting. These descriptions refer to the vast changes that take place as the seemingly helpless newborn grows into a walking, talking, thinking preschooler.

An understanding of how the brain is prepared at birth to be "ready to learn" is crucial to understanding child growth and development during infancy and toddlerhood. As we have discovered, new knowledge about the brain and the power of maturational development and interactions has taken on new meaning. It seems that development has a near-perfect plan for creating the architecture of the brain. It also appears that most of the construction work is accomplished through interactions with the important people in children's lives—their parents, teachers, and friends.

As babies grow, they are able to exert more and more control over their environment. Initially, they have very little physical influence and spend energy learning to control and experience their bodies. Discovering toes and fingers, making sounds, wiggling, and tracking an object visually are all wonderful experiences of discovery.

As babies master fine motor skills, they are able to pick up objects and even turn the pages of a book. As babies master gross motor skills, they are able to roll, crawl, and then, finally, walk. These are exciting physical changes that allow babies to expand their exploration of the world around them.

Problem-solving

Discoveries are the purview of toddlers. During the period from 18 months to 3 years, young children make great strides in discovering how their bodies work and in constructing an understanding of the world in which they live. Meaning is derived from active experimentation with people, the environment, and interactions. Activity levels and intensity of purpose increase dramatically as children figure out that they can make many things happen in their lives and take delight in sticking to tasks until they have mastered them.

Toddlers are adding new physical skills. Physical learning revolves around perfecting gross motor skills, such as running, hopping, balancing, jumping, and coordinating the movements of the arms and legs to the movement of the torso. In the fine motor arena, toddlers focus attention on eye-hand coordination and increasing mastery of the smaller muscles that control the fingers and hands.

The increase in fine motor skills leads to an explosion in learning about mathematical concepts. One and "more than one" are already understood, and "more" becomes interesting to explore. Manipulation of objects, toys, and materials, and emerging preferences for favorite manipulative experiences join to create the ability for toddlers to stay on task in an interesting activity for quite a long time.

Chapter 6 focuses on the knowledge that is important for teachers to understand related to the tasks of moving around and problem-solving. The best practices that emerge from this knowledge are then discussed. The chapter ends by applying this new understanding of theory and practice to a common behavioral challenge.

Knowledge

Brain Development

Everyday we learn more and more about the brain, how it works, and what influences it. McCall and Plemons (2001) suggest that two principles should be considered fundamental with regard to the brain. The first is that the brain influences everything and that changes in behavior change the brain. The second is that there are negative consequences for the brain when there is inadequate stimulation or poor environments.

What influences how the infant and toddler brain develops? Old arguments of nature versus nurture are given little attention these days (Shore, 1997). Advances in neuroscience point to the dynamic interplay between nature and nurture. An intricate dance occurs between what a child is born with and what happens to that potential. As the dance continues, genetic predispositions cannot be separated from what is influenced by experience (Shonkoff and Phillips, 2000).

How Does the Brain Grow?

An understanding of how the brain grows reveals a sequence of overlapping stages, some of which occur in the prenatal stage. The first stage is neural proliferation—the creation of billions of nerve cells called neurons (McCall & Plemons, 2001). The neurological hardware and wiring of the brain is produced during this stage. Brain cells (neurons) begin the process of brain development by connecting to other brain cells. Neurons are designed precisely with this goal in mind. Each cell has an axon and many of hair-like extensions called dendrites (Shore, 1997).

The second phase, called neural migration, is completed during gestation. This process sends out nerve connections throughout the brain and connects them together. The third stage is synaptogenesis—the process of connecting neurons together to form neural networks (see Chapter 2, page 51). Synapses are created when an axon of one brain cell connects with a dendrite of another neuron. This process is repeated millions of times as the young child's brain is developing. During infancy and toddlerhood, the brain creates far more connections than it will ultimately need to process information. The over-development of synapses insures that children are primed and ready for continuing brain development in the early childhood years.

It is during the next step in brain development that these early connections link together to form neural pathways for signals to travel among and between each other, and between other parts of the brain. Neural pathways are activated by things that happen to babies—and the interactive experiences they have with the environment.

There is potential for positive as well as negative influences on synaptogenesis. For example, adequate nourishment provided sensitively to the baby when he or she indicates hunger is an environmental necessity for continued brain development. Yet, if nourishment is withheld or unavailable, or provided by an uncaring and unresponsive adult, the brain's vulnerability is exposed, and brain development may be compromised (Shonkoff & Phillips, 2000).

Neural pathways are strengthened by repeated experiences and by good teaching (Shore, 1997). The goal of this stage of brain development, called selective elimination or degeneration, is to strengthen and reinforce connections between and among neurons to the point that they will always be maintained. This goal is accomplished through repeated interactions—interactions that use the communication links between neurons.

During this period of brain development, neural pathways are pruned and eliminated if they are unused, underused, or if the brain is stressed by environmental factors. Pruning continues throughout the life span, with the brain continually creating synapses as a result of stimulation and abandoning those that are not being used.

The last stage of brain development is called myelination (McCall & Plemons, 2001). Myelination is the process of coating the nerve cells with a fatty substance that insulates the cells and increases the speed and efficiency of connections, which, in turn, increases the ease of communication between neural networks and facilitates coordination among them.

What Affects Brain Growth?

Environmental Conditions Affect Brain Growth—The development of the brain is influenced by many environmental conditions, sometimes positively, sometimes negatively. Nourishment, type and quality of routine care, warm, nurturing interactions, stimulating and interesting surroundings, and stimulation experiences from objects and people in the environment are examples of potentially positive environmental conditions. Maternal depression; trauma; abuse; social deprivation; drug, alcohol, or nicotine use; and institutionalization are examples of potentially negative environmental conditions.

These effects can be immediate (as in drug use during pregnancy) or influence the general direction of brain growth positively or negatively (as in mother-child interactions that are warm and reciprocal). The direction of these effects is pervasive and cumulative, affecting children throughout their lives, not just during infancy and toddlerhood (Bredekamp & Copple, 1997).

Myth or Misunderstanding
A CHILD'S POTENTIAL IS FIXED GENETICALLY AT BIRTH.

As parents peer through the windows to look at their baby in the hospital nursery, some comment on the baby's facial characteristics and how intelligent the baby is. Because the parents and grandparents are intelligent, they expect their baby to be intelligent, too. No one comments on how smart they are going to help their baby become!

The myth here is that innate, genetic characteristics are the most important ones. When babies are born, parents are interested in the baby's physical attributes—are all 10 toes there? whose eye color did the baby inherit? Soon, parents begin to see personality characteristics that they attribute to Dad's side of the family, or maybe to Uncle Don or Aunt Minny.

Families often move on to considering how they can contribute to children's potential. Children's potential is not fixed at birth, it develops through the complex interplay between what the baby is born with and the experiences she or he will have during life. Although eye color won't change, the interactions between the environment and the innate abilities with which a child is born change as a result of the type and quality of the interactions between the baby and the significant others in his social and cultural context.

Make a list of kinds of interactions that might affect brain development positively. Then, do the same for negative interactions.

Normal Maturation Affects Brain Development—Nature equips young children with a mechanism for developing the brain. Developmental maturation is a powerful stimulus that continues the process of connecting neurons, strengthening synapses, and coordinating neural pathways.

Some of these experiences are "expectant" by the developing brain. That is, genetics prepare the brain to receive certain kinds of stimulation that, when received, allows for further organization and development of the brain. There are many expectant experiences during early brain development. An "expectant" experience happens to the brain during the development of visual acuity.

As babies are exposed to variations in natural light and the patterns of early visual experiences after birth, the brain uses these inputs to further normal visual development. Unless something interferes with this experience (like cataracts or strabismus), the brain detects and registers the expected experience and uses the experience to continue to develop the brain's wiring for visual acuity (Shonkoff & Phillips, 2000).

Continued brain development is also "dependent" on experiences. Normal development offers many of these "dependent" experiences. For example, children gain coordination of fine and gross motor skills by repeating the patterns of those skills over and over again, strengthening the communication and coordination between neurons. Babies who do not have experiences on the floor, moving their own bodies, reaching and batting at objects, picking up many different objects, etc., may not receive enough stimulating experiences to increase synaptic coordination and communication.

Understanding that normative development supports brain development is wonderful news for early childhood educators. Teachers have always known that normative assessment is not designed to compare children to each other but instead to monitor emerging skills and abilities. Teachers do so to modify educational experiences to match the child's emerging skills. The crucial importance of monitoring maturation as a teaching activity is validated by brain research. Because normally emerging skills and abilities support experience-dependent synaptogenesis, keeping a keen eye on emerging development is a tool for facilitating continued brain growth. Alert teachers can identify potential interruptions in normal development early enough to apply remediation, preventing interruption of brain development.

Secure Attachments Affect Brain Growth—Intimate, enduring, reciprocal interactions between children and adults in their attachment network are crucial to brain growth. These relationships protect children from the impact of less-than-optimal life experiences, allow children to learn and benefit from life situations that are stress producing, and provide a firm foundation for the natural exploration and experience that continues the wiring of the brain during childhood.

The following characteristics describe relationships that are most beneficial to the brain. The presence of adults in the attachment network who are warm, responsive, caring, and available is the first characteristic. Then, there needs to be a good fit between the interactive style of the adults and gestural and verbal communication of the child, so communication between them can be sent and received efficiently and effectively. Finally, there needs to be an enduring nature to the relationships that children have with adults.

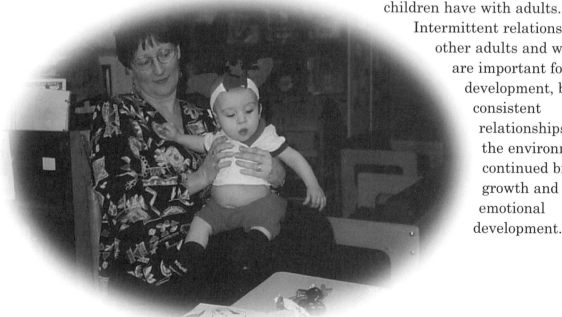

Intermittent relationships with other adults and with peers are important for social development, but consistent relationships create the environment for continued brain growth and emotional development.

Myth or Misunderstanding
CHILDREN BEGIN LEARNING WHEN THEY START "REAL" SCHOOL IN PRE-KINDERGARTEN, KINDERGARTEN, OR FIRST GRADE.

After being involved with the parent committee at World of Children, Alice Jones set up a meeting with the director. At the meeting, Alice let the director know that she was not in favor of the proposed increase in tuition for families and the proposed increase in pay for teachers. Alice told the director that she couldn't justify paying that much in tuition until her child was in "real" school.

The director was disappointed. She felt she had done a good job of communicating the important job that teachers do. Two myths are at work here. One myth is that elementary school is the real beginning of education. The other is that adding "caring" to education lessens the value of the education.

Few argue with the importance of early education but many misunderstand the role of relationships and nurturing in supporting the education process. Ms. Jones' connection of increases in tuition and teacher pay as counterproductive to her being able to afford her child's school illustrates the dichotomy between affordability and quality that forces compromises—either by parents when their fees go up or by teacher turnover when teaching salaries lag even farther behind.

What should happen next? What should the director do? How would you respond to Ms. Jones?

Sensitive Periods Affect Brain Growth—Sensitive periods (also called critical periods and timing effects) are periods when specific structures of the brain are most susceptible to experience. These experiences alter future brain structures and functions. The impact of sensitive periods or timing effects can be positive if they result from normal, beneficial experiences, or negative if they result from abnormal, harmful, or withheld experiences.

There is controversy about sensitive periods. Some neuroscientists say too much emphasis on sensitive periods negates the brain's plasticity and ability to compensate and change, a condition that continues throughout the life span (Bailey, Bruer, Symons & Lichtman, 2001; Shonkoff & Phillips, 2000).

Nevertheless, there is enough evidence to support that there are sensitive periods for certain kinds of brain development to occur.

Most neuroscientists now view sensitive periods as rather long periods for brain development instead of narrow windows. And they view the windows as closing gradually instead of abruptly. Further, opportunities to rewire or further strengthen neural pathways are thought to extend throughout the life span, even though creating and strengthening pathways may not be as easy after these sensitive periods.

What Does Brain-based Care and Early Education Look Like in the Classroom?

Brain-based early education looks like developmentally appropriate early education. It supports teachers in spending time with children to develop close connections. Children's brains work best in the context of healthy relationships. Warm, consistent, responsive care and interactions make brain growth and development proceed as nature planned. So, the time teachers spend connecting, really connecting to children, increasing their understanding of non-verbal cues, observing play, and caring for and cuddling them, is early education for growing brains.

Using warm, responsive touch to stimulate, strengthen, and reinforce neural connections is an important teaching skill in brain-based classrooms. Rough, insensitive touch, however infrequent, puts children at risk for shutting down the emotional connections that are forming between adults and children. This is particularly important when children become more risk-taking in their exploration of the environment by climbing, reaching, and exploring every nook and cranny. When adults view risk-taking as a dangerous activity that should be stopped, the tone of their voices as well as gestures and physical restraint may convey messages that interrupt rather than encourage exploration of new experiences.

Infants and toddlers are highly motivated to explore and discover. A child's world is in the details. Children see and explore minute details that interest them and are able to use a large variety of physical points of view to do so. Brain-based classrooms understand this interest and create environments that are safe to explore from different points of view. Further, teachers view exploration as important and desirable—not an activity to be curtailed or stopped. This doesn't mean that there are no rules for safety or reasonable behavior. It means that the rules and the way the teacher implements the rules are consistent with understanding exploration as a positive stimulation activity, not a negative one.

Talking to and with children is crucial to the future development of language—both the primary language of the family and secondary language of the community or society. Starting at birth with gazing at each other, adults and children begin the communication process and tell each other that messages are being sent and received. Then, using language with children functionally—to get needs met and understand the world around them—is important. Expanding vocabularies help children succeed in their interactions with peers, widening the social world in the process. Finally, the ability to initiate and interact with less support from facilitative adults launches children into the world of language competency.

Stimulation that matches the child's interest and ability without overwhelming or over-stimulating is another part of brain-based early education. This goodness of fit refers to the match between the child's individuality and the actions, interactions, and facilitation of parents and teachers. Individualizing these interactions—making sure there is a match between the child's interest and the teacher's goals and plans—is crucial to brain development. Without this match, there is the risk of interrupting or negating the brain development underway.

Implications of Brain Development for Moving Around and Problem-solving

Knowledge of brain development guides teachers to monitor normative development to make sure experience-dependent and experience-expectant opportunities are maximized. Teachers can also use their careful monitoring of normative development to determine if there are any developmental problems that need intervention.

Embracing repetitive experiences as brain stimulation comes naturally for most teachers. Creating opportunities for repeated experiences that reinforce and strengthen neural pathways must be a curriculum staple.

Knowledge of brain development suggests that teachers keep in mind the cumulative nature of development. This releases teachers from the pressure to accomplish everything at once, forcing activities, experiences, or interactions on children before they are ready for them. There is time—time to individualize responses to children and to plan many more activities and experiences that will contribute to the children's brain development as well as their developmental growth.

Teachers must carefully monitor environmental factors that can affect brain development. Some negative environmental factors are under the direct control of the teacher, such as the amount and type of nourishment provided to the child, the warmth of the interactive relationship with the child at school, and the amount and type of stimulation available in the school environment. Other environmental factors, such as poverty; trauma; abuse; social deprivation; drug, alcohol, or nicotine abuse; and maternal depression may require the teacher to access resources outside the school to help families support the child's well-being.

Investing in relationships seems to have such wide impact that it is mentioned as a strategy for furthering total development. When information about brain development is added to this understanding, the importance of relationships increases. Brain research guides teachers to make investments in forming reciprocal relationships with children—creating the optimum conditions for continued brain growth and development.

Physical Development

Physical development during the early childhood years is an uneven process. This asynchrony shows up in the different growth patterns of different components of the body, as well as in individual children's general growth patterns. Within the body, physical asynchrony can be visible in the size of child's head in proportion to the rest of the body. Because brain growth is rapid during the first three years of a child's life, the head grows faster than the rest of the body, and then it slows down. Other body systems, like the skeletal system, grow rapidly in infancy, then slow down during early and middle childhood, only to return to rapid growth during adolescence.

Cephalacaudal/proximodistal Trend

During infancy and toddlerhood, the child's body changes dramatically. Seemingly helpless newborns grow into physically competent three-year-olds. As with all development, physical development follows predictable developmental patterns even though individual progress may be highly variable.

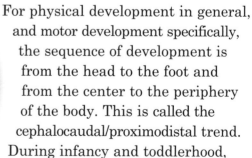

For physical development in general, and motor development specifically, the sequence of development is from the head to the foot and from the center to the periphery of the body. This is called the cephalocaudal/proximodistal trend. During infancy and toddlerhood, children develop their bodies from the top down and from the center out.

For example, most normally developing children can swipe at and hold objects by the age of 5 or 6 months, pick up objects between the thumb and forefinger by about 11 or 12 months, hold a spoon by about 16 months, scribble with a crayon at 18 months, and eat with a fork at about 24 months, illustrating the proximodistal trend. Similarly, normally developing children roll over by about 5 or 6 months, sit without support by about 7or 9 months, pull to a stand by about 10 to 12 months, walk by 12 to 16 months, and walk up stairs at 18 to 20 months, illustrating the cephalocaudal trend.

Both of these trends are affected by all of the components of uniqueness (see Chapter 2, page 50) and the opportunities available for experience and practice of developing skills. Children continue to have an individual pace in acquiring skills, and experience and practice can support or hinder motor development. For example, children who do not have opportunities to be on the floor to develop their motor skills may seem to lag behind those who do.

Gross and Fine Motor Development

The milestones of physical development are usually broken down into two major components—gross motor and fine motor. Gross motor development refers to the large muscles of the legs, arms, and torso, whereas fine motor refers to the smaller muscles of the body including the muscles in the hands, feet, and eyes. Physical development milestones for both gross and fine motor development from birth to age 36 months are listed on page 262.

Toilet Training—Process, Not Magic

Toileting is the physical skill that parents and teachers look forward to children developing. Successful toileting involves learning many physical skills, both for the gross motor muscles of the body and the fine motor muscles of the body. It also involves skill development in other areas including emotional, social, language, and cognition (see chart on page 263).

Four Stages of Successful Toileting—Learning to toilet consistently is a process that begins with an interest in the toilet and what happens in bathrooms and ends with independent toileting. Learning to toilet has four phases. The first phase is toilet play. Many parents and teachers view this beginning stage as readiness for toilet training, when it is actually only the beginning of the whole process. Toilet play is characterized by an interest in the bathroom in general and in what people, particularly parents, do in the bathroom. During this phase, children often like to get on and off the toilet (generally fully clothed!), flush repeatedly, play with toilet paper and wash their hands, and watch what adults do when they are in the bathroom.

Physical Development Milestones

AGE	FINE MOTOR SKILLS	GROSS MOTOR SKILLS
Birth-6 months	• Holds rattle. • Eyes and head follow. • Grasps objects.	• Turns head from side to side. • Holds head and chest up when lying on stomach. • Swipes at objects. • Rolls from back to side.
6-12 months	• Feeds self dry cereal or crackters • Exchanges objects between hands. • Picks up toys and objects. • Points. • Puts objects in containers. • Drinks from a cup.	• Scoots on stomach. • Holds bottle. • Sits without support. • Crawls after ball or toy. • Pulls self to standing position. • Walks with support.
12-18 months	• Uses spoon. • Turns pages of cardboard books. • Stacks blocks. • Scribbles with crayon.	• Walks without support. • Squats down and stands back up. • Carries large objects around. • Kicks a ball.
18-24 months	• Holds cup or glass in one hand. • Unbuttons large buttons. • Turns doorknobs.	• Squats for long periods of time. • Throws large ball. • Carries large objects around. • Dumps out containers of toys or materials.
24-30 months	• Removes shoes, some clothing. • Stacks small blocks. • Fits pegs in pegboard. • Pours and fills containers at sensory table. • Unzips large zippers. • Shows preference for one hand.	• Propels riding toys with feet. • Walks up stairs without alternating feet. • Builds with blocks. • Runs.
30-36 months	• Completes puzzles. • Turns pages of book, though not always one page at time. • Washes hands at sink.	• Walks down stairs without assistance. • Balances on one foot. • Jumps on two feet. • Pedals tricycle.

The second stage of toileting is toilet practice. Getting on and off the toilet without assistance, pulling pants down and up, taking off diapers or pull-up diapers, pretending to wipe after pretending to toilet (or after a coincidental success!), flushing the toilet, and washing hands are all part of the toilet practice stage.

Developmental Skills for Successful Toileting

Body Awareness Skills	Physical Skills	Language Skills	Cognitive Skills	Social-emotional Skills
The ability to delay gratification for a minute: "I can wait for a while, maybe 3 or 4 minutes."	Motor skills such as "I can sit still for a while, maybe 3 or 4 minutes."	"My Mommy and Daddy and I have a set of shared words for elimination--I know what to call what is happening to me."	Prediction skills such as "I may need to potty soon," or "I know what comes next when my body feels like this."	Self-confidence feelings that say, "I can be in charge of my own body!"
"I can tell when my bladder/bowel is filling up and I need to potty" and "I prefer to be clean rather than to be dirty."	Large muscle skills such as "I can pull my pants down and up without assistance from an adult."	"I can tell Mommy and Daddy what I need." "I can access and use the words I need when I need them."	Memory skills so "I won't forget to go potty while I'm busy playing."	Autonomy skills that mean "I can do it myself."
"I can stop what I am doing and go to the toilet in time."	Small muscle skills: "I can regulate the muscles that start and stop the elimination process."		"I understand that I need to think about toileting before I go outside, go down for a nap, etc."	Independence skills that mean, "I want to try to do it myself."
	Motor control skills such as "I can hold my urine or bowel movement while I get to the toilet, pull my pants down, and have a seat!" and "I can wipe my bottom without adult help." Bio-motor regularity skills such as "I have a prolonged periods of dryness, including waking up from sleep (nap or night time) dry."			Self-esteem feelings that mean, "I don't need to make taking care of my body a power struggle."

The third phase is toilet training. The training part comes from cueing children to take a reading of how their bodies are feeling and whether or not there is any bowel or bladder urgency. Some parents and teachers mistakenly think that children are almost trained at this stage and just need to be reminded to go to the bathroom. This is not the case. During the third stage, the aim of training is to help the child who usually becomes increasingly conscious of what is going on internally. Asking children to check their bodies when they wake up, after breakfast, before leaving home, before getting in the bathtub, and before going to bed or nap sets up a pattern of getting in touch with how the body feels that leads to the next stage.

Phases of Toilet Training

Phase 1	Toilet play
Phase 2	Toilet practice
Phase 3	Toilet training
Phase 4	Independent toileting

The last stage is independent toileting. This is the stage that parents and teachers long for—finally, they are not needed to remind or coax a child to toilet. Children take care of their own bodily needs without prompting or reminders. It is the culmination of a process that began with toilet play and ends with parents and teachers who are very proud of the child's accomplishments.

Toileting can be the most problematic developmental issue to understand because of the individual variations in readiness to control toileting and the integrated nature of toileting. Age is a particularly poor predictor of readiness. It is further complicated when parents or teachers approach the process with negative or punitive strategies.

Myth or Misunderstanding
SMART CHILDREN LEARN TO TOILET EARLY.

After Anna started toilet training, the parents of the other children in the classroom started asking when their children would be toilet trained, too. Conversations with parents started to revolve only around toilet training. Parents wanted to know how it was being handled at school and who had made the most progress. It seemed to the teacher that the only conversations she had were about toilet training.

The myth here is that children are all ready to toilet train at the same time. The misunderstanding by parents is that adults can make toilet training happen when they are ready rather than when their child is ready. Components of uniqueness (see Chapter 2, page 50) and alternate developmental pathways (see Chapter 2, page 52) are perhaps the most evident in children's toileting readiness, practice, and success. Some are ready by age two and have relative success with very little practice. Others show no interest at all and are even resistant to practicing precursor skills such as pulling down their pants or getting on and off the toilet. Some have success at school (or at home) and cannot translate the skill to the other setting. Still others get interested, have initial success, then lose interest and refuse to try again. All of these variations (and perhaps a million more) are examples of normal developmental differences in readiness.

Erickson and theorists from the psychoanalytic perspective caution parents and teachers to resist the urge to take charge and control the process. Learning to toilet takes place in the developmental context of experimenting with issues of autonomy and control. Too much pressure or the wrong kind of pressure turns toileting into a control issue rather than an autonomy issue, raising the possibilities that the process will be difficult and unsuccessful.

What do you think the teacher should do next? What kind of resources do parents need to understand the process of learning to toilet? How would you handle a situation where parents want their child to learn to toilet just to limit and control the cost of diapers?

Most children begin this developmental process around the age of two, but few really master toileting until age three or even later. Most children (90%) learn to toilet independently by the end of the third year. Some children master bladder control first; others master bowel control first. Some children master daytime dryness easily, only to struggle with nighttime dryness. Girls may gain control more easily than boys. Most children have accidents well into the third year.

Take the time to understand fully the developmental nature of toileting. When teachers and parents do, children's process through learning to toileting will unfold in an environment of support, encouragement, and in due time, success.

Implications of Physical Development for Moving Around and Problem-solving

An implication for moving around and problem-solving is to be aware of the cephalcaudal/proximodistal trend in individual children. A good indication of the status of children's physical development is the progress being made at controlling the smaller muscles of the arms, hands, eyes, mouth, legs, and feet. Progress in gaining control can be seen in the fine motor skills that interest children and their success in accomplishing them.

Implications for learning to toilet are particularly clear. Toileting is the ultimate developmental task. To become trained, children must accomplish many tasks in all of the developmental domains before success is inevitable. Because this is the case, focusing on successful incremental progress is the best approach. Use the list of skills on page 263 to chart each child's readiness. This careful monitoring of readiness will help celebrate success in getting ready and provide parents with indicators of progress toward the goal of independent toileting.

Accepting the asynchrony of development as normal is another implication for these developmental tasks. The spurts of growth in young children are well documented (Shonkoff & Phillips, 2000). Accepting the spurts and the plateaus that follow as a normal part of growth is a helpful point of view for teachers and parents.

Self-regulation and the Internalization of Self-control

Self-regulation begins with the process of communicating needs and wants to others, then proceeds to developing the capacity to regulate emotions, attention, and behavior. The early childhood years are characterized by an increasing capacity for self-regulation. Parents and teachers can usually see the progress in self-regulation as children become more able to function independently.

Why is self-regulation so important to development? Shonkoff and Phillips (2000) consider self-regulation "a cornerstone of early childhood development that cuts across all domains of behavior" (p.3). Success in achieving self-regulation influences children's lives in many ways. Early in infancy, self-regulation focuses on sleeping, eating, crying, and communicating needs and wants to significant others. Then, children begin to regulate emotions, attention, and behaviors. These highly interrelated dimensions of self-regulation influence each other and children's success in achieving the competencies needed to manage independently.

The acquisition of self-regulatory skills is crucial for children's long-term success. Competent regulatory functioning during infancy and toddlerhood predicts later social competence. It is also related to success in school and self-control during childhood and adolescence (Brunson, 2000).

Several of the theoretical frameworks previously discussed contribute ideas to what we understand about self-regulation and the internalization of self-control. From a psychoanalytic point of view, self-regulation increases as ego strength increases. Both are thought to change in the context of warm relationships and supportive environments. Behaviorists consider growth in self-regulation as the ability to choose larger, yet more delayed rewards for behavior. Social learning theorists think that growth in self-regulation results from observing interactions between others and seeing the rewards and punishments associated with different behaviors. This point of view depends on having good role models, being rewarded for appropriate behavior (or seeing others rewarded for it), and on the internalizing of standards of behavior.

Cognitive developmental theory is the perspective that views the ability to self-regulate as constructed by the child as he interacts with the environment and the things and people in it (Piaget, 1977; Vygotsky, 1978). As children explore and practice behaviors, including emotional behaviors, they increase their understanding of how to control and regulate those behaviors.

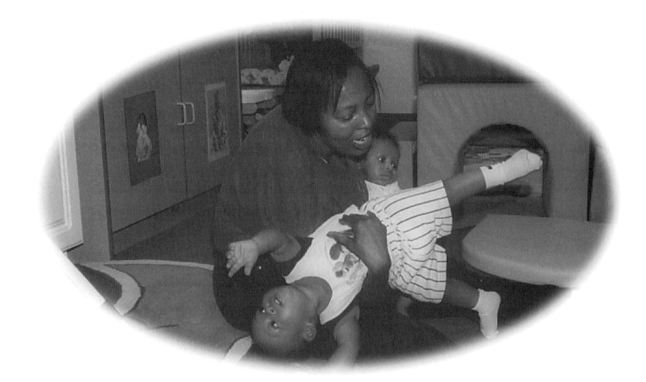

Greenspan (1997) cites increasing evidence from neuroscience for the connection between emotions and cognition. Once viewed as separate and different, cognition and emotions are now considered as connected and interdependent on each other. As children gain control over their emotions, they are increasingly able to focus their attention and behavior—crucial skills for acquiring further cognitive skills and abilities. The reverse of this is also true. If children can't manage their emotions well enough to focus their attention and behavior, they are less likely to be able to benefit from external stimulation of cognitive capacities or teaching from others.

Vygotsky emphasized the role of language in the development of self-regulation. As children learn to communicate thoughts, needs, and intentions through language, they increase their ability to self-regulate. Language serves as a shared experience to give meaning to children's self-regulatory efforts. As children listen to what others say about their behavior, they modify and adjust their behaviors, incorporating what others say into their self-regulation (Mooney, 2000).

Information-processing theories propose that children learn to engage in more organized, efficient, and effective cognitive processes as they develop "executive functions" that control action. Executive function is a term used to describe a collection of interdependent cognitive and attention skills that are necessary for purposeful, goal-directed activity (Shonkoff & Phillips, 2000). These include the ability to self-regulate, sequence behavior, control impulses and delay gratification, and plan and organize behavior.

Most of these skills do not develop during infancy and toddlerhood, but the precursor skills that lay the foundation for executive functions do emerge during this period. Three important precursor skills have been identified. The first is orienting to relevant and important features of the environment while screening out the irrelevant ones. For infants and toddlers, this means choosing the right features of the environment to attend to and screening out unimportant features. Then, the child needs to be able to accurately anticipate what might happen next.

The second skill is being able to plan and implement goal-directed behavior. When infants remove the blanket off of a desired toy, they are indicating planful problem-solving. When toddlers bite to get a toy away from another, they are also exhibiting problem-solving, albeit, a less socially acceptable form. As problem-solving skills grow, infants and toddlers are able to impact and influence what is happening around them. Learning positive and productive ways to problem solve is perfected during the toddler years.

The third precursor skill to executive function is self-control. Self-control is the ability to comply with external expectations, often involving delaying gratification or controlling impulses. Toddlers are often seen struggling to exercise self-control and get better at it during the toddler years. For this reason, we will explore this component of self-regulation further.

The Internalization of Self-Control

The third precursor skill related to executive functions is of particular interest to infant and toddler teachers and their parents. Gaining self-control means that children are making progress in self-regulation and are beginning to understand and adopt the expectations of others for their behavior. Often considered a guidance and discipline issue, gaining self-control is actually a developmental task just like learning to walk or talk.

A continuum helps explain the process of how self-control moves from external control, to adult-assisted self-control, to independent self-control. At each point on the continuum, self-control is supported or influenced by important adults in the child's attachment network in the context of their relationships with the child. Self-control begins outside the child and then moves inside the child through the process of internalization.

Precursor Skills Support the Internalization of Self-control

Some skills are too advanced for infants and toddlers to learn directly. When additional development is needed for children to acquire skills, educators often identify the tendencies that develop in advance of these skills. Called precursor skills, they indicate that the child is approaching or learning the

Internalization of Self-Control

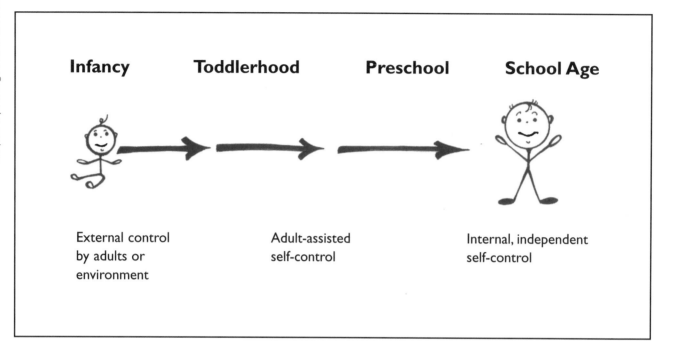

Infancy	Toddlerhood	Preschool	School Age
External control by adults or environment	Adult-assisted self-control	Internal, independent self-control	

subskills or tendencies that come before the actual skill. For example, sharing is often thought by adults to be a positive social skill. But, before children can demonstrate the relatively sophisticated skill of sharing, they are able to demonstrate some skills that will lead to sharing, like taking turns or dividing resources. Taking turns and dividing resources come before and lead to the ability to share.

In order to gain self-control, children need to learn four key precursor skills:
- To control emotional and physical impulses
- To tolerate frustration
- To delay gratification
- To make and implement plans (Marion, 1999)

Controlling emotional and physical impulses is difficult for very young children. So often, the way they feel is the way they act. The ability to step back and examine a situation before acting is a crucial task for young children to learn. As with so many other developmental tasks, this one is learned within the context of important relationships with adults. Positive adult relationships scaffold children's emotional and physical responses, helping them wait just a minute and guiding how they respond.

Tolerating frustration is difficult for children because they are just beginning to experience this intense and challenging feeling. Children feel frustration when there is a discrepancy between what they want and what they get. Many parts of growing up in the first three years are frustrating. Sometimes the frustration comes from not having the necessary skills needed (like wanting to make the scooter go but not understanding how to do so) and sometimes frustration comes from wanting something you know you can't have (like a cookie before dinner). Either way, tolerating these experiences is necessary to the emerging self-control process.

Delaying gratification means postponing participation in a pleasurable activity or experience or delaying getting what you want. Egocentrism in young children makes them want almost everything now, as soon as it occurs to them. By learning to delay gratification, children learn that they can experience and recover from not getting what you want and that life goes on in the process.

A final precursor skill to self-control is the ability to make and implement a plan to get what you want or to solve a problem. The ability to make a plan shows a giant leap in understanding of the social and physical world. Plan making involves thinking of ways to make things happen and then implementing the plan. As children learn that there are ways to get what you want if you can control impulses long enough to make a plan, tolerate the frustration of waiting for the plan to work, and delay gratification while the plan is implemented, their emotional and social worlds become less conflicted and more satisfying.

All of the precursor skills lead to increases in self-control. As children develop these four behaviors, the number of meltdowns, tantrums, and conflicts diminish. But this success is not guaranteed. It takes time and support from adults to practice and perfect these skills. Typically, children are able to voluntarily use these skills in multiple situations as they approach the third year (Vaughan, Kopp & Krakow, 1984).

Implications of Self-regulation and the Internalization of Self-control for Moving Around and Problem-solving

As infants and toddlers make progress in self-regulation, caregivers are reminded to update their expectations. Recognizing progress in self-regulation and validating attempts to practice self-regulatory skills motivates children to improve their self-regulation. But self-regulation must be seen as a process that takes place throughout the early childhood years, not one that "happens" all of a sudden.

Self-control is only one component of self-regulation. The implication of ideas about self-control is that children need adults to help them succeed in acquiring skills of self-control. They are not able to do it alone. Without adult support, self-control cannot be internalized. So, parents and teachers can create experiences that give children the support they need to practice self-control with adult help. Of particular importance is staying close physically to support attempts at self-control, using language to give children ideas about how to stay under control, and identifying the consequences and outcomes of losing control and consistently setting limits and applying consequences.

Guidance and Discipline in Infancy and Toddlerhood

What Are Guidance and Discipline?

Guidance and discipline are part of the process of socialization that leads children to be able to function in the larger social world in which they live. Guidance refers to what teachers do before a problem is present. Discipline is what teachers do after a problem is present. Guidance techniques are preventive in nature; they guide children to maintain self-control without actual intervention by the teacher. Although self-control develops during the early childhood years, children under the age of three still depend on adults to help them maintain control, particularly in situations in which other children are present.

Distraction—The younger the child is, the fewer times he should be expected to comply with verbal requests. For example, infants will frequently pick up food with their hands. Constant verbal reminders to "use your spoon" fail because adults are expecting the child to change his behavior to suit the situation.

A better strategy is to hand the child a spoon. This encourages the child to use a spoon and increases the chance that he might do so by putting the spoon into his hand. It modifies a situation to fit the child.

This guidance technique is called distraction. Distraction involves changing the child's focus from an activity that is unacceptable to one that is acceptable without directly confronting the inappropriate behavior. Distraction works very well with children under the age of three. Use distraction when there is no danger to the child. Distraction also can be used to prevent the escalation of a minor problem into a major one.

Redirection—Redirection is a preventive discipline strategy that requires parents and teachers to be particularly good observers of children. Redirection involves anticipating problems and intervening before they occur. The following are examples of redirection:

- Exchanging an inappropriate toy or activity (like eating dirt on the playground) for an appropriate one (like picking up rattles to shake)
- Quietly singing a song to redirect a child's focus from a separation event to what is going on in the classroom
- Putting something in a child's hand when she is fingering another child's hair (to prevent pulling hair)

Redirection only works when alert parents or teachers get to a situation before it erupts into a full-scale problem. Once children need more intervention, the opportunity to redirect is lost.

Ignoring as a Guidance Strategy—Ignoring inappropriate behavior is a discipline strategy that teachers often forget to use. The school day can be long, and some children exhibit behaviors that are irritating but not dangerous or really problematic.

Ignoring involves removing reinforcement for behavior. For example, infants and toddlers often dump the contents of manipulative toy containers on the floor or tabletops. An observant parent or teacher uses these experiences to model putting things back in the container and to encourage the child to help rather than confronting and trying to change the behavior directly. The strategy is designed to extinguish the inappropriate behavior by limiting the attention or reinforcement the initial behavior gets from adults or peers. Ignoring is not appropriate when children hurt each other or damage toys or the environment.

Positive Discipline

Positive discipline includes disciplinary practices that treat children with respect and dignity. The goal of discipline is to lead children increasingly toward self-discipline or self-control (Swift, 1995). Discipline focuses on teaching children, not just on changing their behavior. It focuses on what the child needs to continue to learn (self-control) rather than what adults need or

Myth or Misunderstanding
ACTIVE CHILDREN ARE PROBLEM CHILDREN.

As Latesha's mother picked her up yesterday, she asked Carl, the teacher, why those hyperactive children had to be in the same class as her child. She also said that everyone knows active children are problem children.

This myth persists throughout both the educational community and the society at large. Although children vary in their levels of activity from low to high as a part of their temperamental personalities, activity level in and of itself is rarely used as a diagnosis for hyperactivity disorders or the related disorders of attention deficits.

Research actually suggests the contrary. Children who are happy, active, boisterous, and aggressive during the toddler years are more successful in their social relationships than calmer, quieter children and than children who are withdrawn and submissive. These children make more attempts to play with others and are more successful in sustaining play. When exuberant children are able to modulate and control their expressions of exuberance, they are valued by others as playmates. Further, children who are highly active and relish novel stimuli are usually not hard to manage and have few, if any, problems with behavior later in life (Shonkoff & Phillips, 2000).

Cultural values influence which characteristics in children are perceived as appropriate, inappropriate, attractive, or unattractive. Teachers, like parents and other adults, need to be wary of labeling particular behavioral characteristics in children as good or bad. Accurate descriptions of characteristics with descriptive labels rather than value labels are important.

What should happen next? How should Carl respond to Latesha's mother? What other concerns may be on Latesha's mother's mind?

want the child to do. A wide variety of positive discipline strategies have been proposed that help children internalize the expectation of their parents, teachers, and the community. Two are discussed here.

Natural and Logical Consequences—Applying natural and logical consequences is a great tool for parents, teachers, and others to use to help children gain self-control. A natural or logical consequence is a consequence that develops from the situation. Consequences help children accept responsibility for their behavior and lead them to choose appropriate behaviors to avoid the consequences of inappropriate ones. This important teaching skill is not one of the easiest ones to learn. And it takes time, practice, and careful response. The following example (below right) illustrates the concept of logical consequences.

Setting Appropriate Limits—Adults have two reasons to set rules and limits. The first reason is to protect children and keep them safe—reason enough for a good set of limits. The second reason parents and teachers set limits is to help children grow toward self-control. Where does a teacher start to establish reasonable limits and rules for the classroom? Rules should have the following elements (Bredekamp & Copple, 1997; Marion, 1999):

Logical Consequences

An infant pulls on your earring as soon as she gets picked up. After you take her hand and remind her to leave the earring alone, the baby pulls again on the earring. You put the baby down, saying, "I can't hold you if you pull on my earring. It hurts!" The logical consequence of not listening to your request is to be put down where she cannot reach your earring.

Notice that there is no power struggle or disapproval in this situation. The consequences come from the situation and are responded to firmly but calmly. As a result, children learn to control their own behavior slowly over time as they are reminded of them both by your words and your actions.

- **First, rules and limits must be humane.** There is no place for rules that are punitive in nature and/or make children feel bad about themselves. Humane rules do not humiliate, embarrass, belittle, or degrade the child. Here is an example of an inhumane rule: "Babies who cry don't get to play." This kind of rule has no place in care and early education settings.
- **Second, limits should not be arbitrary.** Each rule should have several good reasons for existing. The following is an example of an arbitrary rule: "I won't pick you up unless you stop crying."
- **Third, rules should be overt, out in the open, not hidden.** Children, particularly very young children, cannot guess what the rules are. They need to be told, reminded, and reminded again. (Yes, even if it takes thousands of reminders!) For example, if crawling around with a bottle dangling from the child's mouth isn't allowed because he might

fall on his mouth and injure his gums or teeth, then babies need to be reminded about the rule when the adult hands them their bottles. Then, help babies settle into a place to drink them. To determine if rules are overt, simply watch children's behavior. If rules are clear, most children will be learning to follow them when given repeated supportive reminders by adults.

➧ **Fourth, limits should be clearly stated and enforceable.** Rules should refer to the expected behavior and be clear enough for children to know immediately when they have broken the rule. An example of clearly stated rule with a reference to behavior: "Leave the sand in the sandbox or I will have to ask you to play somewhere else." Rules that end in threats such as, "I'll never let you play in the sand again," are ineffective because they are unenforceable, and very young children don't yet have the self-control to resist putting the sand in their mouths.

➧ **Fifth, rules should be accompanied by reasons.** Research has shown that children who are given the reasons behind the rules are more likely to listen and follow the rules later without adult reminders. It is important to be brief and to the point. Children need one good reason for each rule, not three or four. Using the previously stated sand rule, an example might be: "Leave the sand in the sandbox. When you throw it, someone's eyes could be badly hurt."

➧ **Sixth, remember to update rules.** This is particularly important during the first three years when children are maturing and developing so quickly. As children mature, the limits imposed on them should be updated. As new skills emerge, limits should reflect those new skills. As children perfect new skills, for example crawling or taking first steps, update the rules. The teacher might say, "Hold my hand while we walk outside" to a new walker. Then, drop the rule when he becomes steadier on his feet.

➧ **Finally, rules and limits should be firmly enforced** (Brazelton & Greenspan, 2000). As children grow, they will test limits that adults set for them. If parents, teachers, and others use repressive controls like coercion, testing will continue. If adults do not set limits and do not enforce rules, children will heed no adult guidance. Firm, consistent responses to broken rules will result in children who learn to follow the rules set for them by their parents, teachers, and others.

The easiest way to enforce the set limits is to move the child to another setting when out-of-bounds behavior occurs. This technique uses logical consequences to help children remember the rules. If the child is throwing sand, take him by the hand and ask him to find another place to play until he can remember the sandbox rules. If the child is climbing without holding on, take the child off the climbing structure and ask him to find another place to play until he can remember the rules.

Infants and toddlers need frequent reminders of rules and support in complying with them. They are unable to do so just because you say so. Combine your rules with physical action (holding a child by the hand, moving a child to another place), and, later on, infants and toddlers will remember and comply.

Implications of Guidance and Discipline for Moving Around and Problem-solving

One implication of our knowledge of guidance and discipline is that adults need to know a variety of positive discipline strategies for supporting children in behaving appropriately in different situations. Adults need to be flexible in modifying their ideas for guidance and discipline to each child's needs and developmental level.

The idea of "appropriate" deserves careful consideration by teachers. Although children are capable of learning one set of expectations for one setting and another for a different setting, congruence between and across settings increases the likelihood that the child will be able to interpret and adopt the expectations others have for them.

Parents and teachers need to view guidance and discipline as a process that is internalized over time. When viewed as a process, adults are more able to see their guidance and discipline role as a positive, successful one. If compliance is the only goal, adults may feel frustrated and challenged by children at every turn.

Another implication of these ideas is that coming up with appropriate guidance and discipline strategies like redirection and logical consequences is a practiced skill. For most adults, these are skills that adults co-construct as they try out ways to work with different children. As with much of the developmental process, one size does not fit all.

Best Practices

Support Physical Development

Provide Opportunities to Go Outdoors

It is the mantra of the children—outside! One or two trips a day to the outdoors are simply not enough. They are always at the door—clamoring to go outside. This natural interest and tolerance for being outdoors is tied to

expanding skills as well as the autonomy children experience when they are outdoors acting independently as they climb, ride, scoot, crawl, or play.

Trips outdoors provide a change of pace, freedom from being so close to other children, and a constant source of interesting stimuli to look for, examine, and play with. Plan a minimum of least two trips to the outdoors daily, three or four are even more likely to please and stimulate children.

Infants and toddlers are climbers. As they become more interested in the world around them, children become fascinated with climbing, both to try out and practice new skills and to explore the environment from different perspectives. Both indoor and outdoor environments need a place where it is appropriate for children to climb safely and appropriately. Surround climbing structures with approved fall-zone materials.

Parents and teachers can use the appropriate climbing place to take children who are climbing on tables, chairs, and bookshelves, reminding them that the place to climb safely is on the climbing structure. This approach of replacing an inappropriate behavior with an appropriate one is important because it prevents the environment from becoming a place that restricts exploration. Although it will take many reminders, children will eventually climb on appropriate equipment more often than on inappropriate equipment.

Outdoors is where children can really perfect climbing skills. Climbing structures for children need to be sturdy and strong to be safe. Don't forget loose parts for children to arrange in a variety of ways—providing experiences with controlling the environment. Children like to rearrange boxes, blocks, and toys. They also like tents to create places to climb into, under, or around.

Balancing is another exciting skill to explore. Balance beams low to the ground will limit spills to tumbles instead of falls. Investigations of how to balance on a beam compared to balancing on a climber are examples of the way children create their own skill practice when the outdoor environment is conducive to exploration.

Push toys and tricycles to move through space are also popular. With paths through the playground, these important gross motor toys also contribute to dramatic play when paired with play props and supports from the classroom.

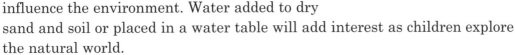

Digging in the sand or soil is another great outdoor activity for children. Not only are the materials stimulating and enjoyable, but also the ability to rearrange sand and soil make children feel powerful and able to influence the environment. Water added to dry sand and soil or placed in a water table will add interest as children explore the natural world.

When children are given ample opportunities to play outdoors, they can practice and experience many developing skills. The ability to impact and influence the environment by riding a tricycle, digging in the sand, climbing on a climber, moving objects around the playground, and playing alongside and with friends, communicates powerful messages of success about the things they can do. It is for this reason that many children love the outdoors—it is a "can do" place.

The fast-paced activity of the outdoors can also be overstimulating and overwhelming. Don't forget to have quiet places for children to cool off or calm down. A blanket in the shade serves nicely, and also can provide a place for children to spend some time with the teacher, refueling and recharging before heading back out to explore the world again.

Bring Indoor Materials Outside

When thinking of outdoor play, many adults think of traditional physical education activities. These, of course, are not appropriate for infants and toddlers. Instead, children need opportunities for sensory and physical stimulation. The very same activities that children need and enjoy inside are appropriate when they go outside. Try some of these:

▶ Books outside provide a special time for reading on a blanket.
▶ Small climbers and low platforms provide opportunities to stretch and move in the fresh air.

◗ Dramatic play takes on a new dimension when activities take place under a shady structure or tree.

◗ Messy art projects that may be difficult to do in the classroom are often easier to clean up outside.

Bringing indoor materials outside helps to provide rich learning experiences for children outdoors. With careful planning and thoughtful interactions, teachers support children as they develop socially, emotionally, physically, and intellectually when they bring indoor toys, materials, and activities outdoors.

Support Health and Wellness

Healthy Babies Should Sleep on Their Backs

Sudden Infant Death Syndrome (SIDS) strikes fear in the hearts of parents and teachers. SIDS is the sudden and unexplained death of an infant under one year of age. SIDS is also known as crib death. As frightening as it is, there are things that parents and teachers can do to make babies safer at home and at school.

New thinking about sleep positions directs us to put babies to sleep on their backs to reduce the risk of SIDS. Both the U.S. Public Health Department and the American Academy of Pediatrics support this recommendation. All children under the age of one should be put to sleep on their backs. Although this information is new and often different from what mothers have traditionally understood, it provides the latest idea about how to prevent crib death.

For more information about sleeping positions, call the "Back to Sleep" campaign at 1-800-505-CRIB (2742) or www.sids-network.org.

Never Shake a Baby

Shaken baby syndrome poses a risk for infants. Over 1,200 cases of injury from shaking are reported annually. Shaking may result in brain damage, blindness, seizures, paralysis, or even death. If you are getting angry, put the baby down in a safe place, and back away. Count to 10 and/or call someone for help. Resist the tendency to play roughly with babies. While the experience may be stimulating at first and start out fun, the risk of serious injury is too great to participate in this kind of activity. Never shake a baby! For more information on shaken baby syndrome go to www.dontshake.com.

Support Self-regulation and Control

There are many techniques that help children control impulses and gain self-control. Here are some strategies that parents, teachers, and others can use to support emerging self-control.

▶ Use physical proximity and touch. Staying close is the best tool to use to provide children with external support for regulating themselves. When you are close, children can use you as an ally and a resource to find solutions to problems and conflicts. When adults are close, they can support children with non-verbal cues (nods and smiles), verbal cues (such as suggestions of what might work), or physical support (like holding the child back a minute while he thinks about what might work or what he might try).

▶ Give children choices. Giving children limited choices is a valuable teaching tool. When children are given choices between acceptable alternatives, they feel independent and successful in solving their own problems. Examples include juice or milk, tennis shoes or sandals, socks or no socks.

▶ Cue children to their lapses in self-control. Many children don't realize they are losing control. Reminders from adults about the likely outcome of the chosen path may help them re-center and regain control. Examples include "I think you are getting upset" or "Take a deep breath and try again."

▶ Give children opportunities to comply on their own or with your help. Sometimes, children need adult support to accomplish their goals. At other times, they need reminders that they can do it, with support from an adult or on their own. Sometimes, just the reminder helps make it happen. For example, "Do you want to do it on your own or with my help?"

Use techniques to help children learn to tolerate frustration.

▶ Empower children to set their own limits in interactions with their friends. For example, when a child takes a toy away, empower the child who lost the toy to ask for the toy back if he isn't ready to give it up. If the child doesn't have the expressive language to ask for himself, do it for him. For example, "Did you want him to take your toy?" "Tell him, 'Mine!'"

⬧ Support waiting by helping children think of alternative activities to do while they wait for a turn or a chance to play. Sometimes tolerating frustration is just a matter of having an important adult recognize that it is difficult to wait. For example, "Let's make a puzzle while we wait."

Use techniques to help children learn to delay gratification.

⬧ Use non-verbal signs to indicate that children are capable of waiting. A hand (like a stop sign), touch (such as a hand on the shoulder), or reminders ("one more minute until your turn") are examples.

⬧ Provide hand-over-hand help for waiting. Hold the child's hands as you remind the child that he or she can wait. Touch communicates to children that you think that they can do it, and sometimes, they can!

⬧ Ask children for ideas about what would help them wait. They may have some good ideas that are worth trying. For example, ask, "Do you have any ideas that might help you wait."

Manage Oppositional Behavior

During the second year of life, children begin to develop a view of themselves as separate and independent from their parents and teachers. Because they have gained control over their bodies, they are now capable of moving away from the adults in their world and exploring and discovering things that were out of reach. Young children can take care of some of their own needs, like eating, drinking, and undressing by themselves. As they try these new skills and abilities and practice being separate and independent, children alternate between being pleased about these newfound abilities and being frightened and overwhelmed by them. Adults see this ambivalence as children handle one situation without problems and the next by falling apart and needing to reconnect with Mom or Dad or teacher before recovering. They also see it when children are tired, hungry, excited, or ill. In these situations, children vacillate between wanting to be independent and separate and wanting to be dependent, cared for, connected, and supported.

Although children are developing a sense of themselves as separate, they are just developing the ability to control their impulses, to wait, or to accurately predict the consequences of their independent behavior. Because of this, they get upset when adults help them control their impulses, ask them to wait, or apply consequences. The result is a kind of meltdown that is the precursor to temper tantrums. Opposition can be very intense and emotional. It can also be upsetting to children and to their parents and teachers.

Psychologists tell us that this is a universal and crucial stage for development that signals emotional growth. If this is the case, what can parents, teachers, and others do to assist toddlers in gaining the psychological and emotional skills they need to move on? Here are some ideas.

Stanley Greenspan and Nancy Greenspan, authors of **First Feelings: Milestones in the Emotional Development of Your Baby and Child** (1989), state that children need three things from parents and teachers to get through this stage. The first is emotional support. Children need emotional support for appropriate behavior and emotional support when they lose control. Adults can provide this by being understanding and empathetic. Empathy implies that you understand and accept the feelings that children have, even when these feelings are negative ones like anger or rage.

The second thing children need is many opportunities to be in control. When you think about it, children have little control over their lives. Parents decide when to get up, when to eat, what to wear, when to take a nap, what food goes on the plate, etc. Adults also decide when to go outside, whether or not particular toys and materials are available, and when to have snack.

Teachers need to work hard to plan things for children to control. Milk or juice? Two cookies or two crackers? Shoes off or on? Giving children meaningful control over these small decisions empowers them to practice controlling what is happening in a positive way. Often, having positive experiences with control will diminish the amount of oppositional or resistant behavior children have.

The third thing that children need is limits. Without limits, children are not sure of where the safe space for experimentation starts and stops. Because children are still unable to manage without the support and protection of adults, a lack of limits feels like being physically and emotionally abandoned. Limits on behavior are crucial to helping children feel competent about separation and independence.

On the other hand, much of what children do is "on the edge." Parents and teachers may feel that they are constantly limiting children's behavior. Good advice at this stage is to make a few non-negotiable rules and use plenty of redirection, distraction, and ignoring of behavior that isn't related to the few important rules. Otherwise, you will feel like you are correcting children all the time. Be realistic. Most oppositional behavior happens when teachers expect children to handle situations that are beyond their ability. Having realistic expectations for children is crucial.

Keep your own feelings under control. If teachers are angry, anxious, or stressed, children will know their behavior is working. Focus on the behavior rather than how you feel about it. This gives children information to use in deciding whether to be resistant or not. Comments such as, "Your feet make noise when you tap them on the floor" instead of "You are driving me crazy with that tapping noise" help children see the impact of their behavior on others.

State directions in positive terms. Tell children what you what them to do rather than saying "No!" or "Don't!" Remember that children are trying to feel competent and independent. No's and don'ts tell them that they have failed.

Changing Negative Statements into Positive Ones

Negative Statement	Positive Statement
Stop running!	Walk! March! Crawl!
Don't throw sand!	Leave the sand in the sandbox.
Don't touch.	Put your hands in your pockets.
Don't whine.	Use a regular voice.
Don't touch the markers.	Put that in my hand.

Be empathetic. Validate what children want even when you don't intend to give in. Children feel motivated to cooperate if they feel like you understood how they were feeling before the resistance sets in. "I know you don't want to stop playing—you're having such a good time." "I know you're upset. We'll go inside soon. It's hard to wait when you are ready to go." "It's upsetting when you have to wait for a turn. Let's cuddle while we wait." Statements like these tell children that you understand their emotions, even if you are not going to give in to the request that accompanies the emotions.

Change the environment. Where children live and play is a minefield for an independence-seeking toddler. Tables and chairs look very much like climbing structures. Doors are there to be opened. Things that cause an action or reaction are fascinating. Rather than deal with constant limit-setting, change the environment. Put safety latches on doors that need them.

Create a place to climb that is safe. Any effort parents and teachers put into this area will make the life at home or in the classroom more calm and less combative.

Finally, be patient. This is a developmental stage. It is part of the process of becoming a competent, independent three-year-old. Viewed this way, a child's stretch for independence and autonomy will give way to increasing skills and abilities and a view of the world that says, "I can do it!"

Handle Temper Tantrums

During infancy and toddlerhood, children struggle to develop a sense of themselves as separate. This process, called differentiation or individuation, actually starts at birth and lasts well into adulthood. It is the process of becoming a separate and successful individual. Adults must view this process as a positive one—even when it seems to present so many difficulties.

An important step in differentiation is related to control—who is in charge of my body, my emotions, my actions, and me? Early in children's lives, adults are in complete charge. As they age, children begin to take charge of some of their own behavior. Development drives children to experiment with when they can take charge and when they can't. This process of transferring some responsibility for control from adults to children usually results in children losing exactly what adults are striving to help them gain—control!

When children feel angry, frustrated, or helpless, they may kick, scream, and flop on the ground. Tantrums are a normal, natural, and inevitable part of growing up. However, that does not make them fun. Make a plan now for how you will handle it when children begin to tantrum.

The first step of the plan is preventive in nature. Help children have some control over their lives. Find ways they can practice and demonstrate emerging competence and emerging control. Start small. Maybe children can help you pick up the toys that are on the floor. Or they can choose between walking outside, crawling like a bug, or marching like a band. Offering choices gives children experience with

Myth or Misunderstanding
CHILDREN WHO TANTRUM WILL GROW UP TO BE PROBLEM CHILDREN.

It seems like every time a parent comes into Martha's classroom, one child or another is having a temper tantrum or recovering from one. Martha is beginning to think that her skills with toddlers may not be up to the challenge of handling tantrums. When children tantrum, Martha feels inadequate as a teacher because she is unable to prevent the trantrums before they start and unable to stop the tantrums once they begin. She is worried that the children who have frequent tantrums will grow up to be problem children later in life.

The myth here is that one behavior, evaluated in isolation, may "bend the twig" or permanently influence children down one path or another. Howes (2000) talks about interactive patterns emerging from frequent rituals and routines, building to provide children with particular feelings and behaviors that become a part of the child. This would indicate that it is not the temper tantrum, per se, that poses a problem for the child. Instead, it is the milieu of the relationship between the child and the adults that matters.

It is the feelings that adults have about tantrums that can be the most problematic. Tantrums can bring out different feelings for different people. Two types of responses are common. One is anger at the child for losing control. The other is feeling inadequate and not knowing what to do to make the tantrum stop. This is one of the times that adults can use their higher order thinking skills to help both themselves and the child to recover from tantrumming. The child's behavior is a result of losing control over a collection of physiological functions—an emotional meltdown—not behavior that is planned or organized. Typically, a tantrum has a course that must be followed to resolve itself. Look at the strategies on pages 285 and 287 for ideas about how to do this.

Prolonged and persistent tantrums can be a problem. Children whose tantrums don't begin to decrease near the third birthday or who don't make progress in learning to mediate and control emotional outbursts may need additional support from helping professionals.

Martha's feelings are not unusual, but they may stand in the way of her helping tantrumming children move on developmentally. Reflect on why Martha feels the way she does, and make some suggestions about what she should do to help children through this normal, yet challenging stage.

making decisions and having them turn out successfully. This experience is crucial in helping children make good choices about whether or not to throw a temper tantrum.

Be sure to reward appropriate progress in taking charge. When a child shows competence in climbing on the climber, eating with a spoon or fork, or pulling on his own socks, reward these early attempts at independence and self-control with hugs, kisses, and encouragement.

Pick a place for children to be out of control. The tantrum place needs to be the place adults will take children for tantrums. Make sure the tantrum place is safe. Then, plan to take children to the special tantrum place when they are out of control. Say calmly to the tantrumming child that he is free to stay out of control as long as he likes—part of this stage is learning that you can take charge of your own behavior. Choosing whether to scream for 1 minute or 10 minutes is certainly taking charge of your own behavior!

Follow through with your response to tantrums. If children get attention from tantrums, tantrums will last much longer than if they have no audience. Removing the audience—yourself and the other children—quickly and calmly when tantrums occur is the best thing you can do to lessen the frequency of tantrumming. Go to another section of the room, far from the tantrumming child. Stay in touch visually, but focus on what is happening with the other children. Tell children who might be interested or fascinated by the tantrum what is going on and that the tantrumming child can rejoin the group when he is finished.

When a tantrum is over, it's over. Accept the child back into family or classroom life as if nothing has happened. Avoid the temptation to lecture or threaten after a tantrum is over. A casual statement such as, "I'm glad you're back under control" is all that is needed. As frustrating as tantrums can be for parents and teachers, a calm, confident approach will go a long way toward helping children grow through the tantrumming stage.

Although temper tantrums are a developmentally normal step in becoming a competent, capable child, they usually peak during the end of the second year of life. Intense and prolonged tantrums may indicate that a child is having emotional difficulty. When tantrums continue to intensify when the suggested strategies are used, teachers need to discuss their concerns with parents and seek support in helping the child move on emotionally and developmentally.

Myth or Misunderstanding
TEACHERS SHOULD NEVER IGNORE
A CHILD'S BEHAVIOR.

As Mrs. Onken, Alessandro's mother, walks in the door to the classroom, she notices that Elisabetta is laying on the floor screaming and crying. She rushes over to her and asks her what is wrong. Elisabetta kicks Mrs. Onken and continues to scream and cry. The teacher, Brooke, goes over to Mrs. Onken and asks to talk with her near the classroom door. Brooke explains to Mrs. Onken that Elisabetta is having a temper tantrum because she wanted Michael's blanket for her baby doll. Michael's blanket is his security item, and as such is protected by the teachers from being used as a toy by others without his permission. When Brooke helped Elisabetta ask Michael if she could play with his blanket, he said "no." As a result, Elisabetta fell apart and the tantrum began. For now, Brooke is ignoring Elisabetta's tantrum because she is too upset. She will process the situation with Elisabetta when she is calm.

Mrs. Onken tells Brooke that she thinks ignoring bad behavior will only make it worse. She tells Brooke to always stop her child, Alessandro, from acting that way. Because Brooke is in the middle of helping Elisabetta and the other children in the classroom, she tells Mrs. Onken that they can discuss this further at a time when she is not so busy and schedules a time to call Mrs. Onken the following day.

The misunderstanding here is that inappropriate behavior must be controlled at all cost—even in the midst of a tantrum. Brooke is showing her knowledge of emotional development by giving Elisabetta a safe place to have an emotional outburst, protecting Michael's security blanket from being used as a toy, and by staying near Elisabetta while she is experiencing the strong emotions. She is not really "ignoring" Elisabetta. She is helping her learn to accept "no" from another child.

This misunderstanding highlights the different points of view of the teacher—who looks at the children as a group of individuals, and the parents—who look at the classroom as their child's classroom. Differences in points of view influence how adults see various situations.

What should happen next? How could Brooke have prevented this kind of misunderstanding with Mrs. Onken? What information does Mrs. Onken need to better understand the school's approach to behavior management and discipline and guidance?

Guide Children to Behave Appropriately

Guidance precedes discipline—and supports children's early efforts at self-regulation and the internalization of self-control. Guidance often comes from room arrangements, from being nearby, and from routines.

Room Arrangement Guides Behavior

The way environments are arranged communicates many messages to children. Classroom arrangement gives children numerous clues about what to do and how to behave. When planned and arranged effectively, classrooms foster self-control and adaptive behavior.

Arrangements for infants and toddlers need to allow for room to play alone, alongside, and with other children, leaving little open, non-functional space. The arrangement should clearly communicate the physical limits of play spaces, regulate children's behavior in each space, and control the use of materials within the space—all without direct intervention from an adult.

For example, if classroom shelves are arranged in such a way that children can identify what toys go in which containers, children will be more likely to put the toys in the containers and the containers back on the shelf. Conversely, if the middle of the classroom has plenty of room to run around, children will use the space to run around, even if you don't want them to do so.

To evaluate whether your classroom arrangement communicates effectively to children, note the location of where children are having trouble "reading" the cues of the environment about what to do in that area. Reassess the arrangement of the physical space in the classroom based on what you discover.

Establish a Few Clear Limits and Enforce Them

Brazelton and Greenspan (2000) consider limit setting and the structure that results from clear limits as one of the irreducible needs of children—what they absolutely must have to grow, learn, and flourish. Children want to please the important people in their attachment networks. Thus, adults, in the context of the meaningful relationships, can put in place a few clear rules to support children's compliance with expectations.

Very young children need just a few rules, combined with plenty of nurturing and supportive guidance, to begin the process of internalizing self-control. But the rules have to be clear and enforceable, and enforced consistently by the adults in the child's world.

When rules are applied intermittently, or when expectations of adults vary or vacillate, children lose touch with a "psychologically safe" place to be. Only when the rules and expectations of adults are clearly defined and consistently applied can children feel safe and secure enough to continue the important exploratory work of childhood.

Respond Consistently to Individual Limit Testing

Children test the limits that adults have for them. When they do, they find out if the rules do or don't apply to each and every situation. Some children can test limits only once and then are able to remember or internalize and follow the rule. Most, however, need repeated reminders and frequent run-ins with limits to make progress in self-regulation of behavior.

Individual children need consistent responses to their own limit testing experiences. When treated individually, adults in their lives can adjust their responses to limit testing to fit the child and the situation.

Invest in a Variety of Teaching Roles

The Teacher as Supporter

The teacher's role in supporting the developmental tasks of moving around and problem-solving is a broad and complex one. She or he must support exploration of the environment, encourage social interaction between children, and support emerging self-regulatory skills. To be effective, this support must be overt, consistent, and regular.

The teacher is also a supporter of safe risk-taking behavior. In order to grow and learn, children must feel safe and secure

Teaching Roles

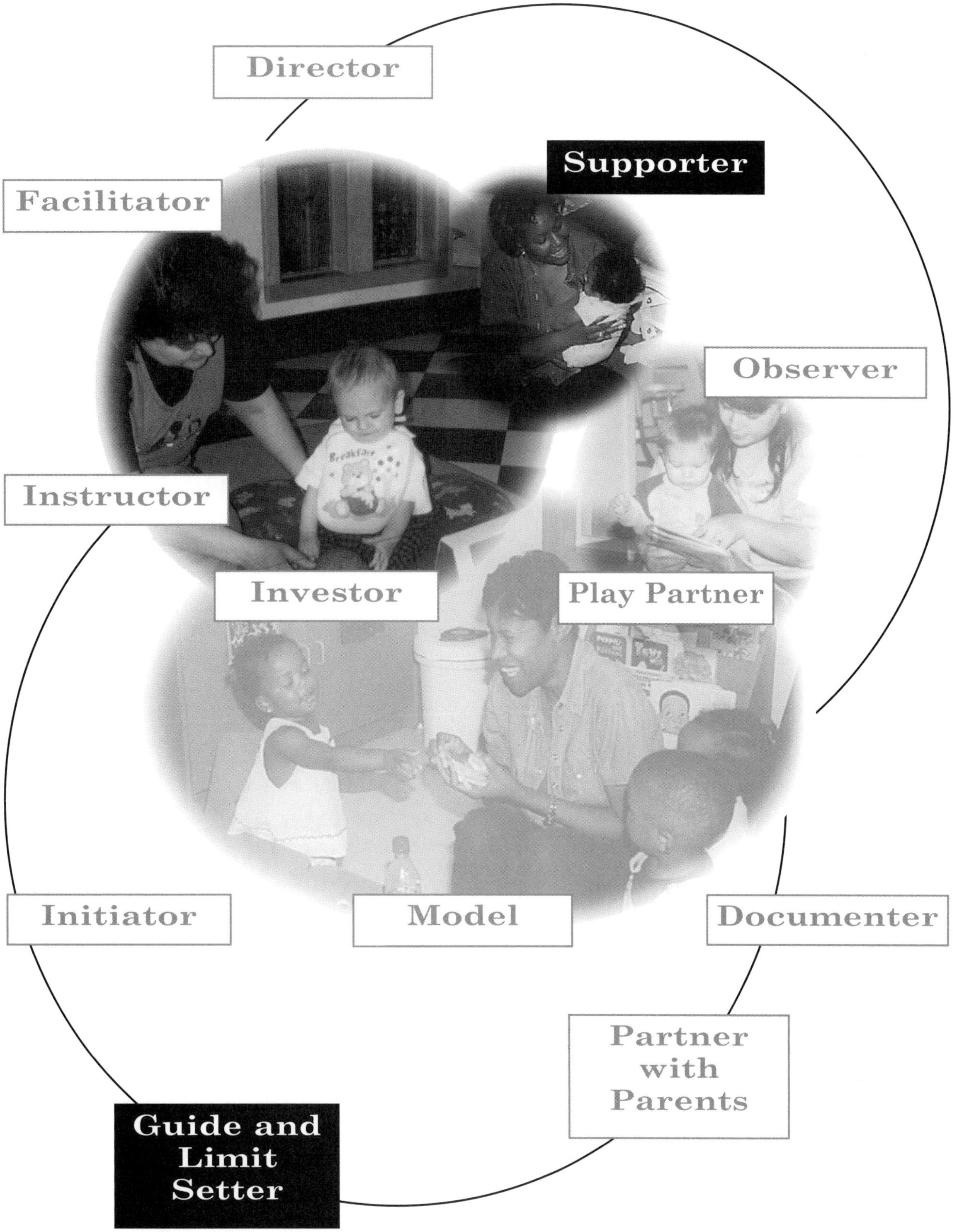

Director

Facilitator

Supporter

Observer

Instructor

Investor

Play Partner

Initiator

Model

Documenter

Partner
with
Parents

**Guide and
Limit
Setter**

enough to try new skills and test their own abilities. Supporting this kind of behavior gives children the feeling that they can try novel experiences and succeed in their chosen activities. Helping children differentiate between risk-taking behaviors is another supportive role. Differentiating between activities that are safe and likely to result in interesting outcomes and those that are dangerous and likely to result in harm to oneself or to others is a learning process for children that needs the teacher's support.

Supporting self-regulatory behaviors is also an important teaching role. Knowing when a verbal reminder is enough or when physical intervention must accompany verbal reminders is a key role for teachers. Children need a great deal of support in practicing the precursor skills to self-regulation including controlling emotions, focusing attention, and controlling behaviors and the self-control skills of delaying gratification, tolerating frustration, and controlling impulses. These supports come from a wide variety of appropriate and interesting activities and experiences as well as directly from the teacher's close and constant physical presence.

The Teacher as Guide and Limit Setter

The role of guide is an important one for infant and toddler teachers. Guiding behavior is much different than directing it. Guiding behavior is a positive discipline strategy designed to improve self-regulation and self-control. Teachers serve as guides when they suggest play ideas for children to enable them to play successfully together, suggest alternatives to strategies that aren't working, and clearly support problem-solving as the strategy for resolving conflicts and disagreements.

The role of limit setter involves making rules and setting limits. These two roles—guiding and limiting—go hand in hand. As a guide, teachers help children understand what is expected. As a limit setter, teachers help children understand when their behavior is not consistent with expectations for behavior. Both of these roles support children's growth.

In the guidance and discipline role, teachers decide when to apply rules and limits and to whom. Because each child is an individual, teachers in this role are constantly modifying their techniques for individual children and individual situations. This dynamic role creates challenges and opportunities to turn almost any interaction into one that helps children acquire more sophisticated self-regulation skills.

Child Abuse Prevention

The four types of child abuse are physical abuse, sexual abuse, emotional abuse, and neglect (Florida Committee for the Prevention of Child Abuse, 1994). Each year over 2,000 children die of physical abuse. Some of the common examples are hitting, burning, biting, and shaking. Often physical abuse is the result of a parent's anger.

Sexual abuse occurs when an adult uses a child under the age of 18 years old for sexual gratification. Examples include indecent exposure, sexual penetration, fondling (by or of the adult), and the use of a child for pornography or prostitution. One out of six boys and one out of four girls are sexually abused by the age of 18 (Florida Committee for the Prevention of Child Abuse, 1994).

Emotional abuse can cause a child to be withdrawn and have very low self-esteem. Children can be emotionally abused by threats, withholding of love and affection, name calling, and humiliation.

Neglect happens when a parent refuses to provide a child with adequate food, clothing, shelter, supervision, nurturing, or health care. A neglected child may be dirty, hungry, or sick. Neglected children may be left alone or in the care of brothers and/or sisters.

Risk factors that may lead to the abuse of children include a previous cycle of abuse, drugs and alcohol, financial problems, marital problems, lack of parental experience and knowledge, immaturity, and social isolation. Parents who were abused are six times as likely to abuse their children than parents who did not experience abuse (Florida Committee for the Prevention of Child Abuse, 1994).

Child Abuse Reporting

The safety and well-being of the children in care and early education programs are a foremost concern and, therefore, child abuse reporting laws must be taken very seriously. Teachers are required by federal law and the Code of Ethical Conduct and Statement of Commitment (Feeney & Kipnis, 1999) to report any suspected child abuse, regardless of who is suspect or where the abuse may have occurred. Judgment of actual abuse is not made by the teacher or the school principal or director. It is the responsibility of the appropriate agency to investigate the allegation and make a judgment. The role of parents and teachers is to report any conditions that indicate the possibility of suspected abuse or neglect.

Documentation of Suspected Abuse

The best way to assure thorough and accurate documentation of suspected child abuse is to have a system for anecdotally recording data on each child in the classroom on a regular basis. Record any and all information related to the child as it comes to a teacher's attention.

Jason arrived at the center at 7:55 a.m. When he took off his hat, a silver-dollar size bump and bruise were noticed above his right eye. His mother reported that he had walked into the corner of the dining room table over the weekend.

For example, if a child arrives in your classroom with a scratch or bump on his cheek, a quick note of the date, time, and description of the scratch is recorded. Facts, not opinions are recorded. Note the example on the left.

This account is accurate and factual and is also non-threatening. It indicates when and where the injury was noticed and establishes the explanation given for the injury. It does not indicate that Jason is abused or neglected.

If Jason had repeated or more serious injuries or seemed to behave in a considerably different way after the injury, a report to the appropriate agency may be necessary. Or, if the teacher noticed a pattern in the injuries that Jason received, reporting might be considered. The better the records, the more likely the child's best interest will be served.

Applying Theory and Best Practices

A large part of professional practice in the field of care and early education is the synthesizing of knowledge, research, and best practices into teaching actions and strategies. A goal of **Innovations: Infant and Toddler Development** is to help teachers apply theory, research, and best practices to real life situations and behaviors in the infant and toddler classroom. Let's take a look at a common behavior to see if the knowledge we have gained, the research we have reviewed, and/or the best practices we have explored give any suggestions of how the behavior might be handled by teachers in the classroom.

Moving around and problem-solving are tasks that encompass almost every domain of development, particularly the physical and intellectual domains. So, let's begin exploring the integration of knowledge, research, and best practices by considering the implications of the topics covered in this chapter for supporting children in learning to toilet.

Possibilities from Brain Development for Learning to Toilet

Every time we consider the possibilities from our knowledge and theories of infant and toddler development, investing in relationships is mentioned. For toileting, the influence of the quality and mutuality of the relationship is evident. Children who are learning to toilet are also individuating—becoming independent and self-sufficient. The drive to do so creates conflicts as children strive to separate from their caregivers. Caregivers who have developed strong, mutual, and enduring relationships with children are able to bridge this important transition, supporting the child in controlling bowel and bladder as an independent activity. Within positive, balanced relationships, caregivers are able to turn control of toileting over to the child.

Knowledge of brain development leads teachers to provide both experience-expectant opportunities (when there seems to be an internal drive to learn) and experience-dependent (when there seems to be an interest in learning) opportunities to learn to toilet. Some toileting skills are the direct result of experience. For example, the ability to pull underwear up and down is necessary before children can toilet successfully. So, providing opportunities and encouragement for pulling pants and underwear up and down is an experience-dependent activity. By comparison, an experience-expectant opportunity might be getting in touch with what a full bladder or bowel feels like so the child is ready when the internal cues become evident. Getting on the toilet and off the toilet often, with many unsuccessful attempts, helps prepare the child to fully anticipate that it is time to go to the toilet. Successful interpretation of the body's cues ("oops, I didn't need to go") leads to a better chance of successfully interpreting being "ready to toilet."

The most significant possibility offered by brain theory is to wait until the child is ready. Ideas about the brain's plasticity means there is plenty of time. Toileting is a significant developmental skill that is tied to all domains of development. But the window of opportunity is wide and closes slowly. Unless there is a physiological problem, most children learn to toilet successfully by end of the third year. Patience is more appropriate than panic.

There are many possibilities for teachers and parents to feel like they are indeed supporting and encouraging toileting. Adults can monitor the child's stage of toileting and match opportunities and experiences to the appropriate stage. By recognizing and validating progress toward successful toileting, teachers and parents are encouraging continued motivation.

Possibilities from Physical Development for Learning to Toilet

The cephalacaudal/proximodistal trend predicts toileting—the muscles that need controlling are far away from the top and the center of the body and come under voluntary control last. Keeping this in mind will insure that possibilities aren't pushed too soon or missed completely.

Provide many opportunities to practice supporting skills such as pulling diapers or pants up and down. Practice at the child's direction—using appropriate play themes and props. Don't forget the possibilities of modeling and imitation. Children often want to "see" what is going on in the bathroom as others learn to toilet. This creates possibilities to match cultural expectations at school with those at home, eliminating conflict between the parental approaches and the school's approaches. Such discussions of approaches need to precede children's readiness so that conflicts don't arise.

An even more important possibility is to accept individual differences in timing. Children will exhibit individual timing of each stage of toileting as well as their readiness and interest in beginning the process of learning to toilet. These timing differences indicate developmental uniqueness, not deviance and should be recognized and accepted. Encouraging parents to view their child's individual pace and sequence of development instead of comparing their child to other children is another important possibility.

Possibilities from Self-regulation and Self-control for Learning to Toilet

The possibility of matching the pace of toilet training to internalization of control offers a good framework for partnering with parents and the child. Children who are just beginning to have success with self-regulatory skills will not be ready to toilet independently. They will, however, be ready for curricula aimed at experiences in the early stages of toileting like toilet play and toilet practice. Sensitive adults recognize these early stages and allow the progress through them to interface with progress in self-regulatory skill acquisition.

Possibilities from Guidance and Discipline for Learning to Toilet

Several theorists indicate concern about the type and intensity of support, guidance, and discipline used by parents about toileting. Erickson (1963) views punitive or coercive techniques as undermining the child's sense of self and threatening feelings of autonomy. Possibilities exist, instead, to use logical consequences to teach toileting skills. For example, giving children opportunities to help with the clean-up process after accidents; change their own clothes; assist with changing wet sheets or soiled clothing, and so on, can be growth producing and developmentally appropriate guidance strategies if used within the framework of a warm, supportive, and reciprocal relationship.

Integrating Theory and Best Practices into Curriculum

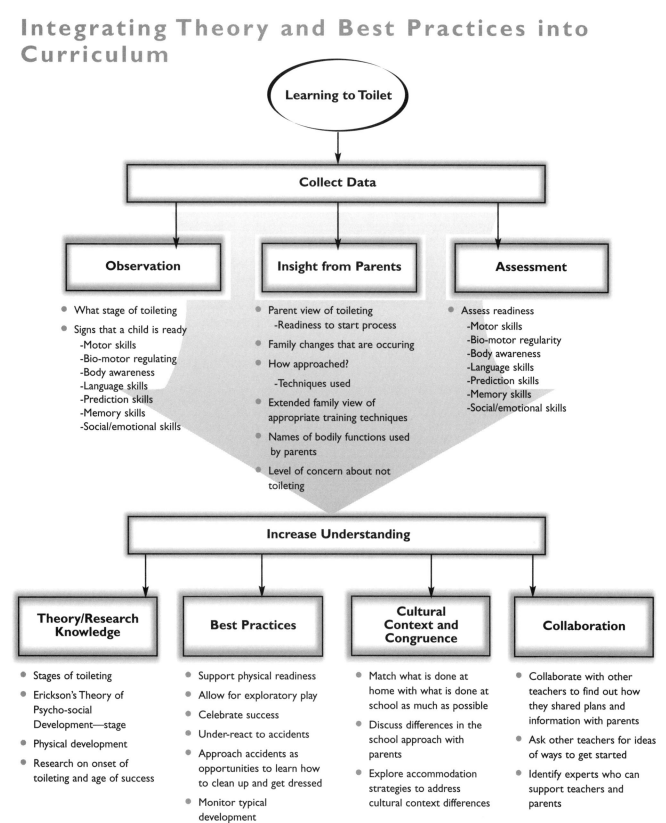

Learning to Toilet

Collect Data

Observation
- What stage of toileting
- Signs that a child is ready
  - Motor skills
  - Bio-motor regulating
  - Body awareness
  - Language skills
  - Prediction skills
  - Memory skills
  - Social/emotional skills

Insight from Parents
- Parent view of toileting
  - Readiness to start process
- Family changes that are occuring
- How approached?
  - Techniques used
- Extended family view of appropriate training techniques
- Names of bodily functions used by parents
- Level of concern about not toileting

Assessment
- Assess readiness
  - Motor skills
  - Bio-motor regularity
  - Body awareness
  - Language skills
  - Prediction skills
  - Memory skills
  - Social/emotional skills

Increase Understanding

Theory/Research Knowledge
- Stages of toileting
- Erickson's Theory of Psycho-social Development—stage
- Physical development
- Research on onset of toileting and age of success

Best Practices
- Support physical readiness
- Allow for exploratory play
- Celebrate success
- Under-react to accidents
- Approach accidents as opportunities to learn how to clean up and get dressed
- Monitor typical development

Cultural Context and Congruence
- Match what is done at home with what is done at school as much as possible
- Discuss differences in the school approach with parents
- Explore accommodation strategies to address cultural context differences

Collaboration
- Collaborate with other teachers to find out how they shared plans and information with parents
- Ask other teachers for ideas of ways to get started
- Identify experts who can support teachers and parents

Possibilities

Parent Possibilities

Teacher-Initiated

Hand out parent postcards on toileting stages
Focus on successes

Parent Participation

Plan meeting with parents to have each share what works, what doesn't, frustrations, successes, and to talk about stages of toileting.
Multiple changes of clothing (including socks and shoes)

Innovations in Environments

Add books about toileting to library
Add bathroom prop box
Check to make sure bathroom environment accommodates children's skills (step stools, easy-to-use soap dispensers) or add these items
Add fine motor activities and materials

Observation/Assessment Possibilities

Observe for signs that child is ready for toileting
Keep track of changes in readiness—update observations
Log frequency of trying/practicing to see who might be ready for next stage
Do checklist of toilet readiness skills
Monitor normative development
Update expectations as changes are made

Interactive Experiences

Use encouragement ("You did it!") after successes, not rewards.
Ask child if he needs to go to the bathroom.
Cue children as adults toilet. "Mrs. Lane is using the toilet." Or, "I'll be back. My body tells me I have to use the toilet."
Develop a schedule of reminders to "check your body" after snack, after lunch, before nap, after nap, etc.
Build reminders into daily schedule for children who are ready.
Focus on progress.
Practice precursor skills.
Monitor environmental factors that influence development.

Plan

Web

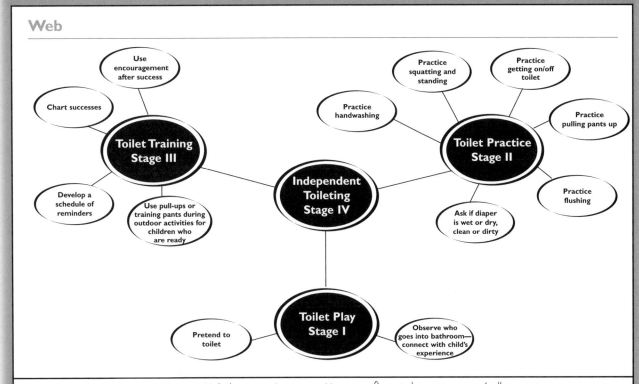

Dramatic Possibilities Add babies in diapers, add props from toileting to area (pull ups, training pants, toilet paper rolls, "pretend" toilet chair, diaper bags)

Art/Sensory Possibilities Bathe dolls

Curiosity Possibilities Add memory games, prediction activities

Music Possibilities Dance to the bathroom and from the bathroom

Movement Possibilities Practice squatting, standing squatting, practice pulling down pants and pulling them up.

Literacy Possibilities Make books of bathroom components with picture file pictures

Outdoor Possibilities Change into training pants before going outside in warm weather

Project Possibilities Chart successes for children in Stage III

Books	Picture File Pictures/Vocabulary
Everybody Poops!, by Taro Gomi I'm Grown Up, by Margaret Miller My Potty Book, by Mary Atkinson Getting Dressed, by Ben Argueta	Children in bathrooms, toilets, sinks, faucets, soap dispensers, toilet paper, potty chairs Give appropriate names to body functions

Rhymes & Fingerplays	Music/Songs	Prop Boxes
Make up toileting rhymes	Look for children's songs about toileting	Toileting prop box

Summary

The infants' and toddlers' brains can be described as amazing, flexible, capable, adapting, vulnerable, complex, and changeable. As young children are developing their fine and gross motor skills, they are developing their brains. As young children interact with adults, each other, and their environment, they are also developing their brains.

Brain cells (neurons) are produced during the prenatal stage to begin the process of brain development by connecting to other brain cells. The axon of one brain cell connects with a dendrite of another neuron. Neural pathways are activated by interactive experiences.

During infancy and toddlerhood, neural pathways are strengthened by repeated experiences and good teaching. Pathways are pruned and eliminated if unused or underused, or if the child is stressed by environmental factors. As coordination between the connections improves, neural pathways become more efficient and capable of handling increased communication.

Environmental conditions (including nourishment, routine care, nurturing interactions, stimulating surroundings, and stimulation experiences from objects in the environment) affect brain growth in a positive way. Other environmental conditions (including maternal depression, trauma, abuse, social deprivation, drug, alcohol, or nicotine use, and institutionalization) are potentially negative.

Additionally, normal maturation affects brain development. Genetics prepares the brain to receive certain kinds of stimulation that allow for further organization and development of the brain. Secure attachments affect brain growth. Intimate, enduring, reciprocal interactions between infants and adults in their attachment network are crucial to brain growth. Sensitive periods (also called critical periods and timing effects) are periods when specific structures of the brain are most susceptible to experience.

Children's brains work best in the context of healthy relationships. Warm, consistent, responsive care and interactions make brain growth and development emerge as nature planned. Talking to and with children is crucial to the future development of language.

Physical development follows predictable developmental patterns. During infancy, children develop their bodies from the top down and from the center out. Both of these trends are affected by all of the components of uniqueness and the opportunities available for experience and practice of emerging skills.

Early development begins the process of learning to manage and depend on oneself. Further, the process of learning self-regulation is greatly influenced by the relationship the child has with the adults in his attachment network. By toddlerhood, children are usually exerting self-control over some of their behaviors some of the time.

Guidance refers to what adults do before a problem is present. Discipline is what teachers do after a problem is present. Adults can help children maintain control by distraction, redirection, ignoring, teaching social problem-solving, and patterning and modeling. Teachers can enhance a child's self-esteem through encouragement instead of through praise.

Best practices concerning moving around and problem-solving include providing opportunities to climb and go outside, putting babies to sleep on their backs, never shaking a baby, supporting self-regulation and control, guiding behavior through environment and clear limits, and protecting children from child abuse.

Questions and Activities

1. Using a specific child, give examples of the cephalacaudal/proximodistal trend.
2. If a classroom consistently has children all together in one group, what critical issues concerning classroom environment would you consider?
3. List five ways you can enhance brain development for infants and toddlers.
4. Tell how you would explain to the mother of an 10-month-old boy that you think he is not yet ready to be toilet trained.

References

Albrecht, K.M. & M. Ward. (1989). Growing pains. **Pre-K Today,** 36, 54-55.

Bailey, C.B., J.T. Bruer, F.J. Symons, & J.W. Lichtman. (2001). **Critical thinking about critical periods.** Baltimore, MD: Brookes Publishing.

Brazelton, T.B. & S.I. Greenspan. (2000). **The irreducible needs of children: What every child must have to grow, learn, and flourish.** Cambridge, MA: Perseus.

Bredekamp, S. & C. Copple. (1997). **Developmentally appropriate practice in early childhood programs.** Washington, DC: NAEYC.

Brunson, M.B. (2000). Recognizing and supporting the development of self-regulation in young children. **Young Children,** 55(2), 32-37.

Erickson, E.H. (1963). Childhood and society. New York: Workman.

Florida Committee for the Prevention of Child Abuse, (1994). **The abc's of child safety awareness: A handbook for providing a safe, nurturing environment for children.** Gainesville, FL: Dial Publishing.

Feeney, S. & K. Kipnis. (1999). **Code of ethical conduct and statement of commitment.** Washington, DC: NAEYC.

Greenspan, S. (1997). **Growth of the mind and the endangered origins of intelligence.** Cambridge, MA: Perseus Books

Greenspan, S. & N.T. Greenspan. (1989). **First feelings: Milestones in the emotional development of your baby and child.** New York: Penguin.

Howes, C. (2000). Social development, family, and attachment relationships of infant and toddlers. In D. Cryer & T. Harms (Eds.), **Infants and toddlers in out of home care** (87-113). Baltimore, MD: Brookes Publishing.

Marion, M. (1999). **Guidance of young children.** Upper Saddle River, NJ: Merrill.

McCall, R.B. & B.W. Plemons. (2001). The concept of critical periods and their implications for early childhood services. In D.B Bailey, J.T. Bruer, F.J. Symons, & J.W. Lichtman (Eds.) **Critical thinking about critical periods.** (267-287). Baltimore, MD: Brookes Publishing.

Mooney, C.G. (2000). **Theories of childhood: An introduction to Dewey, Montessori, Erickson, Piaget, and Vygotsky.** St. Paul, MI: Redleaf Press.

Piaget, J. (1977). **The origins of intelligence in children.** New York: International Universities Press.

Shonkoff, J.P. &, D.A. Phillips (Eds.). (2000). **From neurons to neighborhoods: The science of early childhood development.** Washington, DC: National Academy Press.

Shore, R. (1997). **Rethinking the Brain: New insights into early development.** New York: Families and Work.

Swift, M. (1995). **Discipline for life.** Grapevine, TX: Stairway Education Programs.

Vaughan, B.E., C.B. Kopp, & J.B. Krakow. (1984). The emergence and consolidation of self-control from eighteen-thirty months of age: Normative trends and individual differences. **Child Development,** 55:900-1004.

Vygotsky, L. (1978). **Mind in society: The development of higher psychological processes.** Cambridge, MA: Harvard University Press.

Glossary

Adult-assisted Self-control—The second stage of the process of gaining independent self-control in which children can maintain self-control with the help of adults or external support.

Axon—A nerve fiber that conducts impulses away from the body of the nerve cell.

Cephalacaudal Trend—The tendency for development in general, and motor development specifically, to proceed from the head to the foot.

Child Abuse—Physical abuse, sexual abuse, emotional abuse, and neglect.

Dendrite—The neural branch that receives the signal from the axon of another cell and carries it to the body of another nerve cell.

Differentiation—A child's struggle to develop a sense of himself as separate. Also called individuation, it is the process of becoming a separate and successful individual.

Discipline—Teaching strategies that lead children toward self-control rather than just changing behavior.

Distraction—A guidance technique that changes a child's focus from an activity that is unacceptable to one that is acceptable without directly confronting the inappropriate behavior.

External Control—The first stage in the process of helping children gain independent self-control where adults are fully responsible for supporting the child in staying under control.

Fall Zone—The area around climbing equipment both inside and outside where children can fall without injury.

Fine Motor—Having to do with the small muscles in the body.

Gross Motor—Having to do with the large muscles in the body.

Guidance—A discipline technique adults use before a problem is present that guides children to maintain self-control without actual intervention.

Independent Self-control—The last stage in the process of gaining self-control, in which external expectations are internalized by the child and can be followed without direct support from adults.

Individuation—A child's struggle to develop a sense of himself as separate during infancy and toddlerhood.

Infancy—The time from birth to 18 months of age.

Internalization of Self-control—The process of gaining self-control that begins outside the child and then moves inside the child through the process of internalization.

Logical Consequence—A positive discipline strategy used to help children remember the rules.

Modeling—Showing a child what you want them to do by doing it.

Neural Pathways—The route that a signal takes as it goes from nerve cell to nerve cell to nerve cell.

Normative Assessment—Assessment that provides information on how a child is developing in relation to a larger group of same age children.

Patterning—Hand-over-hand repeating of appropriate behaviors.

Precursor Skills—The tendencies or sub-skills that develop in advance of skill acquisition and indicate advances in development and progress toward the desired skill.

Prenatal—Before birth.

Proximodistal Trend—The tendency for development in general, and motor development specifically, to proceed from the center to the periphery of the body.

Synapse—The space in the brain where the signals go from the axon to the dendrite.

Synaptogenesis—The process of connecting neurons together into neural networks or pathways via synapses.

Temper Tantrums—Loss of physical and emotional control in toddlers.

Toddlerhood—The time from 18 months of age to 36 months of age.

CHAPTER 7

Expressing Feelings with Parents, Teachers, and Friends

Developmental Tasks: Expressing Feelings with Parents, Teachers, and Friends

Children begin expressing their feelings and emotions right after birth. They communicate clearly whether or not an experience is a pleasant one. Infants and toddlers often look like pure emotions when they screw up their faces and begin to cry. As they grow, children begin the process of regulating their emotions, continuing to feel emotions with the same intensity but responding differently to separate emotions and regulating the actions that accompany them.

Learning to express oneself and to identify and understand emotions is a crucial part of growing up. For infants and toddlers, this process is one that changes in the context of other developmental changes.

New interest in the effects of emotions on the developing brain has put the emotional development of infants and toddlers in the spotlight. During the first three years of life, the brain grows to about two–thirds of its full adult size and evolves in complexity at a greater rate than it ever will again. Key learning takes place in several important developmental domains, including emotional learning. Pediatricians, educators, and other specialists emphasize the importance of supporting emotional learning in infants and toddlers right from the start. In addition, experts think emotional development is just as important as physical, cognitive, and language development.

An observable part of childhood is the sincerity and intensity of expressed feelings. Although children begin expressing their feelings and emotions right after birth, it is during the period from 18–36 months that toddlers share the way they are feeling with everyone—clearly indicating whether they are happy, sad, angry, hungry, tired, mad, irritated, or just plain frustrated. Toddlers have learned to differentiate one feeling from another as well as to pair those feelings with physical expressions that convey the differences between one emotion and another. They are beginning the process of managing their emotions.

Chapter 7 focuses on the knowledge that is important for teachers to understand related to the tasks of expressing feelings with parents, teachers, and friends. The best practices that emerge from this knowledge are then discussed. The chapter ends by applying this new understanding of theory and practice to a common behavioral challenge.

Knowledge

Emotional Development

Throughout ***Innovations: Infant and Toddler Development***, the value of enduring, close, reciprocal, and synchronous relationships has been viewed as crucial to early development, not just of emotional development, but also physical, social, and intellectual development. How do these kinds of relationships come about? What can parents and teachers do to develop and maintain relationships that matter for children's continued development?

Relationships and Emotional Development

The nature of interactional experience is responsible for shaping how relationships are co-constructed by children and adults. If the nature of the relationship has certain positive characteristics, it is likely to lead to secure base behaviors that indicate the presence of positive attachment relationships. If the nature of the relationship has certain negative characteristics, the relationship may lead to child behaviors that indicate a disruption in the relationship-forming process.

There is agreement in the field of child development about the characteristics of the relationships that foster optimal growth and development (Howes, 2000; Shonkoff & Phillips, 2000). The characteristics include:

- Contingent, dependable responses from reliable adults
- Warm, nurturing, affectionate, loving interactions
- Sensitivity to cues, including gestural, non-verbal, and verbal cues, by caregivers
- Reciprocal, mutual interest in each other
- Synchronous, perceptive, and insightful interactive styles with a goodness of fit between the child's style and temperament and the caregivers' styles and temperaments
- Protective, caring support
- Dependable, stable, abiding, recursive availability
- Predictable, consistent, believable response from caregivers

Characteristics of relationships that may not foster optimal growth and development include:

- The presence of maternal depression
- Abusive or neglectful parenting behaviors
- Institutionalization of the child
- Disrupted patterns of interactions

➧ Lack of emotional availability

➧ Coercive parenting techniques

➧ Asynchrony in interactive styles

➧ Socioeconomic, relational, and societal stresses like poverty, malnutrition, lack of medical care, limited family support, marital discord, and so on

Myth or Misunderstanding

ONCE THE "TWIG IS BENT" IN EMOTIONAL DEVELOPMENT, IT IS TOO LATE TO INTERVENE.

Research has documented the negative impact of a host of situations and conditions that can disrupt the emotional development of the child (see above). Do these experiences doom the child to a less than optimal future? There is strong support from research and clinical experiences with abused children, orphanage-reared children, and children who are adopted later in life, that removing the negative effects and replacing them with stable, consistent, invested primary caregivers allows most of them to catch up emotionally, socially, and intellectually (Rutter and the English and Romanian Adoptees (ERA) Study Team, 1998; Shonkoff & Phillips, 2000).

Survey your community to discover resources for children who do experience early negative effects. Explore which ones make good referral choices for the children in your school.

Parents and Others

The security of attachment between parents and children influences emotional development more than the relationships children have with other adults and peers in their attachment networks. However, children can develop close relationships with more than one adult. Having a few caring adults who are emotionally dedicated to the child may, in fact, prepare children to deal with the complex world of relationships and people in the broader social context (Howes, 2000). So, while emotional development benefits from secure attachment relationships with parents, having several selective attachments to teachers and extended family members can be beneficial as well (Siegel, 1999).

Siegel (1999) proposes five characteristics of interpersonal relationships that foster emotional well-being and psychological resilience in young children. The first characteristic is collaboration. The ability to develop and maintain collaborative communication and perfect non-verbal communications forms the foundation of reciprocal relationships. Reading cries, interpreting the difference between a request for nourishment and a request for social contact, and anticipating what children might need so they don't have to wait, are all examples of collaborative communication for adults. For children, reading the verbal and non-verbal cues that Mom, Dad, or teacher is going to get the bottle right after the diaper change, reconnecting with Mom, Dad, or teacher after the change is over, and accepting comfort while waiting for the bottle to warm are all examples of collaborative communication for infants. The result is an interpersonal closeness where each individual feels the other can understand his or her emotional point of view.

The second characteristic of interpersonal relationships is reflective dialogue. When parents understand the "states of mind" or internal experiences of the child, they are able to put into words the emotions, thoughts, intentions, and memories of the child. When children learn that these emotional states can be communicated and understood, they are able to share conversations with their caregivers, non-verbally at first, and then verbally. Communication then begins to go both ways, with the child learning to understand the emotions and intentions of important adults. When both members of the attachment pair are involved in reflective dialogues, supporting the emotional experiences becomes the focus of the relationship.

Examples of reflective dialogues for adults include telling the child that you know she is hungry and that you are getting lunch out as quickly as you can; staying close to a tantrumming toddler to reassure her that you will be there to help as soon as she is ready; and, naming and describing emotions that are being expressed to help the child get in touch with the way she is feeling. For children, reflective dialogues are often expressed emotions—crying, screaming, withdrawing, or aggressing. Learning to communicate emotional states and having important adults understand how the child feels is a reflective dialogue that helps children understand they have communicated.

The third characteristic is repair. Disruptions in communication are just as common as collaborative communication in the early stages of emotional development. The ability of the adult to repair these disruptions reconnects the child to attachment figures. Reconnections are important to help children understand that life is filled with misunderstandings and misconnections and that these can be fixed. To be able to repair disconnections, adults must be comfortable with children's intense emotional states and be able to regain control over their own emotions quickly enough to reconnect before damage or negative effects are caused. Reconnecting every few minutes with a child whose crying won't stop, to remind him or her that you are still there; accepting the ambivalence of a toddler who has just finished tantrumming, wants to reconnect, but is still too angry; and accepting that clinging may relieve anxiety in new situations are examples of repair at work.

The fourth characteristic is coherent narratives. "Adults can teach children about the world of self and others by joining with them in the co-construction of stories about life events" (Siegel, 1999, p. 51). Talking about the past, the present, and the future creates shared stories that help children make sense of their experiences. When parents tell their own emotional stories to their children, they are actually creating shared meaning for feelings and constructing a framework for the child's view of reality.

Five Characteristics of Interpersonal Relationships

- Collaboration
- Reflective Dialogue
- Repair
- Coherent Narratives
- Emotional Communication

Adults who tell stories about "when I was a baby" or "when I was your age" are creating narratives. Narratives are also created when adults express their inadequacies and fears ("I don't know what to try next!" or "I wish I could help you go to sleep.").

The fifth characteristic is emotional communication. Adults in close relationships with children amplify and share life experiences with the child—creating moments of heightened awareness that lead to a positive view of self and others. By emphasizing some experiences, and not others, adults help children live in an emotional environment without being overwhelmed by what is happening in it. Adults stay connected to the child emotionally when negative or uncomfortable emotions are present and when soothing intense or negative emotional states. For adults, this means being emotionally available to the child even when the adult's own intense emotions make him or her want to move away from the child.

Stages of Emotional Development

Stanley Greenspan, noted developmental psychologist, describes the stages like this: In the first three months of life, the task at hand is becoming calm, attentive, and interested in the world. As infants learn to calm themselves and control the reflexes with which they are born, they begin to develop a multi-sensory interest in the world (touching, hearing, tasting, smelling, seeing, feeling). It doesn't take long until children are able to express their individual personalities by demonstrating preferences for certain kinds of sensory experiences (Greenspan, 1999).

Stage 1 is important because it forms the foundation of emotional development. When babies are successful in learning to calm themselves and

Myth or Misunderstanding
PARENTS ALWAYS FEEL COMPETENT, CAPABLE, AND READY TO PARENT WHEN THEY HAVE CHILDREN.

Any list of characteristics that support emotional development in children can cause anxiety in parents. Are they sensitive enough? Do they spend enough time with their child? What about the time they got frustrated because nothing helped stop the crying binge? This myth is another one that is encouraged by the images we see of perfect parents in broadcast and print media. Those parents rarely feel overwhelmed, immobilized, frustrated, isolated, or inadequate.

Most parents feel inadequate some of the time and many parents struggle to balance parenting demands and the rest of their lives, including their work and home lives.

Discuss with a colleague or fellow student some of the ways that different parents might show their anxiety, frustration, isolation, and inadequacy. What can teachers do when parents indicate such feelings?

attend to the world, a sense of security emerges. This sense of security forms the foundation of almost all of the higher order social, cognitive, and language skills that children will develop later.

The second stage of emotional development is "a time of falling in love." Stage 2 lasts from months two through seven. During this period, infants develop a joyful interest in the human world, becoming more and more engaged with the important people who care for them. They use each of the senses to engage these important adults in their world in interaction. Although objects in the world are interesting also, infants would much rather respond to an adult, particularly a familiar one. This striking preference for interactions with familiar adults is an important and crucial step in emotional development. It usually results in big smiles and emotional responses that indicate the reciprocity of this stage. It is a mutual falling in love—the baby with the caregivers and the caregivers with the baby.

In the third stage, babies develop intentional communication. They begin to seek a cause-and-effect relationship with the most familiar adults in their lives. In seeking a dialogue with the human world, infants want their caregivers to know, for example, when they are hungry as opposed to when they want to be held. If caregivers are proficient at interpreting children's communication cues and responding appropriately to them, children learn that there are social laws for successful interaction and begin to follow them to get their needs met. As adults respond differently to infant communication cues (feed them when they are hungry and hold them when they need comforting), children learn to distinguish between their own needs and feelings. Stage 3 lasts from months 3 to 10 and overlaps stage 2.

Stage 4, which emerges from months 9 to 18, infants are learning how to solve problems and forming a sense of themselves as separate from their caregivers and others. They are learning how to coordinate behavior with emotions, often acting like they are feeling and clearly communicating the emotion being felt.

Because they are becoming more organized, they are able to use objects and take the initiative. As an organized sense of self begins to emerge, infants begin to link together units of cause and effect into chains. The child will grab Mommy's hand and take her over to the refrigerator, point to the bottle, and say "muk" instead of merely crying for something to drink. Greenspan (1999) calls this type of interaction "circles of communication." From opening and closing many circles of communication with people, toys and materials, and the environment children begin to cope successfully with their emotions, think scientifically, develop a sense of right and wrong, and refine their sense of self as unique and different from others.

Stage 5, from 18 months to 30 months of age, finds children discovering a world of ideas. They are developing an ability to create their own mental images of the world and to use ideas to express and communicate emotions. Not only can they conjure up an image of their last interaction with a teacher or parent when they are no longer present, but they can also "make believe" or pretend. This shows that toddlers at this stage are truly "thinking" in the traditional sense. A child of this age can play out her emotional dramas and can begin to internalize rules.

The emerging ability to pretend and use language is an important leap in emotional development. As children play with real things and begin to use imagination to enrich and extend play, they are creating and expanding their thinking as well as communicating those ideas to others.

During stage 6, between 2 1/2 and 4 years, children expand their emotional capacities. They develop the ability to build bridges between ideas. This is emotional thinking—distinguishing between different emotions and the behaviors that go with those emotions, and understanding how feelings relate to one another.

In addition to a stage theory of emotional development, Greenspan offers another new idea. He proposes that all intelligence is emotional, that is, each intellectual skill or ability is first organized by the emotional interaction that accompanies it (1997). It is the emotional interaction or reaction that creates the ability to apply that cognitive skill or ability to the interactive world. This view of intellect and emotion as integrated, not separated, fits within the developmental and interactional views of how children grow and learn. It also challenges the widely held view of focusing so heavily on cognitive skill acquisition over other domains. Greenspan views emotions as the "architects, conductors, and organizers of the mind" (Greenspan, 1999, p. 9). Viewed this way, emotions work in an integrated way with cognitive, language, social, and physical skills. Without the emotional connection, individual skills within domains cannot be accessed and applied.

Other Ideas about Emotional Development

Emotional development is often addressed within other theories of child growth and development. We previously discussed several stage theories that included emotional components. These ideas offer insight into the realm of emotional development and will also be mentioned here.

Erickson's Theory of Psycho-social Development (see Chapter 3, page 98), uses labels for the stages of development that carry clear emotional connotations. In fact, Erickson organized each stage around an emotional issue that is expressed in gestural, non-verbal language, through play, and, then, through the skills and abilities (Hyson, 1994). It is easy to see how Erickson's theory applies to emotional development and contributes to social development. As children experience life, the quality, quantity, and timbre of their

experiences affects current development as well as influences the path of future development. If they are mostly positive, Erickson's crises are resolved positively. If they are predominantly negative, the crises are resolved negatively. If they are sometimes positive and at other times negative, then the crises are not resolved and the child cannot move on to the next stage.

Maslow's Hierarchy of Needs, discussed in Chapter 2, page 45, also contributes to our knowledge of emotional development. The overlap between Greenspan's stages (discussed in this chapter) and Maslow's Hierarchy, are easy to see. For example, learning to calm oneself (Greenspan's Stage 1) is similar to level one (Maslow's survival and well-being) needs while learning how to solve problems (Greenspan's Stage 4) is similar to level four needs (self-esteem and self-worth). When theories support each other's ideas, our understanding of emotional development is enriched, expanded, and improved.

Implications of Emotional Development for Expressing Feelings with Parents, Teachers, and Friends

The emotional realm of a child's development is usually an important consideration for teachers. Ideas about relationships and emotional development support teacher's efforts to incorporate the positive characteristics of relationships into their interactions with each child in their classroom.

Greenspan's stages give clear hints about the type of activities that facilitate each stage of emotional development. Teachers can plan to incorporate experiences that match the emotional stage of each child in their classroom curriculum.

Maslow and Erickson's theories offer a powerful tool for teachers to use in the role of observer. Observing carefully for the "direction" of children's crisis resolutions and level of needs gives teachers important information about how children are perceiving the interactive environment. Ideas for the kinds of experiences children need, both at school and in the home, can be incorporated into the classroom and shared with parents to insure positive outcomes. With this information, teachers can refer families with children who are having difficulty viewing the world positively and as meeting their needs to professionals for further evaluation.

Aggression

Aggression between and among children in school gets frequent media coverage. Toddlers can be so aggressive that teachers wonder if there is something seriously wrong. To be able to help children learn to manage aggression, it is important to understand what aggression is and how children learn to manage it.

Kinds of Aggression

Aggression is defined as any behavior that injures or diminishes a person or thing or damages or destroys property. All aggression is not the same. There are three different types (Marion, 1999). Accidental aggression is aggression that occurs during the process of sensory exploration, play, or interactions. It is not intended to hurt another child. Children often bump into each other, knock over play materials, crawl over hands, and accidentally step on each other as they play. When these acts are not intentional, they are called accidental aggression.

Instrumental aggression is aggression aimed at getting something you want, either a toy, a space on someone special's lap, or an experience. Typically, instrumental aggression has no deliberate intent to hurt the other person, they just happen to be in the way or between the child and the toy, lap, or experience that is desired. For example, when one child pushes another out of a favorite caregiver's lap, she is not really intending to hurt the other child, but she is intending to take her place in the caregiver's lap. If the other occupant falls and hurts her shoulder, the aggression was instrumental to accomplishing the child's goal, not aimed at hurting.

Hostile aggression is aggression that is intended to harm another person. There are usually two types: overt aggression and relational aggression. Overt aggression is physical aggression that is intentional. The child who wants a toy, bites the child who has it so she will drop it, and then runs away to play with the toy, is exhibiting overt aggression. It is this type of aggression that seems to bother parents and teachers the most. Overt aggression seems deliberate, focused, and intentional. Although research shows that overt aggression peaks between two and three years of age and then begins to decline (Shonkoff & Phillips, 2000), toddler teachers and parents are still very concerned about this kind of aggression, both when their child is the aggressor and when their child is the one who is hurt. Overt aggression declines as children acquire larger repertoires of skills including the ability to use language to solve problems and the ability to delay gratification.

Relational aggression is designed to modify relationships between peers or between children and adults. Relational aggression occurs as children gain an understanding of other children's motivations and discover that they are often in conflict with their own motivation (Berk, 1999). Toddlers use relational aggression near the end of toddlerhood when they call their friends mean names. Relational aggression is more often seen in the early preschool years. For example, when a child tells others they can't come to her birthday party, she is using relational aggression to change the play relationships between her playmates.

How Aggression Develops

Theories of how aggression develops focus on the influences of the family, peers, society, and the media. These ideas come from ecological systems theory (Bronfenbrenner, 1979, see Chapter 3, page 95), which looks at children in the context of the systems that impact their growth and development.

The family is one of the most important systems that influences children's growth and development, and therefore, their behavior. Aggression typically develops within families when children are exposed to violent and aggressive behaviors and see solutions to problems addressed in aggressive ways. Then, children model the behaviors they see in the context of the family to solve their own interactive problems. Sometimes aggressive behaviors in the family are directed at other family members (like spouses, other children, or extended family), and at other times they are directed at children.

Families learn many of their behaviors for coping from the context of the culture, community, and society in which they live. When a culture or community accepts violent behaviors as normal, aggressive behaviors are likely to increase. As families accept the norms of the culture and community, they pass on what they have learned to their children. So, cultural behavior that allows or encourages aggressive solutions to problems will teach children to solve problems aggressively.

Peers also influence aggression. When peers have similar experiences with aggressive behaviors, they use the aggressive behaviors that they have observed to work out problems in the context of their friendships. As peers use aggressive behaviors to solve problems, children's aggressive responses are reinforced and become patterns for responding.

Children also learn aggressive behaviors from observing them in broadcast, print, and video media (Levin, 1998). Because of the way children construct their ideas of how the world works, children try to make sense of their media viewing in their own way. Young children are not good at distinguishing fantasy from reality, making logical causal connections, and they focus on one aspect of a situation at a time. As a result, the many acts of violence and aggression that are viewed in cartoons, commercials, and video and television programming influence them in many ways. Children learn from these sources that fighting is an acceptable way to solve problems, conflict is normal, that violence is fun and exciting, and that the world is a dangerous place so fighting is necessary. None of these lessons match most children's real situations.

Aggression Is Normal

For children under the age of three, some aggression is normal—a byproduct of growing, becoming in control of and responsible for one's behavior, and of being in a group of peers at school. Children construct their knowledge from others of how to respond to aggression as well as what to do when aggression doesn't work for them. Both are part of learning to interact with peers and siblings.

Continuum of Aggression—As children grow, they usually go through a continuum of aggressive behaviors in the process of constructing their knowledge of how aggression works or doesn't work. At one end of the continuum is indiscriminant aggression—aggressive responses that are directed at everyone and everything in the child's environment, both people and things. Then, children usually direct their aggressive behaviors at others—adults and peers with whom they share the interactive world. The next point on the continuum is aggression that is limited to things—the toys and the environment. Finally, children learn to control their aggressive behavior and substitute words and language as the means of expressing aggression.

Myth and Misunderstanding
ONCE AGGRESSIVE, ALWAYS AGGRESSIVE.

This myth seems real for parents and teachers of infants and toddlers. The entire infant and toddler period is the time in which aggressive behaviors are the most frequent. Do children who act aggressively during the infant and toddler years stay that way?

The answer for most children is no. Most children outgrow aggressive responses to problems as they learn more skills and abilities to handle the situations in which they act aggressively or experience aggressive responses from their peers. They do so, though, with the support of adults who help them learn more appropriate behaviors over time, who do not tolerate hurting by intervening and focusing on the victim rather than the perpetrator. They also do it in circumstances where parents and teachers are on the same page about how to address these inappropriate behaviors. If one significant adult says, "Hit 'em back," and another says "Don't," children will have difficulty figuring out how to respond.

When children live in situations where violence and aggression, either from media or from real life, are a regular experience, they need more support than just learning skills to use instead of aggression. Children need help managing the stress and anxiety that living in such situations causes. Their families need help limiting their exposure to violence and aggression. Both school and home need to work with children to reduce the role of violence and aggression in their lives and to counteract the negative lessons children are learning from these behaviors (Levin, 1998).

Discuss the school's role in limiting exposure to media violence.

At each point on this continuum (on page 319), children can learn or be taught other strategies to cope with and solve their problems. Learning non-aggressive strategies and being taught problem-solving strategies to address problems replaces aggression with more appropriate and more acceptable behaviors and strategies.

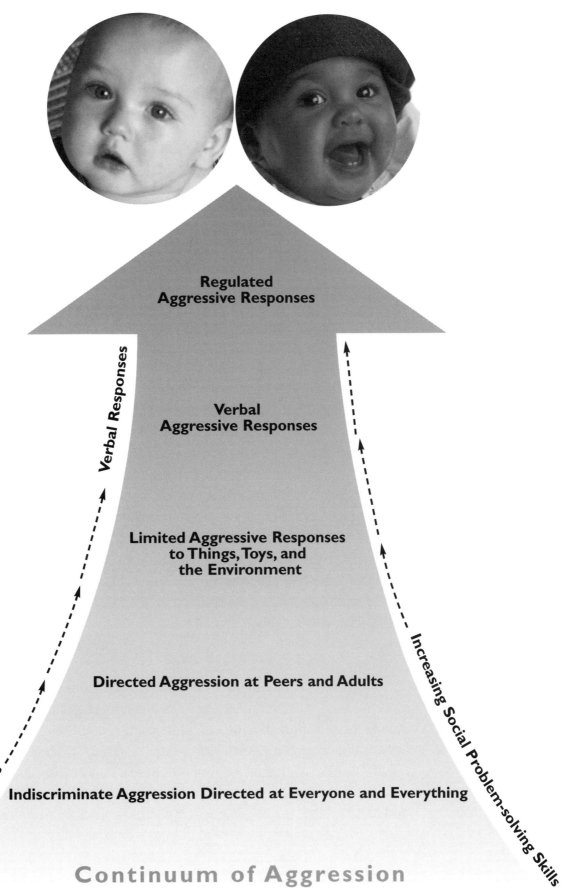

**Regulated
Aggressive Responses**

Verbal Responses

**Verbal
Aggressive Responses**

**Limited Aggressive Responses
to Things, Toys, and
the Environment**

Directed Aggression at Peers and Adults

Indiscriminate Aggression Directed at Everyone and Everything

Physical Responses

Increasing Social Problem-solving Skills

Continuum of Aggression

Managing Normal Aggression

Aggression is a normal part of young children's experiences. Aggression results from powerful emotions that are not yet under the child's direct control. Children hit, pinch, bite, slap, and grab when their emotions cause them to act before they can think about doing something else.

Children learn to manage aggression when supportive adults help them learn other skills and connect consequences with aggression. Using aggression to stop aggression only teaches children that they must submit to adults who are bigger and more powerful. It does not help children gain control over aggressive behavior or replace it with more appropriate skills. Replacing aggressive behavior with more sophisticated skills is a process—just like learning to express feelings appropriately is a lifelong task. Children take the first steps in the first three years.

The following are some examples of ways supportive teachers can meet aggression with consequences from the earliest stage.

- Set clear limits for your classroom about aggression. If children know you will not tolerate aggressive behavior as a way to get what you want, they will feel safe enough to work on developing other strategies.
- Teach social problem-solving. Help children learn to call for help, trade, take turns, walk away, use words, and make plans (see Chapter 4, page 165).
- When a child grabs a toy away from a friend, explain that the friend had the toy first and return the toy to the friend. Offer another idea about how to get the toy back. Tell the child to put out her hand, asking the friend with a gesture to put the toy in her hand. If the child falls apart when you do this, remove her from the situation until she is calm enough to return to play.
- Give children the words to use when they are having trouble communicating with each other. When a child screams for help because she lost a toy to a friend, focus your help on the child who is unable to use language, whether gestural or expressive, to get her needs met. Go over near the child, showing her that you are her ally and will help her work it out. First explore the situation by asking, "What's happening?" Offer a suggestion about what she might try to get her needs met. If the child is unable to use gestures or language, then you provide the words for her. You might say something like "Did you want her to take your toy?" If the child says no, then help her say no to the child who took the toy. "Then tell her with words, I don't want you to take my toy. Give it back to me!"

◆ Recognize cooperative behaviors. When children are successful in working things out without losing control, make sure to encourage them to continue to do so and to recognize their success. When children fail to work things out, remind them that they did it once before and that you expect them to do it again next time.

◆ Apply appropriate consequences to situations where aggression is used. With help, children will find out that they don't get what they want when they use aggression, and that there are consequences for acting aggressively. Early experiences with the consequences of aggression help children learn over time that  aggressive behavior doesn't accomplish much. After this lesson is learned, children can begin the process of becoming assertive enough to prevent being victimized and becoming authoritative enough to be seen as a leader. Both of these important lessons will never be learned unless both teachers and parents help children learn to manage normal aggression and convert it into constructive assertion and problem-solving.

Implications of Aggression for Expressing Feelings with Parents, Teachers, and Friends

It is important for teachers and parents to view managing aggression as a normal part of emotional development and growing up. Viewing aggression as an opportunity to teach seems the most helpful way to approach it. Teachers and parents also need to expect that children will learn to manage aggression with the help of caring adults. Children can learn to use other problem-solving strategies.

Teachers can work with parents to understand the amount of exposure children have to violence and aggression, from media and in the family and community setting. Then, they can help parents limit exposure to media violence and aggression. When violence and aggression are pervasive in the child's culture, teachers may need to get assistance and support for families from helping professionals.

Observing for increasing skills in managing aggression, and sharing observations about growth and developing skills with parents is important. Seeing progress from parenting and teaching interventions points to success down the road.

Perhaps the most important thing to do is to establish that aggression has no place in your classroom and will not work as a way to get what you want. Helping children see that aggression does not succeed at accomplishing goals is crucial for encouraging other skills.

Best Practices

Invest in Relationships

Throughout **Innovations: Infant and Toddler Development**, the importance of the relationships that children have with significant others has been discussed. The following best practices give specific insight into teaching strategies that support developing relationships between teachers and children.

Help Children "Feel Felt"

Recognizing, identifying, labeling, and validating feelings in young children are important teaching strategies for supporting emotional development in young children (Albrecht & Forrester, 2001). For teachers and parents, this means being able to put word labels on feelings.

When children feel like their emotional expression is understood, an interpersonal closeness develops that supports development in all domains, not just the emotional domain. This concept, called "feeling felt" (Siegel, 1999) allows children to join with adults in experiencing primary emotions like happiness, sadness, anger, frustration, and irritation. Children then come to understand, through signals communicated verbally and non-verbally, that someone understands exactly how they feel. Knowing that their emotions are perceived and understood by another is one of the ways that adults help children accomplish the important task of understanding and controlling emotions.

Teachers and parents don't have to fix emotions. It would be a mistake to try to eliminate or remove emotions from the child's experience, or to assume that adults have the responsibility for taking away intense and powerful feelings in young children. Emotions are feelings—and as such do not need amending or fixing. When emotions are recognized, identified, labeled, and validated, children are more able to handle the intense feelings that some emotions create.

It is when emotions are attached to behaviors or physical action that parents and teachers are called on to do something. Intervention often takes the form of keeping children from hurting themselves or others, giving children time to recover from the intensity of emotional expression in order to talk about and work on a solution or resolution, or comforting children until they recover emotionally. The following are examples of words and phrases that parents and teachers can use as they recognize, label, and validate feelings with children.

Helpful Words and Phrases for Recognizing, Identifying, Labeling, and Validating Feelings in Young Children and Their Messages to Children

Helpful Words and Phrases	Skills or Abilities Being Learned or Practiced	Message to the Child
I think you are feeling …(sad, happy, mad, angry, irritated, frustrated, bothered, pressured, excited, etc.).	• Identifies and labels feelings; • Models the ability to talk about feelings; • Shows children how to think about feelings.	• Validates feelings and helps children "feel felt" by others; • Supports the development of emotional self-regulation.
I bet that feels yucky.	• Identifies and labels feelings.	• Modulates emotions by recognizing them.
You are a boy (or girl) who can tell me how you are feeling.	• Models the ability to talk about feelings.	• Validates feelings and helps children "feel felt" by others; • Supports differentiation of self from others.
Shucks!	• Tells children that they can control themselves even when they feel intense emotions.	• Shows non-judgmental concern about feelings; • Helps children "feel felt" by others.
I am not sure how you are feeling.	• Supports children's ability to label their emotions.	• Modulates emotions by helping identify and label them.
It makes you mad (sad, frustrated, lonely, upset, happy, etc.) when …	• Connects one's feelings to the actions of others.	• Acknowledges the behaviors that cause feelings; • Clarifies emotional responses; • Supports reflection about past and future behaviors.
This is hard for you.	• Labels intense feelings.	• Acknowledges the feelings underneath behaviors.

Practice Floor Time

Floor time is a teaching practice that supports children's emotional development (Greenspan, 1999). Floor time looks something like this. The teacher prepares an area of the classroom with an attractive display of toys and materials, either taken from the regular toys and materials or specially planned for floor time. One or two children who are ready to play are invited to join the teacher in an area of the classroom that is set up for floor time. The teacher starts the practice of floor time by watching, listening, and being with the children as they begin to play with the toys and with each other. She or he lets the child or children direct the time together. If a child smiles at the teacher, the teacher smiles back. If the children include the teacher in the play, she responds by joining in the play. Following the child's lead is the important part of floor time.

When a child picks up toys, the teacher expands and extends the play to enhance the child's experience. For example, if the child is driving miniature cars on a roadway, the teacher might describe what she or he sees happening and smile at the child to encourage her to continue.

Interactions like these support interest in the social world and validate that the teacher is going to support being a part of it. These interactions also fill children with feelings of competence. Once initiated through a supportive adult, the child will be able to reconnect with the feeling without the adult's support at a later time.

Teachers may find it hard to identify time when they can practice floor time with just a few children. Try some of the following ideas:

▶ Pick a time of day that naturally lends itself to calm play. Some ideas might be the beginning of the day as children are arriving one by one, or after naptime as the first few children wake up, or even during the time spent in self-selected activities in the classroom or the end of the day as children are leaving and the group size is decreasing.

▶ Try to spend floor time with one or two children per day during the week. You might even want to keep track of who has had floor time each week—indicating it on your curriculum plan after it occurs, so you know who hasn't had special time with the teacher.

▶ When children are having developmental difficulties or are experiencing stress from other sources (like a traveling parent or recovering from an illness), give them extra floor time. Stress increases children's need to feel connected to their primary caregivers. The child who is demanding the most attention may be able to cope better on his own if he gets what he needs—a feeling of being filled up with attention and connected through play to his teacher.

▶ Enlist the help of others. Invite parents, students who are studying early childhood education, and grandparents to spend some time on the floor playing with children in your group or helping in the classroom so that you are freed up to practice floor time.

Provide Experiences that Facilitate Emotional Development

Babies from birth through three months need to have opportunities to learn to calm themselves and to receive and respond to stimulation from the world. Learning to calm oneself does NOT mean that babies need to cry for a while before their teachers respond to them. On the contrary, they need prompt attention to distress, so they can begin to feel the difference between comfort and discomfort. At this stage, a crying baby will continue to cry for a minute after being picked up because she does not recognize the change right away. Babies need practice determining when something has changed their situation and will learn to respond more quickly to the change.

Babies need plenty of sensory stimulation—seeing, hearing, touching and being touched, and smelling. Create and produce these experiences for infants. For example, mount an unbreakable mirror in the crib to catch indirect light and reflect the baby's face or a mobile overhead to attract visual attention. Give infants things that make noise when they are touched such as certain rattles, soft grab toys, and crib gyms. Music is important during this period, however, it must be more than just background noise (babies can't tune it out as well as adults can).

Babies need teachers who talk to them, touch them, snuggle them close, and challenge each of their senses to respond. In preparation for the next stage, very young infants need many real interactions with teachers, particularly the teachers with whom they will spend a major part of the day.

Because emotional stages tend to overlap, infants begin to develop an intense interest in the human world while interacting with adults during this first stage. If children don't demand the adults' attention, it needs to be available anyway to stimulate social-emotional development.

From two months to seven months, babies need someone to fall in love with at the school—a special, caring, interesting, consistent person who woos the child's love and interest. Assigning a primary teacher is the first step in making sure the child at this stage has her needs met and her social-emotional growth facilitated. The rest comes naturally for most children. Ira Gordon (1970) calls the interaction during this stage "ping-ponging." The teacher smiles at the baby—the baby smiles back—the baby coos—the teacher talks back to her or him. This type of interaction forms the best environment possible to help infants continue to develop.

Senses need to be involved in stimulation, too. Touching, tasting, smelling, hearing, and seeing the world are a very important part of this stage for infants. Opportunities to do so should be numerous and repetitive so that infants have many sensory experiences. By this stage, children should spend very little time in their cribs except when they are sleeping. Time awake should be spent near adults, watching, hearing, touching, smelling, and tasting them and the things adults offer children.

From 3 months to 10 months, babies need plenty of opportunities to see what happens if.... They are beginning to seek out cause-and-effect relationships, and the classroom should be full of them. Push-pull toys, squeak toys, adults who play hide-and-seek, water to pour, blankets to pull, and so on. Babies also need alert, attentive teachers who don't wait until the infants are too tired to go to sleep or too hungry to eat. They need adults who can read their non-verbal cues and anticipate their needs. If adults can learn to do this, children also will learn it as they mature.

Getting a copy of the baby's regular schedule from her parents will help you develop sensitivity to her cues. If you know a baby is likely to be hungry about 11:00, you can make sure the bottle is warmed and ready about 10:50 so that there is no waiting when the hunger bells go off. The same is true of elimination, sleeping, irritability, and so on. This is why primary teachers want to know everything about a baby that her parents can share. It makes the job of reading cues so much easier.

From 9 to 14 fourteen months, the organized sense of self begins to show itself in assertive exploration of everything. The child begins to test limits and attempts to control and manipulate the world around her—including the adults in it. Firm, consistent limits are important even in situations when children are practicing being the boss or testing their independence. Notice once again the overlapping of stages. This stage is emerging between 9 and 18 months.

Children need opportunities to test and experiment with the range of feelings they have. They are learning to understand a little bit of what another child feels (called empathy) but cannot yet really take the role of the other person in their interactions (called altruism). During this stage, children begin to internalize the rules adults have had for them during infancy and need less frequent reminders about old rules. New rules, though, take a period of constant reminding before they begin to be followed. Facilitating emotional development during this stage means making rules clear and reminding children often of what they mean and what the consequence is for breaking each rule.

A dependable, familiar primary teacher is still important—particularly during times of stress or when intense negative emotions are present. Toddlers need someone to read non-verbal cues and anticipate needs just like babies do. Now, toddlers are able to think about more abstract things than when they were younger. Concentration emerges during this stage, and teachers will see children play for longer periods of time at activities that interest them or test their skill. And, play becomes more complex, often including experiences observed in the broader world of the family, school, and community.

Dramatic play is so important during this stage. Toddlers need dramatic play spaces and props that allow them to continue to express the complete range of emotions that they feel—not just the positive ones. They need practice acting out anger, fear, hostility, and eagerness, as well as empathy, altruism, curiosity, and so on in acceptable ways that do not cause conflict. In play, they practice the roles they see adults using in the real world. They also begin to separate what is real from what isn't and begin to understand when and how to switch from fantasy to reality.

Teachers who foster dramatic possibilities plan exciting, interesting, and changing dramatic play spaces. They play along with children as they act out these experiences, facilitating and enhancing the experience.

And, they spend lots of time observing children as they play, watching for emerging interests, new abilities being practiced or tried out, and for ideas about what play themes can be expanded or supported. Teachers change the themes and props available to children to refresh play ideas and offer variety. They always view play from the point of view of the emotional development of the child.

Use a Variety of Teaching Roles

The Teacher as Problem-solver

In this role, teachers approach problems in interactions as opportunities to teach children social problem-solving strategies. Interactions that don't work or end in aggression are viewed, not as major crises, but as platforms for helping children see the consequences of their behaviors for others, opportunities to help children assess whether behaviors should be used again, and openings to consider more appropriate alternatives.

Being a good model of appropriate social problem-solving for children to see is an important teaching role. Children imitate and model the behaviors they see others use. As teachers interact with parents and other adults in appropriate and positive ways, children get ideas they may be able to use in their interactions with others.

Teachers also provide important scaffolding of children's efforts to solve problems. When teachers help children solve problems that are too complex by being near, offering suggestions about what might work, and supporting attempts even if they don't work, children are often able to solve problems that are beyond their ability to solve on their own.

Teaching Roles

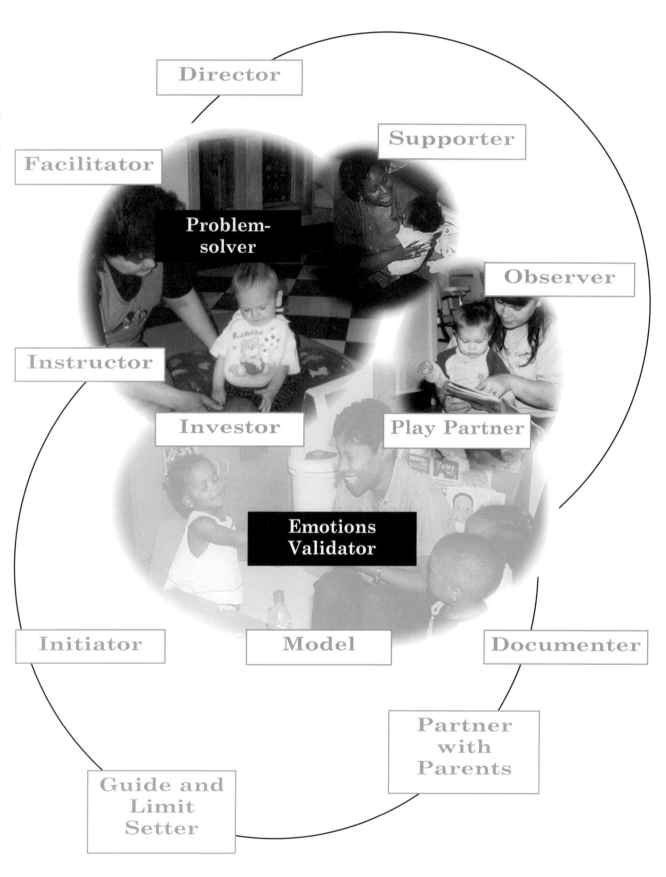

Director

Supporter

Facilitator

Observer

Problem-solver

Instructor

Investor

Play Partner

Emotions Validator

Initiator

Model

Documenter

Partner with Parents

Guide and Limit Setter

The Teacher as an Emotions' Validator

When teachers identify, acknowledge, and validate feelings for infants and toddlers, children's emotional development is encouraged and supported. This important teaching role is ongoing—it happens all day long in many different settings and within many different interactions. Soon, children are able to label their own feelings and share with their peers how interactions make them feel. Teachers also have to monitor their own impressions of the emotional climate of their classrooms, avoiding under-recognizing feelings. Some children's emotions are more subtle than others, yet are just as important for identification and validation.

Differentiating between feeling and doing for children is a role that supports socialization and emotional development. Helping children separate the feeling from behavioral action begins the process of feeling, then thinking, then responding appropriately—a difficult process to learn.

Teachers also support children when intense emotions are present. One of the most difficult times for children in school is when their emotions overtake and overwhelm them. Teachers serve as a cushion when this occurs, providing support to weather the storm and connections that help children move on when the storm subsides. They understand that intense emotions need an outlet—and support appropriate outlets whenever possible.

Create Environments that Support Emotional Development

When internal regulation of emotion or behavior is low, as it is during toddlerhood, external regulation of structural components of the environment need to be ritualized and predictable (Albrecht & Forrester, 2001). Structural components of the environment are the predictability of the environment, the familiarity of schedule, and the appropriateness of individual schedules.

Repetition increases structure to support emotional development. The more often an activity is repeated in a predictable format, the more likely children will take comfort from the structure of it. Try creating structures for separations, reunions, what happens before and after naptime, and when the primary teacher leaves.

Ritualize routines and transitions. If hectic times, like transitions outdoors, transitions indoors, snack time, or lunch time are ritualized, children take comfort from the ritual to give them indications of what comes next and how to act or behave as the routine or transition occurs.

Give children choices among appropriate alternatives. When children are trying out new autonomy behaviors, trying to do things on their own, giving them choices among appropriate alternatives works for everyone. For

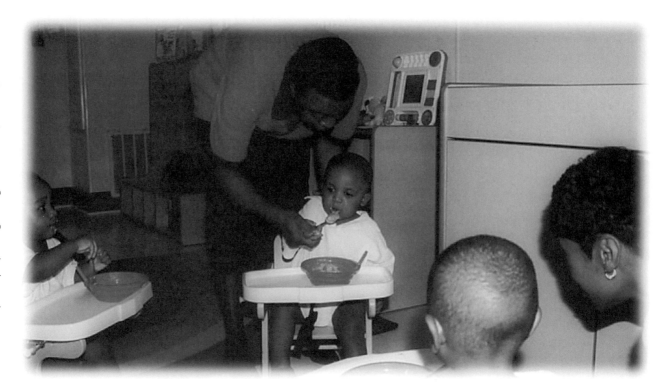

example, "Do you want saltine crackers or graham crackers for snack today?" gives children a choice between two acceptable ones. Children benefit from practicing making decisions like these as they perfect decision-making skills.

Say "Yes" more than "No." This simple strategy for supporting children's emotional development tells them that they will get to do what they want. For example, if a child wants to go outside during snack time, say, "You can go outside, AND we will finish our snack first." Notice the AND. When adults use "but" with children, children often take it as saying "no." Using "and" instead of "but" says that children will get their wish and tells them when it will happen.

Applying Theory and Best Practices

A large part of professional practice in the field of care and early education is the synthesizing of knowledge, research, and best practices into teaching actions and strategies. A goal of *Innovations: Infant and Toddler Development* is to help teachers apply theory, research, and best practices to real-life situations and behaviors in the infant and toddler classroom. Let's take a look at a common behavior—aggression—that is a part of most children's experience in care and early education settings to see if the knowledge we have gained, the research we have reviewed, and/or the best practices we have explored give any suggestions of how aggression might be handled by teachers in the classroom.

Integrating Theory and Best Practices into Curriculum

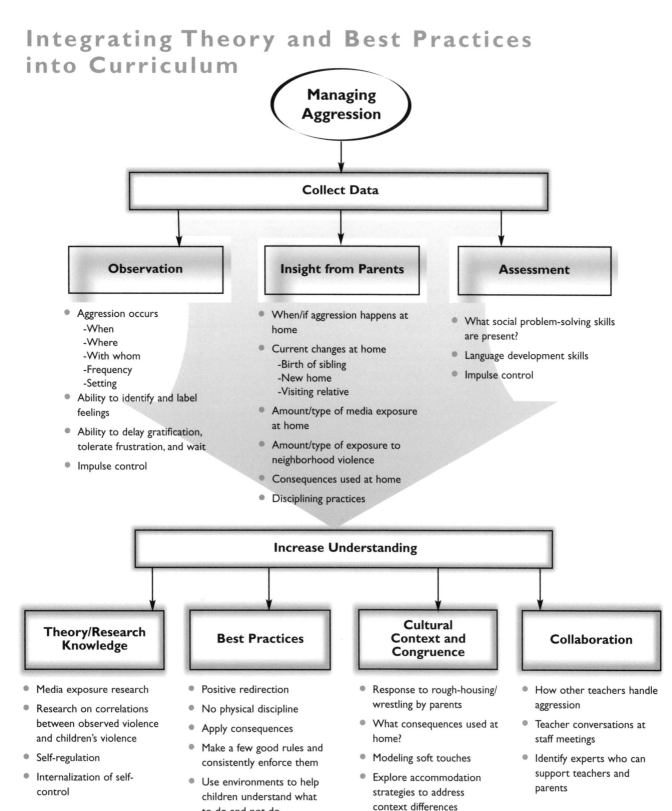

Managing Aggression

Collect Data

Observation

- Aggression occurs
  - When
  - Where
  - With whom
  - Frequency
  - Setting
- Ability to identify and label feelings
- Ability to delay gratification, tolerate frustration, and wait
- Impulse control

Insight from Parents

- When/if aggression happens at home
- Current changes at home
  - Birth of sibling
  - New home
  - Visiting relative
- Amount/type of media exposure at home
- Amount/type of exposure to neighborhood violence
- Consequences used at home
- Disciplining practices

Assessment

- What social problem-solving skills are present?
- Language development skills
- Impulse control

Increase Understanding

Theory/Research Knowledge

- Media exposure research
- Research on correlations between observed violence and children's violence
- Self-regulation
- Internalization of self-control

Best Practices

- Positive redirection
- No physical discipline
- Apply consequences
- Make a few good rules and consistently enforce them
- Use environments to help children understand what to do and not do

Cultural Context and Congruence

- Response to rough-housing/wrestling by parents
- What consequences used at home?
- Modeling soft touches
- Explore accommodation strategies to address context differences

Collaboration

- How other teachers handle aggression
- Teacher conversations at staff meetings
- Identify experts who can support teachers and parents

Possibilities

Parent Possibilities

Teacher-Initiated
Support parents' feelings about aggression.
Support parents in limiting exposure to media violence.

Prepare parents for aggression by talking about how to handle it before it happens.

Parent Participation Plan parent get-together to share strategies, ideas, frustrations

Innovations in Environments

Review structural components of the environment—schedule, predictability, and routines
Spread children out in environment—duplicate popular areas
Add a peace table to the classroom—send children to sit across from each other and solve problems with teacher's support
Add soft elements to classroom
Make sure to have duplicates of toys

Observation/Assessment Possibilities

Which social problem-solving skills are present?
Ability to delay gratification, ability to tolerate frustration
Chart where, why, when, with whom, and how aggression occurs

Interactive Experiences

Model the recognition and expression of feelings
Pattern appropriate strategies for getting needs met
Plan curriculum activities to facilitate emotional development and positively influence crises.
Say "Yes" more than "No."
Ritualize transitions
Give choices among acceptable alternatives
Support intense emotions
Differentiate between feeling and doing

Plan

Web

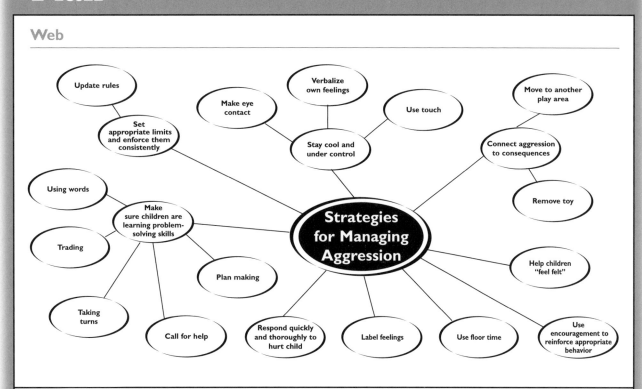

Dramatic Possibilities   Puppet theatre, add peace pack prop box

Art/Sensory Possibilities   Shared sensory tubs, scribbling on wall-size paper, tearing paper

Curiosity Possibilities

Music Possibilities   Calm, classical music

Movement Possibilities   Simon Says

Literacy Possibilities   Add emotion face chart to wall (with expressions of emotions)

Outdoor Possibilities   Provide full range of options

Project Possibilities   Repeated stomping feet painting

Books	Picture File Pictures/Vocabulary

Will I Have a Friend? by Miriam Cohen
Nobody Likes Me, by Raoul Krischanitz
That Toad is Mine, by Barbara Shook Hazen
Alexander and the Terrible, Horrible, No-Good,
    Very Bad Day, by Judith Viorst
The Grouchy Ladybug, by Eric Carle
	Pictures of expressed emotions:
	   Mine!
	   Don't hit me!
	   Walk away!
	   Help!

Rhymes & Fingerplays	Music/Songs	Prop Boxes
Five Little Monkeys	"If You're Happy and You Know It" "As I Was Walking" "Rain, Rain Go Away!"	Peace pack with egg timer, digital timer, dial timer, etc.

Summary

Learning to express oneself and to identify and understand emotions is a crucial part of growing up. For infants and toddlers, this process is one that changes in the context of other developmental changes.

New interest in the effects of emotions on the developing brain has put the emotional development of infants and toddlers in the spotlight. The nature of interactional experience is responsible for shaping how relationships are co-constructed by children and adults. The security of attachment between parents and children influences emotional development more than the relationships children have with other adults and peers in their attachment networks. However, children can develop close relationships with more than one adult.

Siegel (1999) proposes five characteristics of interpersonal relationships that foster emotional well-being and psychological resilience. These characteristics are collaborative communication, reflective dialogue, repair, narratives, and emotional communication.

Greenspan describes the stages of emotional development as:

- **Stage 1**—from birth to two months, the foundation of emotional development when babies learn to calm themselves and gain a sense of security
- **Stage 2**—from months two to seven, a time of falling in love and having a joyful interest in the human world
- **Stage 3**—from months 3 to 10, a time to seek a cause-effect relationship with the most familiar adults
- **Stage 4**—from months 9 to 18, a time to learn how to solve problems and form a separate sense of self
- **Stage 5**—from months 18 to 20, when children discover a world of ideas
- **Stage 6**—from years 2 ½ to 4, when children are able to first build bridges between ideas – emotional thinking

Aggression is any behavior that injures or diminishes any person or thing or damages or destroys property. The three different types of aggression are accidental aggression, instrumental aggression, and hostile aggression (including overt aggression and relational aggression). For children under the age of three, some aggression is normal—a byproduct of growing up and becoming in control of and responsible for one's behavior and being in a group of peers at school. Learning non-aggressive strategies to address problems and being taught problem-solving strategies to address problems, replaces aggression with more appropriate and more acceptable behaviors and strategies.

Children learn to manage aggression when supportive adults help them learn other skills and connect consequences with aggression. Using aggression to stop aggression only teaches children that they must submit to adults who are bigger and more powerful. It does not help children gain control over aggressive behavior or replace it with more appropriate skills. Replacing aggressive behavior with more sophisticated skills is a process—just like learning to express feelings appropriately is a lifelong task. Children take the first steps in the first three years.

Questions and Activities

1. Explain the major points you would like to include in a parent conference about an 18-month-old child who is karate chopping other children in the classroom. How will you approach the subject of media violence?

2. How can the teacher use different techniques to help children who are in involved in the three different types of aggression?

3. When teaching in your toddler classroom one day, a substitute is assigned to work with you. When two children are struggling over the same toy, Winston hits Joshua. Then you hear the substitute say, "Hit him back!" What do you do?

4. Why does a teacher need to give attention to the child who is hurt instead of the child doing the hurting? Likewise, how can the teacher teach children that aggression does not work for a child to get his/her way?

5. Create a system for the classroom to assure that all children get a scheduled "floor time" during the week.
6. What is so important about emotional development for children from two to seven months old?

References

Albrecht, K. & M. Forrester. (2001). Unpublished project report.

Berk, L.E. (1999). *Infants and children.* Boston: Allyn and Bacon.

Bronfenbrenner, U. (1979). *The ecology of human development: Experiments by nature and design.* Cambridge, MA: Harvard University Press.

Gordon, I. (1970). *Baby learning through baby play.* New York: St. Martin's.

Greenspan, S.I. (1997). *Growth of the mind and the endangered origins of intelligence.* Cambridge, MA: Perseus Books.

Greenspan, S.I. (1999). *The six experiences that create intelligence and emotional growth in babies and young children.* Reading, MA: Perseus Books.

Howes, C. (2000). Social development, family, and attachment relationships of infants and toddlers. In D. Cryer, & T. Harms (Eds.), *Infants and toddlers in out of home care.* (87-113). Baltimore, MD: Brookes Publishing.

Hyson, M.C. (1994). *The emotional development of young children: Building an emotion-centered curriculum.* New York: Teachers College Press.

Levin, D.E. (1998). *Remote control childhood? Combating the hazards of media culture.* Washington, DC: NAEYC.

Marion, M. (1997). Research in review: Guiding young children's understanding and management of anger. *Young Children,* 52(7), 62-67.

Marion, M. (1999). *Guidance of young children.* Upper Saddle River, NJ: Merrill.

Rutter, M. & the English and Romanian Adoptees (ERA) Study Team. (1998). Developmental catchup, and deficit, following adoption after severe global early deprivation. *Journal of Child Psychology and Psychiatry.* 39(4), 465-476.

Shonkoff, J.P. & D.A. Phillips. (2000). *From neurons to neighborhoods: The science of early childhood development.* Washington, D.C: National Academy Press.

Siegel, D.J. (1999). Relationships and the developing child. *Child Care Information Exchange.* 130, 48-51.

Glossary

Accidental Aggression—Occurs during the process of sensory exploration, play, or interactions.

Aggression—Any behavior that injures or diminishes a person or thing or damages or destroys property.

Coherent Narratives—Shared stories that help children make sense of their emotional experiences.

Collaboration—Communication between children and their caregivers in which non-verbal cues are read and interpreted accurately, both by the child and the adults.

Ecological Systems Theory—Theory by Urie Bronfenbrenner that looks at children in the context of the systems that impact their growth and development.

Emotional Communication—Communication between children and their adult caregivers that is characterized by accurate interpretation and response to emotions and emotional behavior.

"Feeling Felt"—When children are joined by adults in experiencing primary emotions like happiness, sadness, anger, frustration, and irritation.

Floor Time—A teaching practice that supports children's emotional development by opening and closing circles of communication during play led by the child.

Hostile Aggression—Aggression intended to harm another person.

Instrumental Aggression—Aggression aimed at getting something you want, either a toy, a space on someone special's lap, or an experience.

Intentional Communication—Communication from babies that has a specific message for caregivers.

Overt Aggression—One of two types of hostile aggression. Overt aggression is physical aggression that is intentional.

Reflective Dialogue—Communication that exchanges information about the child's state of mind or internal experiences.

Relational Aggression—Aggression designed to modify relationships between peers or between children and adults. Relational aggression occurs as children gain an understanding of other children's motivations and discover that they are often in conflict with their own motivations.

Repair—Ability of attachment figures to repair disruptions in communication and reconnect emotionally with the child.

Appendix

Master List of Best Practices

Appendix

- Conduct Gradual Enrollments
- Create Supportive Environments
- Invest in Observation
- Observe for Temperamental Differences
- Validate What Moms and Dads Know
- Actively Facilitate Adjustment
- Use a Variety of Teaching Roles
- Identify and Respond to Individual Differences
- Maximize Interactions during Basic Care and Routines
- Respond Promptly to Crying
- Invest in Establishing Relationships
- Implement Primary Teaching
- Provide Continuity of Care
- Facilitate Attachment within Attachment Networks
- Create Home-school Partnerships
- Establish Two-way Communication with Parents
- Employ Family-centered Practices
- Facilitate Interactions between Children
- Help Children Make Friends
- Create Appropriate Environments
- Teach Children to Use Prosocial Behaviors
- Teach Social Problem-Solving
- Add Mirrors to the Environment
- Create Opportunities to Explore Roles
- Support Children's Role Exploration
- Observe to Support Exploring Roles
- Talk to Children Often Using Language Stimulation Techniques
- Build Vocabulary
- Support Linguistic and Cultural Diversity
- Provide Cognitively Stimulating Environments
- Support Emerging Literacy
- Use Multi-age Grouping
- Identify Developmental Challenges
- Support Physical Development
- Support Health and Wellness
- Support Self-regulation and Control
- Manage Oppositional Behavior
- Handle Temper Tantrums
- Guide Children to Behave Appropriately
- Establish a Few Clear Limits and Enforce Them
- Respond Consistently to Individual Limit Testing
- Protect Children from Abuse and Neglect
- Invest in Relationships
- Provide Experiences that Facilitate Emotional Development
- Create Environments that Support Emotional Development

Parent Communication

Parent Postcards as an Essential Component of Partnerships with Parents

Innovations: The Comprehensive Infant Curriculum and ***Innovations: The Comprehensive Toddler Curriculum*** contain a useful tool for facilitating communication between school and home about developmental, parenting, and educational issues. Called Parent Postcards, these short, topical notes are designed to introduce an idea to parents. Postcards in these resources are shared as parents show an interest in the topic, as developmental issues arise, or at appropriate times during the child's tenure at school. In addition, teachers are encouraged to supplement the ***Innovations***' Postcards with articles from other professional literature, ideas from teaching practice and experience, and from other sources, creating a resource that grows as the teacher's knowledge of and relationships with the parents of her or his children change and grow.

To give a feel for the application of Parent Postcards, sample Postcards on a frequent topic of concern for parents—biting—are duplicated here. Teachers are encouraged to apply and modify this strategy of sharing developmental and educational information with parents to fit their school or classroom's developmental, educational, and cultural needs.

Help! My Child Got Bitten!— Understanding Exploratory Biting

All parents dread the time when the teacher tells them their child has been bitten at school. The parent feels helpless for not being there to protect the child from the biter. And the parent wonders why the teacher couldn't or didn't prevent it.

Why does biting seem to occur among children at school? The simple answer to this question, according to noted psychologists Louise Ilg and Florence Ames, is that children bite because they lack language and social skills. They say biting is a developmental phenomenon—it happens at predictable times for predictable reasons tied to children's ages and stages.

For children between early infancy and about 14 or 15 months, biting is often part of the investigation and exploration that defines babies' play. They are curious about things that get put into their mouths. They want to see how things taste and feel. They are interested in exploring everything with their mouths.

Children are also teething during this period. When gums are sore and ache, chewing on something relieves the pressure and feels good! Very rarely at this stage is biting purposeful or intentional.

TO

TO

Action/Reaction Biting: Help! My Child Got Bitten, Again!

Again? You thought it was over when your child's friends finished teething and started playing with objects instead of putting them in their mouths. Well, not so. Investigative/exploratory biting, which usually occurs from infancy to around 14 or 15 months, is followed by biting to get a reaction (action/reaction biting).

Why does biting seem to occur among children in groups at school? The simple answer to this question, according to noted psychologists Louise Ilg and Florence Ames, is that children bite because they lack language and social skills. They view biting as a developmental phenomena—it happens at predictable times for predictable reasons tied to children's ages and stages.

This predictable stage is called action/reaction biting. When you bite down on the finger that is gingerly exploring your face, it gets a big, loud reaction from the other child and from the adults in your classroom. The ruckus that is created is interesting, different, and, yes, even fun.

Children between 9 and 20 months are beginning to connect actions with reactions. They are exploring interesting combinations of actions to see what reactions they might discover. Other children provide a wide array of interesting reactions to being bitten, whether purposefully bitten or accidentally bitten. As a result, biting may be quite an interesting activity!

Oh, No! Not Again: Handling Purposeful Biting

By now you may be wondering if biting will become a way of life for children in your child's group at school. It may seem to you that every time you turn around children are entering another biting phase. And, now, your child will tell you all about when the bite happened, who did it, and why (although reports may bear little relationship to the facts!). Helpless feelings associated with your child's first bite may resurface, and you may be a little concerned that your child is biting, too.

Why does biting seem to occur among children in groups at school? The simple answer to this question, according to noted psychologists Louise Ilg and Florence Ames, is that children bite because they lack language and social skills. Biting is a developmental phenomena—it happens at predictable times for predictable reasons that are tied to children's ages and stages. This stage, which occurs around 18 months, is called purposeful biting. It often seems mean and malicious to adults. Further, the bites received during this stage may even leave marks.

What is going on, and what should parents do? The first step is to remember that investigative biting and action/reaction biting have come and gone. As serious as these forms of biting seemed at the time, your child passed through the stage of being bitten through investigation and biting by investigation. Then, your child also passed through the stage of being bitten for a reaction and biting for a reaction. Purposeful biting will pass as your toddler's language and social skills mature.

TO
_____
_____
_____

What Can Teachers Do to Prevent Purposeful Biting?

Let's take a look at what your child's teacher will be doing to anticipate, prevent, and handle purposeful biting. Understanding why children bite is the first step in preventing biting. Biting does not mean the child is "bad" or "cruel." Children bite because they lack interaction, language, and social skills. They are not yet able to say, "Leave me alone," or "That's my toy." As soon as they learn to tell their friends to leave them alone, to move away when they get too close, and to negotiate turns, the frequency of purposeful biting diminishes.

Prevention and anticipation are two ways your child's teacher will deal with biting. She or he has created an environment that spreads children throughout the available space. Toddlers tend to be "groupie" in nature. They are wherever the teacher is. Teachers arrange the classroom to limit children's ability to see everyone and everything. If children are unable to see the toys others are playing with, they will be less likely to want to play with those specific toys and less likely to bite to get them.

Your child's teacher will also focus on anticipating biting. She or he will observe when, where, and with whom biting occurs. She or he will observe when, where, and with whom biting occurs to provide the basis for anticipating biting episodes. Your child's teacher limits the development of situations in which biting occurs by separating a regular biter from his or her most frequent target, anticipating tired or fussy times that will likely result in conflict, and rearranging play pairs.

The teacher will also use substitution to help biters learn to control biting. During some ages, sore gums that need rubbing can be the cause of biting behavior. The nearest available object to soothe sore gums just might be the arms or fingers of another child. Soft rubber manipulative toys are offered to children who are cutting teeth.

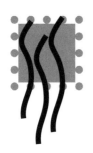

TO

Additional Steps to Prevent Purposeful Biting

Sometimes, prevention, anticipation, and substitution are not enough. When a toddler bites three or more times in one day, additional steps need to be taken. Your child's teacher will follow a three-step plan to deal with a biter once there are no more preventive measures to try. All three steps help children understand the logical consequences of biting.

The first and most important step is one your child's teacher has been using for some time—responding to the child who is bitten. If the conflict is over a toy, she or he will position herself or himself between the biter and the child who was bitten and pick up the toy. Without moving away from the biter, the teacher will comfort the toddler by holding the child near, stroking his or her back, or saying comforting things like, "I bet that hurt," or "It upsets you when Jenny bites you." This step is usually enough to help older toddlers learn that biting gets neither the toy nor attention from the teacher. In fact, the logical consequence of biting is that the other child gets attention, and the biter gets left out. Often this step is all that is needed to help a child gain control over biting.

Your teacher also has been narrating to your child. Narration is an on-going monologue of what is happening in the child's world. Teachers talk about what children are doing, how they are interacting, and how children are responding to each other's actions. Narration helps children learn to pick up cues about other children's feelings and reactions.

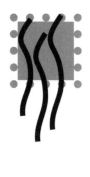

TO

Additional Steps to Prevent Purposeful Biting (continued)

If the biting persists, your child's teacher will take the next step. She or he will plan a place to isolate the biter, removing him or her from the play setting and restricting the toddler's ability to play. When a child bites, the teacher will simply say to the child, "It hurts when you bite." Then the teacher will pick up the child and put him or her in the isolation place. The teacher won't be angry or disapproving, just matter-of-fact, communicating that biting just didn't work. The message the teacher is sending the biter is that you don't get to play freely in the classroom for a few minutes when you bite.

Because playing is much more fun than watching others play, the biter quickly gets the message that he or she is in control of whether or not he or she can continue to play. After a minute or two, the teacher helps the biter return to play. If the child cries or is upset by the removal, the teacher will wait a minute or two for him or her to gain control. Isolation won't be very long. Toddlers have little perspective on time and will get the point after even a brief separation.

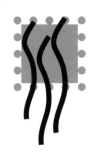

TO

Teaching Social Skills to Toddlers to Reduce Biting

Now is also the time that your child's teacher will teach social skills to help children increasingly control their own behavior. Because most conflict during this stage occurs over limited resources (toys, crayons, blocks, manipulatives, the teacher's lap), the first social skill a child needs is the ability to wait just a moment. This is called delaying gratification, and it is a particularly difficult skill for a child to master.

Then, the teacher will teach children to use their words. The teacher will start with "Mine!" As language grows, the words will get more specific ("I want the truck, please."). Then the teacher will teach children to walk away from a problem, or to ask the other child to walk away and leave them alone. This skill makes children feel powerful and capable of solving their own problems some of the time. Next comes asking for what is wanted instead of grabbing it. "Please put that in my hand," often works very well. The next step is trading a toy you don't want for a toy you do want. "Trade me a yellow car for the blue one," makes both children winners. Finally, your child's teacher will help your child accept "no" for the answer when all of these strategies don't work.

Taking turns (first me, then you) comes next, followed finally by actually sharing. As children master these skills, expect biting specifically and aggression in general to reduce.

Children who are biting frequently (for example, three or more times a day for three or more consecutive days) may need increased supervision throughout the day. Shadowing the child or limiting his or her freedom within the classroom by having the child hold the teacher's hand reinforces the idea that biting will be controlled in your child's classroom.

TO

What Can Parents Do to Prevent Purposeful Biting?

The first thing you can do is to continue responding promptly when your child is hurt by another child or a sibling. Then, never let your child bite you without getting a negative reaction. Tell your child that you don't like it when he or she hurts you. Remind your child that you always touch him or her softly. Then walk away for a minute or two to communicate that biting won't get your attention; in fact, it will make it disappear. Don't forget to reinforce and reward appropriate behaviors your child has and to show your child how you would like him or her to act. Finally, use the continuum of strategies above to help your child add these important social skills to his or her skill collection.

You should also plan to work closely with your child's teacher if biting is occurring at home and your child's classroom. Teachers are open to working with you to make sure biting does not exploit anyone at school. But, expect biting to come and go. It is a developmental phenomenon that will be replaced by more mature skills as your child grows and learns. Remember these important points:

◆ Respond quickly when your child is hurt by another child or a sibling.

◆ Biting is a developmental phenomena that comes and goes.

◆ All children bite occasionally at various ages and stages.

◆ Your child's teacher will quickly comfort hurt children who are bitten, hugging and cuddling them until they are calm.

◆ Expect your teacher to talk to you about biting incidences.

◆ Expect to see a written report.

◆ Biting disappears and is replaced by more mature skills as your child grows.

◆ Be your child's first teacher about biting. Don't let him or her bite you without getting a negative reaction from you.

◆ Give your older toddler lots of attention and hugs for positive social behaviors with friends and siblings such as touching softly or taking turns.

What Can Parents Do to Prevent Purposeful Biting? (continued)

▲ Talk about what your child is doing and describe his or her actions and reactions, and the actions and reactions of others as they happen.

▲ Model behaviors you want your child to use such as talking softly, saying "please" and "thank you," and holding your hand in dangerous situations.

▲ Verbal children often identify the wrong child as the biter. Or, they may attribute every right and wrong in the classroom to one child. Check out the facts with your child's teacher.

▲ Prevention, anticipation, and substitution take care of most biting incidences.

▲ Help your child learn to wait for just a moment.

▲ Teach your child to use words, walk away, trade, and take turns.

▲ Shadow your child in new situations to prevent biting.

▲ Parents of older children can be a resource to help in understanding biting.

▲ Who did the biting is not as important as the teacher's plan for handling it.

▲ Talk to your child's teacher if you have any concerns about any of your toddler's behaviors.

▲ Bites rarely cause problems from a health perspective. Concerns about infection or contracting HIV are usually unfounded.

TO

Communication Sheet

INNOVATIONS

CHILD'S NAME _____ **FOR THE WEEK OF** _____

DAY	BREAKFAST	TOTAL HOURS SLEPT	BEHAVIOR CHANGES NOTICED	PARENT COMMENTS/INSTRUCTIONS	FOODS EATEN SOLIDS	FOODS EATEN LIQUIDS	DIAPER CHANGES WET	DIAPER CHANGES BM	NAPTIME START	NAPTIME WOKE	TEACHER COMMENTS
M	YES / NO		YES / NO								
T	YES / NO		YES / NO								
W	YES / NO		YES / NO								
Th	YES / NO		YES / NO								
F	YES / NO		YES / NO								

INNOVATIONS

Accident/Incident Report
(for school records)

Name of injured child

Date of accident/incident

Location of accident (address)

Site (place in school)

What happened? Describe what took place.

Why did it happen? Give all of the facts—why? where? what? when? who? etc.

What should be done to prevent this accident from recurring?

If the accident involved a child, how were the parents notified and by whom?

What was the parent's reaction?

What has been done so far to correct the situation?

With whom was this accident discussed, other than the child's parents?

Reported by   Date

The American Montessori Society Bulletin
American Montessori Society (AMS)
150 Fifth Avenue
New York, NY 10011
www.nccanet.org

The Black Child Advocate
Black Child Development Institute
1463 Rhode Island Avenue NW
Washington, DC 20001
www.nbcdi.org

Center for Early Childhood Leadership
National-Louis University
6310 Capitol Drive
Wheeling, IL 60090

Child Care Information Exchange, The
Directors' Magazine
Exchange Press, Inc.
PO Box 3249
Redmond, WA 98073
www.ccie.org

Child Health Alert
PO Box 388
Newton Highlands, MA 02161

Child Welfare Journal
Child Welfare League of America, Inc.
(CWLA)
440 First Street NW
Washington, DC 20001
www.cwla.org

Childhood Education
Association for Childhood Education
International (ACEI)
17904 Georgia Avenue, Suite 215
Wheaton, MD 20832
www.udel.edu/bateman/acei/

Children and Families
National Head Start Association
1651 Prince Street
Alexandria, VA 22314

Developmental Psychology
American Psychological Association
1200 17th Street NW
Washington, DC 20036

Dimensions of Early Childhood
Southern Early Childhood Association
Box 5403 Brady Station
Little Rock, AR 72215

Early Childhood News
PO Box 608
Vandalia, OH 45377

Early Childhood Research Quarterly
National Association for the Education of
    Young Children
Elsevier Sciences, Ablex Publishing Company
100 Prospect Street
Stamford, CT 06904-0811
www.udel.edu/ecrq

Early Childhood Today
Scholastic
Office of Publications
2931 East McCarty Street
PO Box 3710
Jefferson City, MO 65102-3710

Educational Research
American Educational Research Association
(AERA)
1230 Seventeenth Street NW
Washington, DC 220036

ERIC Clearinghouse on Elementary and
    Early Childhood Education
University of Illinois at Urbana-Champaign
Children's Research Center
51 Gerty Drive
Champaign, IL 61820-7469
www.ericeece@uiuc.edu

ERIC/EECE Newsletter
805 West Pennsylvania Avenue
Urbana, IL 61801

Exceptional Children
Council for Exceptional Children
1920 Association Drive
Reston, VA 22091

Gifted Child Quarterly
National Association for Gifted Children
4175 Lovell Road, Suite 140
Circle Pines, MN 55014

International Association for the Child's
    Right to Play (IPA)
Dr. Rhonda Clements
Hofstra University
278 Swim Center
Hempstead, NY 11549-1000
or
c/o Mr. Robin C. Moore
North Carolina State University, School of
Design
Box 7701
Raleigh, NC 27695-7701

**Journal of Research in Early Childhood
    Education International**
11501 Georgia Avenue, Suite 315
Wheaton, MD 20902

National Association of Child Care Resource
    and Referral Agencies (NACCRA)
905 School House Lane
Dover, DE 19904
www.nara-licensing.org

The National Child Care Association
1016 Rosser Street
Conyers, GA 30012

Texas Child Care
PO Box 162881
Austin, TX 78716-2881

United States Association for Child Care
3606 NE Basswood Drive
Lee's Summit, MO 64064
www.usachildcare.org

Young Children
NAEYC
1509 16th Street NW
Washington, DC 20036-1426
www.naeyc.org

The Innovations Model

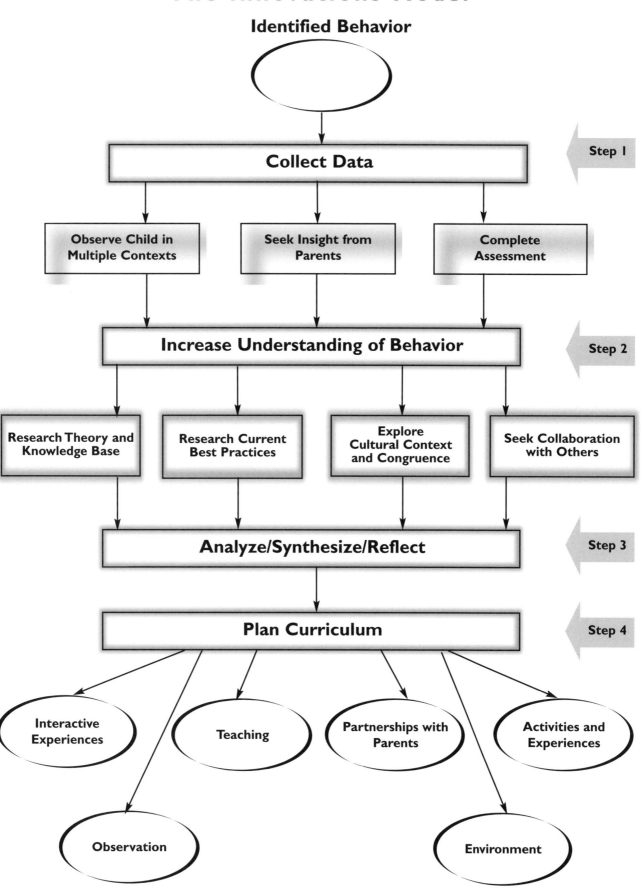

Identified Behavior

Collect Data — Step 1

- Observe Child in Multiple Contexts
- Seek Insight from Parents
- Complete Assessment

Increase Understanding of Behavior — Step 2

- Research Theory and Knowledge Base
- Research Current Best Practices
- Explore Cultural Context and Congruence
- Seek Collaboration with Others

Analyze/Synthesize/Reflect — Step 3

Plan Curriculum — Step 4

- Interactive Experiences
- Teaching
- Partnerships with Parents
- Activities and Experiences
- Observation
- Environment

Possibilities

Parent Possibilities

Teacher-Initiated

Parent Participation

Innovations in Environments

Observation/Assessment Possibilities

Interactive Experiences

Plan

Web

Dramatic Possibilities

Art/Sensory Possibilities

Curiosity Possibilities

Music Possibilities

Movement Possibilities

Literacy Possibilities

Outdoor Possibilities

Project Possibilities

Books	Picture File Pictures/Vocabulary

Rhymes & Fingerplays	Music/Songs	Prop Boxes

Appendix

References

Ainsworth, M.D.S., M.C. Blehar, E. Waters, & S. Wall. (1978). *Patterns of attachment: A psychological study of the strange situation.* Hillsdale, NJ: Erlbaum.

Albrecht, K. & L.G. Miller. (2000). *Innovations: The comprehensive infant curriculum.* Beltsville, MD: Gryphon House.

Albrecht, K. & L.G. Miller. (2000). *Innovations: The comprehensive toddler curriculum.* Beltsville, MD: Gryphon House.

Albrecht, K., M. Banks, G. Calhoun, L. Dziadul, C. Gwinn, B. Harrington, B. Kerr, M. Mizukami, A. Morris, C. Peterson, C., & R.R. Summers. (2000). The good, the bad, and the wonderful: Keeping children and teachers together. *Child Care Information Exchange,* 136, 24-28.

Albrecht, K., L. Dziadul, C. Gwinn, & B. Harrington. (2001). The good, the bad, and the wonderful: Keeping children and teachers together (part 2). *Child Care Information Exchange,* 137, 90-93.

Albrecht, K.M. & M. Ward. (1989). Growing pains. *Pre-K Today,* 36, 54-55.

Bailey, C.B., J.T. Bruer, F.J. Symons, & J.W. Lichtman. (2001). *Critical thinking about critical periods.* Baltimore, MD: Brookes Publishing.

Bell, S.M. & M.D.S. Ainsworth. (1972). Infant crying and maternal responsiveness. *Child Development*, 43, 1171-1190.

Berk, L.E. (1994). Vygotsky's theory: The importance of make-believe play. *Young Children*, 50 (1), 30-39.

Berk, L.E. (1999). *Infants and Children*. Boston: Allyn and Bacon.

Berk, L.E. and A. Winsler (1995). *Scaffolding children's learning*. Washington, DC: National Association for the Education of Young Children (NAEYC).

Bernhardt, J.L. (2000). A primary caregiving system for infants and toddlers: Best for everyone involved. *Young Children*, 52(7), 12-15.

Bloom, L. (1998). Language acquisition in the context of development. In W. Damon, D. Kuhn, & R. Sigler (Vol. Eds.), *Handbook of child psychology: Cognition, perception, and language*. 5, 309-370. New York: John Wiley.

Bowlby, J. (1982). *Attachment and Loss: Attachment* (Vol. 1), New York: Basic Books.

Brazelton, T.B. (1992). *Touchpoints: The essential reference*. Reading, MA: Addison-Wesley.

Brazelton, T.B., & S.I. Greenspan. (2000). *The irreducible needs of children: What every child must have to grow, learn, and flourish*. Cambridge, MA: Perseus Publishing.

Bredekamp, C. & C. Copple (1997). *Developmentally appropriate practice in early childhood programs, Revised edition*. Washington, DC: National Association for the Education of Young Children (NAEYC).

Bronfenbrenner, U. (1979). *The ecology of human development: Experiments by nature and design*. Cambridge, MA: Harvard University Press.

Brunson, M.B. (2000). Recognizing and supporting the development of self-regulation in young children. *Young Children*, 55(2), 32-37.

California State Department of Education. (1990). *Flexible, fearful, or feisty: The different temperaments of infants and toddlers*. Videotape. Sacramento, CA: Department of Education.

Cassidy J., S. Kirsh, K.L. Scolton, & R.D. Parke. (1996). Attachment and representations of peer relationships. *Developmental Psychology*, 32, 892-904.

Cherry, C. (1976). *Creative play for the developing child: Early childhood education through play*. Belmont, CA: Fearon.

Chess, S. & A. Thomas. (1987). *Know your child*. New York: Basic Books.

Chomsky, N. (1957). *Syntactic structures*. The Hague: Mouton.

Cooper, P. (1993). *When stories come to school: Telling, writing, and performing stories in the early childhood classroom*. New York: Teachers and Writers.

Cryer, D. & T. Harms. (2000). *Infants and toddlers in out of home care*. Baltimore, MD: Brookes Publishing.

Curry, N.E. & C.N. Johnson (1990). *Beyond self-esteem: Developing a genuine sense of human value*. Washington, DC: National Association for the Education of Young Children (NAEYC).

Curtis, D. & M. Carter. (2000). *The art of awareness: How observation can transform your teaching*. St. Paul, MI: Redleaf Press.

Edwards, C., L. Gandini, & G. Foreman. (1998). *The one hundred languages of children: The Reggio Emilia approach to early childhood education – Advanced Reflections*. Norwood, NJ: Ablex.

Elkind, D. (2001). Thinking about children's play. *Child Care Information Exchange*, 139, 27-28.

Erickson, E.H. (1963). *Childhood and society*. New York: Workman.

Feeney, S. & K. Kipnis. (1999). *Code of ethical conduct and statement of commitment*. Washington, DC: NAEYC.

Fein, G.G., A. Gariboldi & R. Boni. (1993). The adjustment of infants and toddlers to group care: The first six months. *Early Childhood Research Quarterly*, 8, 1-14.

Florida Committee for the Prevention of Child Abuse, (1994). *The abc's of child safety awareness: A handbook for providing a safe, nurturing environment for children*. Gainesville, FL: Dial Publishing.

Gandini, L. & C.P. Edwards. (2001). *Bambini: The Italian approach to infant/toddler care*. New York: Teacher's College Press.

Gandini, L. & J. Goldhaber. (2001). Two reflections about documentation. In L. Gandini & C.P. Edwards (Eds.), *Bambini: The Italian approach to infant/toddler care*. 121-145. New York: Teacher's College Press.

Gardner, H. (1983). *Frames of mind: The theory of multiple intelligences*. New York: Basic Books.

Gerber, M. (1979). *Resources for infant educarers: A manual for parents and professionals*. Los Angeles: Resources for Infant Educarers.

Gerber, M. & A. Johnson. (1997). *Your self-confident baby*. New York: Wiley.

Goleman, D. (1995), *Emotional intelligence*. New York: Bantam Doubleday Dell.

Goleman, D. (1998). *Working with emotional intelligence*. New York: Bantam Doubleday Dell.

Gordon, I. (1970). *Baby learning through baby play*. New York: St. Martin's.

Greenman, J. & A. Stonehouse. (1996). *Prime times: A handbook for excellence in infant and toddler programs*. St. Paul, MN: Redleaf Press.

Greenspan, S.I. (1997). *Growth of the mind and the endangered origins of intelligence*. Cambridge, MA: Perseus Books.

Greenspan, S.I. (1999). *The six experiences that create intelligence and emotional growth in babies and young children*. Reading, MA: Perseus Books.

Greenspan, S.I. & N.T. Greenspan. (1989). *First feelings: Milestones in the emotional development of your baby and child*. New York: Penguin.

Greenspan, S.I. & N.T. Greenspan (1989). *The essential partnership*. New York: Penguin.

Helms, J.H., S. Beneke & K. Steinheimer. (1997). *Windows on learning: Documenting children's work*. New York: Teacher's College Press.

Hitz, R. & A. Driscoll. (1988). Praise or encouragement? New insights and implications for early childhood teachers. *Young Children*, 43(5), 6-13.

Hostetler, L. (1984). Public policy report: The nanny trap: Child care work today. *Young Children*, 39(2), 76-79.

Howes, C. (1988). Peer interaction of young children. *Monographs of the Society for Research in Child Development*, 53 (1).

Howes, C. (2000). Social development, family, and attachment relationships of infant and toddlers. In D. Cryer & T. Harms (Eds.), *Infants and toddlers in out of home care* (87-113). Baltimore, MD: Brookes Publishing.

Howes, C. & C.E. Hamilton. (1992). Children's relationships with caregivers: Mothers and child care teachers. *Child Development*. 64, 859-866.

Howes, C. & C.C. Matheson. (1992). Sequences of the development of competent play with peers: Social and pretend play. *Developmental Psychology*, 28: 961-974.

Howes, C., D.A. Phillips, & M. Whitebrook. (1992). Thresholds of quality: Implications for the social development of children in center-based care. *Child Development*, 63, 449-460.

Hyson, M.C. (1994). *The emotional development of young children: Building an emotion-centered curriculum*. New York: Teachers College Press.

Jalongo, M.E. (1987). Do security blankets belong in preschool? *Young Children*, 42(3), 3-8.

Katz, J.R. & C.E. Snow. (2000). Language development in early childhood. In D. Cryer & T. Harms (Eds.), *Infants and toddlers in out of home care* (49-87). Baltimore, MD: Brookes Publishing.

Katz, L.G. (1998).The benefits of the mix. *Child Care Information Exchange*, 124, 46-49.

Katz, LG., D. Evangelou, & J.A. Hartman. (1990). *The case for mixed-age grouping in early education*. Washington, DC: NAEYC.

Katz, L. & P. McClellan (1997). *Fostering social competence: The teacher's role*. Washington, DC: National Association for the Education of Young Children (NAEYC).

Kirsh, S.J. & J. Cassidy. (1997). Preschoolers' attention to and memory for attachment-relevant information. *Child Development*, 68: 1143-1153.

Korner, A.F. & E.B. Thoman. (1972). Visual alertness in neonates as evoked by material care. *Journal of Experimental Psychology*, 10. 67-68.

Kovach, B.A. & P.A. Da Ros. (1998). Respectful, individual, and responsive caregiving for infants: The key to successful care in group settings. *Young Children*, 53 (3), 61-64.

Laible, D.J. & R.A. Thompson. (1998). Attachment and emotional understanding in preschool children. *Development Psychology*, 34(5): 1038-1045.

Lally, J.R. (1995). The impact of child care policies and practices on infant/toddler identity formation. *Young Children*, 51 (1), 58-67.

Leavitt, R.L. (1994). *Power and emotion in infant-toddler day care*. Albany, NY: State University of New York Press.

Leiberman, A.F. (1993). *The emotional life of a toddler*. New York: The Free Press.

Lowman, L.H. & L. Ruhmann. (1998). Simply sensational spaces: The multi-S approach to toddler environments. *Young Children*, 53(3), 11-17.

Mahler, M.S., F. Pine, & A. Bergman. (1975). *The psychological birth of the human infant: Symbiosis and individuation*. New York: Basic Books.

Marion, M. (1997). Research in review: Guiding young children's understanding and management of anger. *Young Children*, 52(7), 62-67.

Marion, M. (1999). *Guidance of young children*. Upper Saddle River, NJ: Merrill.

Maslow, A. (1954). *Motivation and personality*. New York: Harper & Row.

McBride, S.L. (1999). Family centered practices. *Young Children*, 54 (4), 62-68.

McCall, R.B. & B.W. Plemons. (2001). The concept of critical periods and their implications for early childhood services. In D.B. Bailey, J.T. Bruer, F.J. Symons, & J.W. Lichtman (Eds.), *Critical thinking about critical periods*. (267-287). Baltimore, MD: Brookes Publishing.

McMullen, M.B. (1998). Thinking before doing: A great step on the road to literacy. *Young Children*, 53(3), 65-69.

McMullen, M.B. (1999). Achieving best practices in infant and toddler care and education. *Young Children*, 54 (4), 69-75.

Mooney, C.G. (2000). *Theories of childhood: An introduction to Dewey, Montessori, Erickson, Piaget, and Vygotsky*. St. Paul, MI: Redleaf Press.

National Association for the Education of Young Children. (1998). Learning to read and write: Developmentally appropriate practices for young children. *Young Children*, 53(4), 30-36.

Neuman, S., C. Copple, and S. Bredekamp. (2000). *Learning to read and write: Developmentally appropriate practices for young children*. Washington, DC: National Association for the Education of Young Children (NAEYC).

Paley, V.G. (1981). *Wally's stories*. Cambridge, MA: Harvard University Press.

Parten, M.P. (1932). Social participation among preschool children. *Journal of Abnormal Psychology*, 27, 243-269.

Pellegrini, A. S. & C.D. Glickman. (1990). Measuring kindergartners' social competence. *Young Children*, 45(4), 40-44.

Perry, B.D. (2000). Emotional development: The developmental hot zone. *Early Childhood Today*, Nov./Dec.

Piaget, J. (1962). *Play, dreams, and imitation in childhood.* (C. Gattegno & F.M. Hodgson, Trans.) New York: Norton.

Piaget, J. (1977). *The origins of intelligence in children*. New York: International Universities Press.

Post, J. & M. Hohmann. (2000). *Tender care and early learning*. Ypsilanti, MI: High/Scope Press.

Powell, D.R. (1998). Reweaving parents into the fabric of early childhood programs. *Young Children*, 53 (5), 60-67.

Raikes, H. (1996). A secure base for babies: Applying attachment concepts to the infant care setting. *Young Children*, 51 (5), 50-67.

Reisenberg, J. (1995). Reflections on quality infant care. *Young Children*, 50 (6), 23-25.

Rogers, C.S. and J.K. Sawyer. (1988). *Play in the lives of children*. Washington, DC: National Association for the Education of Young Children (NAEYC).

Rubin, Z. (1980). *Children's friendships*. Cambridge, MA: Harvard University Press.

Scanlon, P. (1988). In search of excellent training: Tuning into right brain/left brain thinking. *Child Care Information Exchange*, 63, 7-11.

Schweinhart, L., H. Barnes, D. Weikart, W.S. Barnett & A.S. Epstein. (1993). *Significant benefits: The High/Scope Perry Preschool study through age 27*. Monographs of the High/Scope Educational Research Foundation, No. 10. Ypsilanti, MI: The High/Scope Press.

Shonkoff, J.P. & D.A. Phillips (Eds.). (2000). *From neurons to neighborhoods: The science of early childhood development*. Washington, DC: National Academy Press.

Shore, R. (1997). *Rethinking the Brain: New insights into early development*. New York: Families and Work Institute.

Seigel, D.J. (1999). Relationships and the developing child. *Child Care Information Exchange*. 130, 48-51.

Sroufe, L. A., & J. Fleeson. (1986). Attachment and the construction of relationships. In W.W. Hartup & A. Rubin (Eds.), *Relationships and development* pp. 51-71. Hillsdale, N.J.: Erlbaum.

Stern, D. (1985). *The interpersonal world of the infant: A view from psychoanalysis and developmental psychology*. New York: Basic Books.

Stonehouse, A. (1988). *How does it feel?: Child care from a parent's perspective*. Redmond, WA: Exchange Press.

Swift, M. (1995). *Discipline for life*. Grapevine, TX: Stairway Education Programs.

Tabors, P.O. (1998). What early childhood educators need to know: Developing programs for linguistically and culturally diverse children and families. *Young Children*, 53(6), 20-26.

Vaughan, B.E., C.B. Kopp & J.B. Krakow. (1984). The emergence and consolidation of self-control from eighteen–thirty months of age: Normative trends and individual differences. *Child Development*, 55:900-1004.

Vygotsky, L. (1978). *Mind in society: The development of higher psychological processes*. Cambridge, MA: Harvard University Press.

Wardle, F. (1995). How young children build images of themselves. *Child Care Information Exchange*, 104, 44-47.

Index